THE STOLEN CHILD

THE
STOLEN CHILD

ASPECTS OF AUTISM AND
ASPERGER SYNDROME

ANN HEWETSON

FOREWORD BY SUSAN J. MORENO

BERGIN & GARVEY
WESTPORT, CONNECTICUT • LONDON

Library of Congress Cataloging-in-Publication Data

Hewetson, Ann.
    The stolen child : aspects of autism and Asperger syndrome / by Ann Hewetson;
foreword by Susan J. Moreno.
      p.   cm.
    Includes index.
    ISBN 0–89789–844–3 (alk. paper)
      1. Autism.   2. Asperger's syndrome.   I. Title.
RC553.A88H49   2002
616.89'82—dc21   2001043015

British Library Cataloguing in Publication Data is available.

Library of Congress Catalog Card Number: 2001043015
ISBN: 0–89789–844–3

First published in 2002

Bergin & Garvey, 88 Post Road West, Westport, CT 06881
An imprint of Greenwood Publishing Group, Inc.
www.greenwood.com

Printed in the United States of America

The paper used in this book complies with the
Permanent Paper Standard issued by the National
Information Standards Organization (Z39.48–1984).

10 9 8 7 6 5 4 3 2 1

All the information provided in this book is for informational purposes only, and the author
and publisher cannot be held liable for any errors or omissions or actions undertaken as a result
of using it. Reference to any intervention, treatment, or therapy does not constitute an
endorsement by the author or publisher of that intervention, treatment, or therapy, and they
assume no responsibility for the use made of any information published in this book. At all
times it is the individual's care giver, medical advisor, or other qualified professional who should
decide on intervention options or therapies.

Excerpts from B. Singer, "Jonathan at Forty," *The Early Years of the MAAP*, p. 128. MAAP, P.O. Box 524, Crown Point, IN 46308.

Excerpts from S.L. Smalley, J. McCracken, and P. Tanguay, "Austism, Affective Disorders, and Social Phobia." *American Journal of Medical Genetics* 60 (1995): 19–26. Reprinted by permission of Wiley-Liss, Inc., a subsidiary of John Wiley & Sons, Inc.

Excerpts from H. Asperger (1944), "Autistic Psychopathy in Childhood" in *Autism and Asperger Syndrome*, edited by U. Frith (Cambridge: Cambridge University Press, 1991).

Excerpts from U. Frith, "Asperger and His Syndrome" in *Autism and Asperger Syndrome*, edited by U. Frith (Cambridge: Cambridge University Press, 1991).

Excerpts from L. Wing, "The Relationship between Asperger's Syndrome and Kanner's Autism" in *Autism and Asperger Syndrome*, edited by U. Frith (Cambridge: Cambridge University Press, 1991).

Excerpts from D. Tantum, "Asperger Syndrome in Adulthood" in *Autism and Asperger Syndrome*, edited by U. Frith (Cambridge: Cambridge University Press, 1991).

Excerpts from L. Wing, "Asperger's Syndrome: A Clinical Account," *Psychological Medicine* 11 (1981): 115–129. Reprinted with permission of Cambridge University Press.

Excerpts from L. Wing, "The Autistic Spectrum," *Lancet* 350 (December 13, 1997): 1761–1766. © by The Lancet Ltd. 1997.

Excerpts from W.B. Yeats, "The Stolen Child" and the entire poem entitled "He Wishes for the Cloths of Heaven." Reprinted with permission of A.P. Watt Ltd. on behalf of Michael B. Yeats.

Policy statement number thirty-nine: "Secretin in the Treatment of Autism." Reprinted with permission of the American Academy of Child and Adolescent Psychiatry.

Excerpts from "A Family History Study of Neuropsychiatric Disorders in the Adult Siblings of Autistic Individuals" 29, 2 (1990): 177–183; "Psychiatric Disorders in the Parents of Autistic Children" 30, 3 (1991): 471–479; "Asperger's Syndrome and Autism: Neurocognitive Aspects" 29, 1 (1990): 130–136; reprinted with permission of the American Academy of Child and Adolescent Psychiatry.

The author would also like to thank: Dr. Simon Baron-Cohen, Dr. Dorothy Bishop, Dr. Edwin Cook, Mrs. Mary Anne Coppola, Dr. Carl H. Delacato, Dr. Angel Diez Cuervo, Dr. Stephen Ehlers, Dr. Pauline Filipek, Dr. Eric Fombonne, Dr. Uta Frith, Dr. Christopher Gillberg, Dr. Temple Grandin, Mr. Charles A. Hart, Mr. Perry Hoffman, Dr. Robert Katzman, Mr. Barry Neil Kaufman, Dr. Thomas L. Kemper and Dr. Margaret Bauman, Dr. Ann-Mari Knivsberg, Mrs. Susan Moreno, M.A.A.B.S., Dr. Nickola W. Nelson, Dr. Edward M. Ornitz, Dr. Clara Claiborne Park, Mr. Richard Pollak, Dr. Kathleen A. Quill, Dr. Isabelle Rapin, Dr. Bernard Rimland, Dr. Clive Robbins, Dr. Oliver Sacks, Dr. Eric Schopler, Mrs. Bernice Singer, Dr. Leon Sloman, Dr. Susan L. Smalley, Mrs. Annabel Stehli, Dr. Peter Szatmari, Dr. Digby Tantum, Dr. Jane Taylor McDonnell, Dr. Luke Tsai, Dr. Fred R. Volkmar and Dr. A. Klin, Mrs. Louise Warren, widow of the late Dr. Reid P. Warren, Dr. Lorna Wing, Dr. Sula Wolff, and Ms. Polly A. Yarnall, M.Ed.

To all those who live in the eye of the storm

&

To those who walk beside them.

CONTENTS

PART III. SOME QUESTIONS

PART IV. SOME PEOPLE

FOREWORD

In my work, I am asked to read and review many books on autism. It is wonderful that so many books now exist on the subject and that many more are being written. When my daughter was young, there were very few books on autism in general and only one about children who were more advanced. However, with the burgeoning number of books available, it becomes increasingly difficult to know which ones to recommend to parents, professionals, family members, and individuals with autism. I am happy to say that Ann Hewetson has written a work that I would recommend to anyone. Both a scholar and the parent of an individual with Asperger syndrome, Ann gives us accurate and insightful information.

If I am to describe this book in its most essential terms, I would call it poetically accurate. Ann Hewetson is eloquent in her similes and metaphors. She takes the uninitiated by the hand and leads them through the world of autism. From gripping and sensitive descriptions of three individuals who have autism, but who present an array of manifestations remarkably distinct from one another, to a good history of the professionals who influenced thought about autism, to basic coverage of accounts of the syndrome by individuals with autism and their parents. A seasoned academic, Ann Hewetson has impeccably researched her subject materials. She possesses a thorough grasp of autism in all of its facets, both current and historical. As a parent, she presents the wrenching emotions and challenges faced by families who cope with autism.

For those like myself, who live in the United States, it is important to realize that many parts of the world are still emerging from the "mother did it" misinformation on autism. Ann Hewetson's description of a young family's first, futile attempts to receive a diagnosis and attain direction in seeking help struck a too-familiar chord. In my work, I hear hundreds of similar stories. But again, Ann is profound in her description. She refers to "having to give an account of their [the family's] stewardship, while the spotlight was focused firmly on the parents, *not* on the child."

Throughout her descriptions of the symptomatology of autism, Ann Hewetson vividly presents the rationality of irrational behaviors. Her discussion of the *logic* of pronominal reversal is truly brilliant. She says, "in Bryan's case, it was just another example of his associational thinking." . . . "If you are constantly called 'you,' and told that things are 'yours,' then you begin to associate the words 'you' and 'yours' with yourself. If the other person always refers to themselves as 'I,' and says 'that's mine' and 'give me that,' then the 'I,' 'mine,' and 'me' become associated with the other person." Ann describes a child using his family's primary language as attempting a foreign language. She explains his halting during speech as a search for "neurotypically acceptable form."

In Western cultural terms, I would call Ann Hewetson the Margaret Mitchell of Autism. Not since Ms. Mitchell made the red clay of Tara and the drama of the Civil War come to life for us in *Gone With the Wind* has anyone so immersed us in a subject and a set of experiences. This is most vividly evident in her description of bullies. Here is but a morsel of her words on the subject: "Like the predators they are, they feed off the emotions of their prey and cause untold misery during the vulnerable years of formation. They roam the jungle of the school yard seeking whom they may devour."

I could go on and on, but I am detaining you from the privilege of learning about autism through the eyes of a brilliant, scholarly, and truly sensitive author. In my opinion, she is the most eloquent one you'll have read in years—or perhaps ever.

Susan J. Moreno, M.A.A.B.S.
Parent
President and Founder, Maap Services, Inc.

PREFACE

This book looks at autism in the twentieth century, charting its checkered course from the first diagnosis of the condition in 1943 by Leo Kanner, through the slow stagnation of the second half of the century, to watch it accelerate to the exciting pace of millennium research. The condition is seen from two vantage points—the personal and the professional. The first of these depicts the life experience of the person who has autism and of the parent living with autism. The second traces the disorder as seen through the eyes of some of the professionals who have worked and are working in this field.

While there are many questions about autism, there are as yet few clear fundamental answers because all the factors involved in the autistic equation have not yet been assembled and identified. Now, however, the tools of neuroscience and molecular genetics are beginning to be applied to autism and the mist is beginning to disperse. It is expected that the early years of this twenty-first century will begin to yield some long awaited answers. As will emerge from the pages of *The Stolen Child* there is, however, one very important fact already in the public arena: intensive special education intervention in the very early years of life, in addition to behavioral approaches, can hold promise for improving the aptitude of the autistic child to learn and acquire language.

The expression of autism is wide, and over the years because of the lack of clear fundamental answers, many theories have emerged about the cause of autism. In fact the first of these theories, which surfaced in the mid-1940s and was propagated for over a quarter-of-a-century, was the psychogenic theory of autism (having its origin in the mind rather than in the body). This theory held that the parents themselves were the cause of autism. One of the theories about methods of treatment put forward in that era was to treat the mothers with psychotherapy and if this was not successful then to remove the child from home and place him in foster care.

Since that time further theories about causes have given rise to further theories about methods of therapy or treatment. Methods of therapy are a controversial field in autism and this field is strewn with examples of therapies or treatments that were based on firmly held beliefs rather than on strict scientific evidence. Consequently, when tried, they were found to fall short of expectations. A number of current therapies or treatments are discussed in the book and every effort is made to give a balanced picture, drawing where possible on the available scientific evidence and advice. However, it must be pointed out that these are not intended to be comprehensive statements of available therapies or treatments. Rather they are more in the nature of an overview.

At all times it is the reader who is responsible for the choice of therapy or treatment. It must be kept in mind when reading that the knowledge given here is for informational purposes only and does not constitute an endorsement by the author or publisher of any therapy option or treatment, and they assume no responsibility for the use made of any information provided in this book. As previously mentioned, the individual's care giver, medical advisor, or other qualified professional should make these decisions.

ACKNOWLEDGMENTS

I am taking this opportunity to say "Thank you" to Sharon, without whom this book could never have been begun; to Brian, without whom it would never have been finished; to James, always willing to share his computer expertise; to Roisin and Fionnbharr, for editorial assistance; and above all to Mark R., John K., and Bryan O'B. without whom there never would have been a book.

ABBREVIATIONS

AD	Autistic Disorder
AS	Asperger Syndrome; also spelled Asperger's Syndrome
ASD	Autistic Spectrum Disorder
APA	American Psychiatric Association
ASA	Autism Society of America
CDC	Centers for Disease Control and Prevention, United States
DSM-IV	Diagnostic and Statistical Manual of Mental Disorders, Fourth Edition
ICD-10	International Classification of Diseases: Tenth Revision
HFA	High-Functioning Autism
MAAP	More Advanced Individuals with Autism, Asperger's Syndrome, and Pervasive Development Disorder
NAS	National Autistic Society, United Kingdom
NIH	National Institutes of Health, United States
PDD	Pervasive Developmental Disorder
PDDNOS	Pervasive Developmental Disorder Not Otherwise Specified

PART I

SOME INSIGHTS

For he comes, the human child,
To the waters and the wild
With a faery, hand in hand,
From a world more full of weeping than he can understand.

"The Stolen Child," William Butler Yeats (1865–1939)

CHAPTER 1

❧❧❧

BEGINNINGS

The lines from William Butler Yeats' "The Stolen Child" capture the essence of autism, revealing a bewildered child who does not appear to understand the world into which he has come and therefore is unable to comprehend his own state of mind or the state of mind of another. What he cannot understand he can neither relate nor adapt to, and if he cannot assimilate the concrete world, he will not succeed in coming to terms with the world of the abstract.[1]

The theme of the lost child stolen by the faeries and the changeling left in its place is not a new one in autism. Clara Park, in describing her artistic daughter, Jessy, in her illuminating book *The Siege* written more than thirty years ago, documents some similarities between the mythical image of the faeries and some aspects of her daughter's autism.[2] Jane Taylor McDonnell, writing more recently about her son Paul, muses again on the Irish legend of the changeling. She ends her book with a Swedish version of the story indicating that the well-being of the real child depends on the nurturing of the changeling. In the end the stolen child is returned to his parents and becomes one with the changeling, having survived only because the changeling had been so loved and cared for. His return had been a measure of gratitude for the exhaustive care and devotion of his mother.[3]

The remoteness, the inaccessibility, the other worldliness of children with autism is mirrored in the language of Yeats' poem. Outwardly they carry no sign of their devastating inner disability. Being guileless, they have no malice;

being victims, they are not perpetrators. Because of cognitive defects they are thought to have impaired "theory of mind," and so they cannot understand the human experience, and what they cannot understand they can neither relate to, nor empathize with. They live in our world but can do so withdrawn, isolated, and remote, thus belonging in their own world while struggling to come to terms with ours.

Even though the condition of autism (see glossary) was first diagnosed by Leo Kanner in 1943, it did not arise for the first time in that century.[4] There are many descriptions of autistic-like persons in the records of medical history going back to the Middle Ages. It is a condition that has always attracted popular attention, and a web of myth has grown up around it. The image of the beautiful child locked away behind the closed doors of his intelligence with perhaps untold talents waiting to be developed has been strengthened by the extraordinary achievements in art, music, and mathematics by a small number of autistic people with savant talents; about 10 percent of the autistic population possesses these extraordinary "islets of ability" in the midst of so much disability. In this climate of opinion it is hard to separate fact from fantasy, image from impression, myth from reality. But what *is* the reality of autism and living with autism?

Imagine a house where one cannot move freely around because most of the floor space is occupied by long lines of toys; toys that will never be used for constructive play. They just remain on the floor for months on end gathering dust in parallel lines. If they are removed or displaced the screaming tantrums will continue until they are put back again. *Sameness is sacrosanct.* Every time one goes out the front gate of this house one must turn left or else run the gauntlet of having to cope with the same devastating reaction. *Repetition becomes routine.* The predictability of repetition and routine form the external structure providing the outer framework to bulwark a life of inner chaos. They are the landmarks in a dangerous sea of uncharted territory.

There are no handles on the doors. The nonverbal three-year-old has discovered the art of the screwdriver and the manual dexterity of the acrobat. With the sureness of an expert he removes the handles from every door in sight. At night while he sleeps they are replaced by the authority figures. The following morning the pantomime begins again and by nightfall not a door is left with a handle intact. *Compulsions are commonplace.* Any attempt to intervene and stop the process will bring on the same screaming tantrums. To alleviate distress, a conscious decision is made not to replace the handles and the doors remain open; peace at a price. But the obsession remains and the perseveration tendency to use the screwdriver is now turned on plugs of electrical appliances. Fortunately the sockets are high up out of reach. A number of dummy plugs and dummy sockets on extension leads going nowhere supply the outlet for the fixation. Later the obsessive, compulsive, fixated, behavior will find another outlet. What drives the obsession? It is hard to guess. The sheer constructive energy involved, could it be put to practical use, is talent indeed. But it dismantles rather than assembles. It cannot be redirected. *The fixated attention is awesome and yet ominous.* It is locked into the task at hand to the exclusion of all other stimuli. There will be no reaction even to a fire alarm; no startle reflex. Is it possible that the attention centers of the cerebellum run in single grooves and cannot easily shift gear?

These deft actions are carried out by a child who looks through people as if they were made of glass. His unfocused eyes are constantly fixed on some vague point beyond the horizon. Yet this same child will spot a pin head on the floor and remove it with all the speed and accuracy of a hawk swooping for the kill. The fovic cells in the retina of the eye record and magnify minutiae. His fragmented vision sees everything without appearing to look at anything. His eyes scan; they record but do not view; fastening on detail, ignoring the global. *Vision without apparent viewing.* He does not feel pain, nor does he seem to know when he is too hot or too cold, thirsty or hungry. Never tiring, he just keeps going, finally dropping from exhaustion. As if he lacks the ability to monitor his own internal environment and does not seem to know how he feels. It is striking, this lack of self-perception. Where does the fault lie? In the sensory receptors or in the brain itself? Whatever the answer, it is obvious that there is *no sense in sensation.* He never points or gestures. If he wants something he will simply grasp the hand nearest to him and use it as an artificial limb. As if he could neither see nor feel his extremities, or was not aware of the position of his limbs or that they belonged to him. Does he suffer from a lack of knowledge of his own body boundaries? Perhaps he has no internal brain map, no body percept by which to navigate his body and chart his course. *Absence of bodily awareness.*

His speech is echolalic. One lives with the echo reverberating in the mind. Every question, every statement, bounces back through the eerie silence of the ether without comprehension. There is no comfort in this silence, no hope for companionship. It expresses no need for closeness, rejecting not connecting. A crescendo of silence deafening in its ability to isolate. *Comprehension makes contact; echolalic speech does not.* It gives no insight into the mind of another; connects with no internet for the two-way interaction process of communication; gives no glimpse into the interior; leaves the questioner without any awareness of even where to begin. This self-absorbed, self-complete, self-isolated, small human being will regularly disappear behind the thick folds of a blanket and shut out the light, retreating from a world that is obviously too much with him. He slips away, this human child, into his own space, escaping from a land that for him may not always be "more full of weeping than he can understand." It would appear he goes into recovery time. Later he will reemerge and continue his routines. *Oversensitivity to stimulus sensitizes.*

All around him average children of the same age are engaged in normal, varied, constructive play, reminiscent of all children, in all ages, and all climes, and designed to help them process the concrete concepts of their environment and orientate themselves properly in it. The autistic child, if he is active at all (so many are passive and unmotivated, quietly rocking; unwilling or unable to interact with their environment), is mired with un-varied routines and rituals as these vital early formative years pass by. These are the key years when the process of absorbing sensory information and organizing the sensations in the brain is of vital importance because it is now that the internal picture of the body, the body percept, is being built up inside the brain.[5]

This same house that we imagine has a vacuum cleaner, but it sits idly in a closet while the house cleaner sweeps the floor with a brush. There is an electric mixer standing unused on the counter top while nearby the cook mixes a Christmas cake with a wooden spoon. All fluorescent lights have been removed and replaced by old-fashioned bulbs. *Sensory overload over-whelms.* Every effort is made to reduce the impact of unnecessary stimuli on all five senses.

Rigidity and rituals rule. Only the child is allowed to answer the phone or doorbell. One wonders why. Otherwise a family member is likely to get knocked down in the stampede. At mealtimes the child must be the last to sit at the table. If not, the screams begin again. Perhaps some abstruse math-ematical calculation would be disturbed, some associational meaning shat-tered, if the order were reversed. As if the lack of order inside had to be compensated for by a strict adherence to order outside. How does one ac-count for the extreme reaction? Once an event has been scheduled for the day it has to be carried out. There is no room to maneuver; no possibility of a change of mind; no negotiation; no last minute plans; predictability at all costs.

Motion begets measurement. The washbasin is filled with water exactly thirty times and the plug pulled to watch the flow. A stopwatch records the time and the number of tries. Nothing unusual, except this routine continues for months until replaced by the next ritual. Over time this compulsion to meas-ure runs the full gamut of the varying physical phenomena; height, depth, car speed and wind speed, rainfall, temperature, barometric pressure, sound intensity. The meter stick, the speedometer, the ventometer and their equiv-alent become the playthings. The files of figures grow larger. Perhaps if you cannot understand the world and its environs, then quantifying them will help to make sense of them. Perhaps if you pin things down and reduce them to concrete figures, they then become more tangible and easier to assimilate. If you cannot absorb concepts intuitively, perhaps you can do so intellectually. *Autism confronts the abstract by absorbing the concrete.*

This picture of a fixated, obsessive child can represent autism in the early years. But the picture is not static. Any artist depicting an impression of autism will need different canvasses and different brushes. On his palette of primary colors he will need to mix many shades of color; many nuances of tint, tone, and hue, because autism is not a condition that reveals itself uniformly. Rather, it runs the gamut of many facets and behaviors, all of which shade into each other and change over time and environment, pointing to multiple causes.

There is enormous variation in the autistic spectrum. It is described as follows:

The autistic spectrum consists of a group of disorders of development with life-long effects and that have in common a triad of impairments in: social interaction, communication, imagination, and a narrow and repetitive pattern of behaviour. The spectrum includes, but is wider than, the syndromes originally described by Leo Kanner and Hans Asperger. The triad can occur on its own but is often accompanied by other features. It can be found together with any level of ability, from profound general learning disability to average or even superior cognitive skill in areas not directly affected by the basic impairments. It can occur with any other physical, psychological, or psychiatric condition. . . . The spectrum overlaps with but covers a wider range than the category of pervasive developmental disorders in the tenth edition of the International Classification of Diseases (ICD-10). . . . The fourth edition of the American Psychiatric Association's Diagnostic and Statistical Manual (DSM-IV) has definitions of pervasive developmental disorders and subgroups that are almost the same as those in ICD-10.[6]

At the present time there is neither a medical test nor a biological marker to unequivocally diagnose autism. The diagnosis is based on behavior. It is made "by obtaining a detailed developmental history (from infancy), from parents or other informants, with particular emphasis on the elements of the autism triad and repetitive behavior."[6] The terms *autism, autistic*, and *autistic spectrum disorders* are used interchangeably throughout this book to refer to the broader umbrella of pervasive developmental disorders (PDD).

In autism the most important predictor of outcome in future life has been found to be the child's initial level of nonverbal IQ. Next in importance ranked the ability to develop useful speech by the age of five years.[7] The three life histories described below under pseudonyms cover many aspects of the autistic spectrum.

CHAPTER 2

MARK R.

Mark R. was born with severe distortion of sensory perception. In contrast to the average child his perception of time and space was not synchronized with that of the world in which he lived, resulting in his internal time/space measurements coming into conflict with the reality of what surrounded him, causing him to constantly misjudge his environment. His concept of distance and depth being illusory, he tried to walk off the end of every wall not seeming to notice the sharp drop below him. When maneuvering himself down from a chair he tried to walk out onto the air as if it were at ground level. When he fell his skin never looked bruised and neither pain nor temperature appeared to register with his sensory receptors. His bright blue eyes never clouded with tears, even in the very worst of the tantrums never a tear would fall. Being hyperactive, he slept little. Periodically throughout the night, without waking up, he rocked on all fours in his crib, gyrating it around the room, sometimes jamming it in the doorway. Finally the crib had to be bolted to the floor.

Every few months the bars of the crib were raised higher and higher, until one night watching Mark managing to maneuver himself to the top of the bars and ready to crash five feet onto the floor below, it was decided that low was better than high. After that he slept curled up on two mattresses in a corner. From then on there was no formal bedtime, no tucking up, no bedtime story. After his bath he stormed around the room collecting toys from all quarters to make a large pile in the center. When exhaustion finally overcame him, he climbed onto the pile, and, oblivious to the hard edges of wooden blocks and metal cars, he slept. It was then possible to put him to bed on his mattresses, and there was peace for a few short hours.

There appeared to be few boundaries in Mark's perception and little concept of the limit of things. When out walking at dusk, breaking away from whoever held his hand, he ran out onto the road to touch the lights of oncoming cars, oblivious of their motion, focused only on their headlights. When night fell and the lighthouse flashed several miles across the bay, he leaned far out of his bedroom window, straining to touch the light. In neither case did his space parameters take cognizance of the distance. In the swimming pool the instructor invariably had to call out "Stop" when he reached the end of the pool. Otherwise he would knock his head against the tiles. He ran into the sea and the lakes fully clothed, his illusions of scale in conflict with that of the land and water around him.

He appeared to see objects in parts only and not as a whole. Could it be that the same eye or part of the brain, which for Mark magnified the head of a pin and made it seem so easy to remove, constantly magnifies certain aspects of the world, distorting it and fragmenting it? Could it be that what is seen is not seen as the sum of its component parts but only in terms of its individual components; as if the "uniting cohesive central force" that should draw it all together is missing?[7A]

The first noticed example of this seeming fragmentation of vision was seen in his obsession with the windshield wipers of cars. At the age of two Mark developed the first of his many obsessions. It was with windshield wipers. He sat for hours ecstatically fixating on the hypnotic rotating action of the wipers, when he seemed to enter his own Elysian fields; reclusive and remote, he was lost to the world around him. When he could not entice the driver to use the "ripers," he swished his hands from side to side in imitation and fixated on those instead. Once, slipping away from supervision in a parking lot, he did a rapid tour of the parked cars, standing all wipers out from the windshield like sentinels on duty. The cars did not seem to exist for him, yet the wipers had a life of their own. When looking for him during this period either in the house or garden, all one had to do was follow the trail of windshield wipers made out of sticks, stones, grass, pencils, and straws. They led unerringly to where he was to be found, putting the last set in place.

Then he discovered railway tracks and the trails of wipers gave way to parallel lines of Legos leading in, around, and out of every room in the house. These had to be left permanently in place; any attempt to remove them led to the most frightening tantrums. In an effort to turn this obsession into a more constructive pursuit, he was given a sizeable set of automated trains and tracks, but nothing would induce him to play with them in the normal way by running the trains on the tracks like his six-year-old peers did. He simply lined up the carriages as well as the tracks in two parallel lines and added them to the trails already occupying most of the floor space in the house. This type of *anxiously obsessive desire for the maintenance of sameness* was one of the defining features of autism for Leo Kanner.[4]

The same scenario was played out with any gifts of Legos that Mark was given. The set inside contained all the pieces necessary to make the aircraft or car attractively pictured on the box, but Mark never made the slightest attempt to put the pieces together in any constructive way. If the car or aircraft was made for him, the minute he got his hands on it he just dismantled it down to its basic pieces, adding these to the trails already on the floor. He appeared to have no capacity for pretend play and seemed incapable of playing with toys in a normal manner. Even though he had an intense interest in aircraft, this interest lay in a fixation with their shape and cataloguing their specifications. Never did he run around the room with a toy aircraft in his hand, simulating flight, like the average six-year-old.

Because the outward manifestation of autism can mean different behaviors at different ages but with a constant stereotyped pattern running through them, five years later the lines of tracks on the floors had given way to a life-size representation of the cockpit of an aircraft filling one corner of Mark's bedroom. As a special treat for his eleventh birthday a visit was organized to an aeronautics museum. Here he joined the line to sit for a few short minutes at the controls of a De-Havilland Rapide aircraft. When his turn came he took his seat at the controls and seemed to look into space with eyes unfocused, giving the impression that he saw nothing. But in reality he was scanning, recording, storing, filing away all details for future reference and within two days an exact representation of the interior of the cockpit had been reproduced in the corner of his room where it remained for three years. Every so often the data on the controls and dials was changed to simulate take off, landing, and many different flying conditions. This entailed constant changes in oil pressure, temperature, revolutions per minute, altitude, air speed, and so forth. Mark quite obviously had "special islets of ability," but they were stranded in an ocean of disability. This was a talent in isolation. Being automatic, this talent did not seem to be integrated into his whole personality but remained aloof, to be turned on and off at will, that will applying only to his obsessions. It was never possible to get him to use it for any constructive purpose other than that which interested himself. It could not be expanded or channelled.

To digress for a moment and ponder further the question of "savant talents," we go to the work of Professor Oliver Sacks. In discussing the nature of savant talents he considers them to be "a genuine intelligence, but intelligence of a peculiar sort, confined to limited cognitive domains." They are not just an expression of rote memory. He also writes that they "provide the strongest evidence that there can be many different forms of intelligence, all potentially independent of each other." In the past, he considers, there had been a tendency to write off savant talents as "freakish." More recently they tend to be regarded as "normal" intelligence but different in that they are highly specialized and developed to an advanced degree and, of course, in that they are isolated and not integrated with other intelligences, with personality, and emotions. To quote again, "It may be that savants have a highly specialized, immensely developed system in the brain, a 'neuromodule', and that this is 'switched on' at particular times—when the right stimulus (musical, visual, whatever) meets the system at the right time—and immediately starts to operate full blast."[8] At the philosophical level this explanation would equate well with the concept of inspiration.

Sacks indicates that savant talents do not appear to follow the pattern of normal development. They are fully fledged from their beginnings, "pre-set and ready to go off." Also they have an automatic quality about them as they do not occupy the mind or concentration fully, and they do not connect to the rest of the person as normal talents do. He suggests that this indicates a different "neural mechanism" from the one underlying normal talents. Also savant talents can disappear forever as suddenly as they appeared the first time. Normal talents, he holds, do not appear and disappear in this fashion. They develop gradually, integrating themselves with the rest of the mind and personality. They are not isolated units, incapable of being influenced from outside. In discussing the global power of the mind, Sacks suggests that the mind is more than just a series of talents; rather it is global in encompass, and that it is this global power of the mind "that allows us to generalize and reflect, to develop subjectivity and a self-conscious self."[8] He points out that Kurt Goldstein called this the "abstract attitude of the mind." In this connection it is interesting to note that the more "normalized" Mark became, that is, the more he developed "the global power of his mind," the more his "special islets of ability" seemed to become submerged or disappear; as if it was not possible to maintain both at the same time, as if one had to be developed at the expense of the other.

To return again to the story of Mark, later he moved on to a compulsive interest in weather conditions, amassing large files of figures on daily recordings of barometric pressure, temperature, rainfall, cloud cover, and wind speed and direction. During this period he also developed an intense interest in converting degrees centigrade to Fahrenheit with drawings of thermometers, both scales side by side and showing the conversion ratio, littering the available floor space. All his recorded figures were correlated, plotted, pie charted, graphed, and bar graphed; every forecast was recorded, and the walls of the den were festooned with the results. But again the focus was too narrow, too specific, the details too repetitious; there was never a cut-off point where the results could be analyzed and conclusions drawn. So the amassing of facts became an end in itself and not a means to an end. It was not possible to move Mark on to broaden the concept, to generalize it and apply it. He appeared to have no capacity for analysis of the findings, as if he could not bridge the gap between perception and cognition, as if he was stuck in repetitive mode. So the data remained forever unprocessed.

But we move ahead too fast. To return again to the younger years, Mark finally progressed from wipers to speedometers and revolution counters and by the age of eight was scouring the scrap yards for speedometers and other spare parts, amassing the best collection in the neighborhood. It was during this period also that a set of disused wipers appeared at the base of every window in the house.

During his very early years his inability to see things as a whole was not confined to objects. On one memorable visit to the zoo, on his third birthday, he stood at the elephant enclosure on a quiet Monday afternoon, a beautiful day in May. It was feeding time, and Jill, the eight-year-old elephant, was being hand-fed her after-dinner treat of sliced bread by her keeper. Mark watched, fascinated, quivering with excitement as Jill deftly swung the slices of bread, six to eight at a time, from the tip of her trunk to her mouth, coiling and uncoiling her long trunk, swinging it up and down. Seeing his intense interest, the keeper invited him to feed Jill and he was led across the enclosure. Fearlessly he fed the giant elephant a total of six large loaves as she gently took the bread from his small hands, swinging the tip of her trunk to her mouth back and forth. Mark watched, *fixated and utterly absorbed*. A mother standing nearby with an older child, remarked sharply to her offspring "Why are you afraid of the elephant? Look at that brave little boy, and you're much older!" Mark of course, was not being brave. He never actually saw the elephant. With his perception difficulties he was incapable of focusing on such a large creature and taking in the total picture. What he saw was the hypnotic rotating action of the trunk. The animal behind the trunk did not exist for him.

In the early years up to about age six, Mark showed all the classic features of *extreme autistic aloneness* described by both Leo Kanner and Hans Asperger as the cardinal feature of autism. People did not seem to impinge on his consciousness. In fact, he never appeared to see them except when, very occasionally, he sought them out to satisfy his basic needs. Instead he peopled his world with objects—first with windshield wipers and speedometers, then with dials and gauges, power tools, trimmers, lawnmowers, chainsaws, cars, flashing lighthouses. These were his fascinations and they absorbed him utterly. As for the house lights, they were flicked on and off ad infinitum. As long as the object either moved, made sound, or lit up, he became fixated with it. He gave the impression that he did not miss the human race, in fact he did not even seem to know it existed. In those early years standing beside him became something of an occupational hazard because he never appeared to even sense the presence of another person, let alone see them. Being a sturdy toddler and moving with speed, when he brought his head or his fist up fast, one was likely to get anything from a black eye to a dislocated jaw.

The challenge then was to get him to notice the human race and, having achieved that, to make it interesting enough for him to want to join it. His strong reaction to sound provided the key to this. From an early age Mark could be distracted from most undesirable behaviors by sound; either a song, a whistle, a high note, a very low note, a hum, an off-pitch key, an animal sound. Any new sound, song, piece of music, lullaby, or something he had never heard before worked. Music was used constantly to capture his attention, and having got it, to keep it focused on the singer. Gradually this made him aware of the people around him, and more and more he tuned in to speech. He learned to sing speech before saying it. It seemed easier. His strong reaction to music was very evident late one evening when a friendly visitor to the house volunteered to sing the bedtime song to a tantruming Mark with a view to calming him and settling him for the night. Unfortunately the visitor was tone deaf, and his spirited rendition of "Old Man River" was not *music* to Mark's ears! He was stunned into silence, and then the first and only real tears seen in his young life streamed down his face.

Eventually he learned to echo speech, and at age four, when asked one day "Mark, where are you?" back came the echo "Mark, where are you?" an exact mimic of the voice asking the question. Echolalia (see glossary) had begun. He did develop one constructive phrase that was used for every contingency—"Want ut-Have ut." Never pointing or gesturing, if he needed anything, simply catching the arm nearest to him he swung it in the direction of the object, using it as a lever. He had two very important strengths that were later to be of great benefit in teaching him to speak. One was an outstanding ability to mimic sound and the other an excellent rote memory. At three he could recite verbatim "The Lord's Prayer" in three different languages, English, Irish, and Latin; word perfect, but without comprehension. When taken to the eye specialist for a test at age two-and-a-half, he astonished the doctor by reading accurately every letter on the eye chart down to the last line. Apparently he had grasped the letters of the alphabet from having them pointed out to him on his building bricks as he lined them up along the floor. But this feat of memory was an exercise in shape recognition only. The meaning of the letters and what they stood for had not registered.

Mark's speech problem then, was not one of phonation. Rather it lay in the area of attaching meaning to words and in the lack of the ability to spontaneously produce words and phrases that had not already been introduced to him by ear in a given sequence. By age five it was possible to teach him speech as one would teach a very rudimentary course in a foreign language; that is, to fit words to a situation. He was able to mimic the stock phrases needed to cope on a daily basis, learning that the formula needed to get a drink was "I'm thirsty" and to get food "I'm hungry." Later this was expanded to "I want water," "I want orange," "I want bread and jam," and so on, to cover all the normal contingencies he was likely to meet with. Because of his excellent rote memory the magic words needed to produce the desired results were never forgotten. His diction was perfect. Every word was enunciated clearly because he was not producing the words spontaneously like the average five-year-old; he was just repeating learned phrases. But this enabled him to take a place in the world of his peers. He was, however, ten years old before he grasped the concept of "yes" and "no."

Just as Mark's internal concept of space was in conflict with that of his environment, so also was his concept of time. For him, time as we know it had little meaning. It was illusory, its passage an enigma, and it appeared to consist of disconnected fragments each an eternity in itself. Yesterday, last month, last year, a few minutes ago were all kaleidoscoped. His existence seemed to be lived in the ever-present now. Consequently, having neither a vision of hindsight nor foresight, his response to every situation was one of totality. When he was tired and upset there was no point in saying "We'll be home soon" because for him there was no concept of soon. There was only now.

As he grew from his second into his third year, Mark's parents, being extremely concerned about his lack of language, gradually began to see their son's difficulties with his environment in terms of a time/space perception deficit. They decided it was time to seek professional help. This proved to be both a futile and a painful process because at that time the parental culpability theory of autism still attracted support. A year later they emerged from the experience without even a diagnosis. As a fraught Mark rampaged his way through the offices of a number of clinics, his equally fraught parents found themselves having to give an account of their stewardship, while the spotlight was focused firmly on the parents *not* on the child. When the verdict was finally handed down, Mark's parents were found to be severely lacking in parental skills.

Disillusioned, they turned next for help to the literature, but could find no mention of even the existence of perception problems in children, let alone any solution. Eventually they came across a reference to some advanced work taking place in Australia on the lack of speech development in children. This research was of the opinion that a child had to have the ability to orientate himself properly in his environment both in time and space before he could develop language. If he did not have this ability, it could be developed with intense input and then spontaneous language would follow. This precept was based on the work of Dr. Jean Piaget. Piaget, the Swiss psychologist and the great observer of cognitive intellectual development in children, devised one of the most influential theories concerning the ways in which children come to know and understand the world around them by actively engaging with it. He lists space and time as two of the principal categories that intelligence uses to adapt to the external world, and he concludes that "It is by adapting to things that thought organises itself and it is by organising itself that it structures things." Piaget also suggested that before the brain can assimilate the abstract world, it has to have the capacity to absorb the world of the concrete.[1] More recently, in commenting on the connection between perception and conceptual thought in the young child, Sacks suggests that before language can make sense to the young child it has to correlate with his own individual experience, gained through his senses, of the world around him. If this does not happen then he will not be able to create meaning from language because he will not be able to internalize it. Consequently he will not be in a position to transcend perception and move to conception. The creating of this meaning is dependent upon his own sensory experience of the world.[9]

To return again to the story of Mark: Armed with their Australian reference of about ten lines in all, Mark's parents set out to correct this time/space perception deficit in their son. Joining their endeavor were a Montessori teacher and a swimming instructor. The process continued for years, and it was trial and error all the way. If something worked they stayed with it. If it did not, it was abandoned and the next feasible technique undertaken. Travelling uncharted territory the craters were many, but time brought results and slowly but surely Mark stopped walking off walls and hitting his head on the swimming pool tiles. He no longer ran out onto the road to meet cars nor had to be fished out of ponds. Much of this work was carried out in the swimming pool. Under the eagle eye of his swimming coach and with a parent always in attendance, Mark learned to swim; first the width of the pool and later the length. On completion of his first length he earned the green twenty-five-meter badge, which he proudly wore stitched onto his jacket. His next goal was the blue, two-length, fifty-meter badge. In time a row of colored badges lined both sides of the jacket as he swam his way up to ten lengths of the pool. He became so at home in his new medium that eventually, diving like a dolphin, he zoomed through the water gaining concrete experience of the phenomenon of depth.

His interest in measurement was harnessed to reinforce the work being done in the swimming pool. From an early age, having a natural interest in finding out how big or small and how high or deep things were, he had begun the task of quantifying his environment. The meter stick was his favorite tool, joined by the measuring tape and the ruler, and many a brick and stick were put between the jaws of the callipers. Maps were poured over using the map scale or just a simple piece of thread laid along the route and later run off against the scale. He experimented with the four components of shape, size, color, and location with exercises in "find the blue ball under the cushion on the chair" or "hide the small round box under the table." He was a natural experimentalist and in time worked out his own answers. Work in the sandbox gave him the opportunity to experiment with different textures; he loved to run the grains of sand through his fingers. He loved the feel of smooth marble alternating with rough sandpaper and of cold ice against his fingers contrasted with the warmth of water. In all of these experimental ways he began the task of improving his ability to correctly perceive the world around him through his senses, to synchronize his internal space illusions with the reality of what surrounded him, to gauge correctly, to develop stable judgment, and so to learn how to orientate himself in his environment in space.

By contrast, developing a sense of time was a long, slow, tedious process with few rewards along the way. There were even fewer signs of progress as there are no ground rules for gauging another's concept of the passage of time. He did not grasp it intuitively like others do. At this stage of development he had little faculty for abstracts and had to be given a yardstick to measure them by. That yardstick was a watch. With a fantastic eye for detail and prodigious memory, mastering the technique of using the watch or clock offered no difficulty. From the age of six he constantly wore a watch and always had two spare watches in readiness in case one broke down. When this happened panic set in until a spare watch was produced. In the meantime life came to a standstill. Often two watches were worn, one on each wrist, both very accurate. As long as he could hear the ticking of the watch, he felt secure, and slowly, imperceptibly, over the years a sense of the passage of time, the present, and future began to develop.

Stopwatch in hand, he timed everything, from the time it took the sound of the train to pass the house, to the time of the chime of the grandfather clock, as if he had an inbuilt knowledge of what he lacked and was building up a reservoir of time to draw on, automatically replacing the abstract with the concrete. Lining up his collection of egg timers, he loved to watch the grains of sand run out as the stopwatch clicked the seconds away. But it took him a long time to grasp the concept that time moved in one direction only. There was no going back. He could never return to his childhood because time had marched on and yesterday would not come again. Eventually he grasped this abstract concept by thinking of time in terms of a train on a single track, travelling across the plains but going in one direction only. Once he got this image he held it firmly in his mind and thoughts of returning to live in the past were fewer. Eventually he accepted the concept and stopped asking such questions as "When I'm three again will we go to the zoo again to feed the monkeys?"

One incident stands out in the mind. It pinpoints the difference between grasping the concept of time intuitively, and so establishing an intrinsic evaluation of it, as other children do, and learning it intellectually, as Mark was beginning to do. It was Halloween and a small friend, two years his junior, came to visit on Sunday afternoon as usual. This Sunday the clocks had been put back an hour as summer time had ended the night before. On leaving the house at the usual time this small visitor showed his surprise at the darkness outside: "Why is it dark at this time tonight when it was never dark at this time before?" Mark, whose concept of time was based on the dial on his wrist, had never even noticed the difference; intrinsic evaluation was lacking.

The sequencing of pictures in time was another big stumbling block for him. When faced with a series of pictures of, for example, the sequence of harvesting apples in an orchard in the autumn, he was very nonplussed, being quite likely to put the picture of the gardener returning the ladder to the shed first, long before the apples had ever been picked. Old comic strips were useful to work through this difficulty and to give him a sense of ordering events logically in time. When the comic strips ran out, pen and paper came to hand, and then he could give free rein to his impression of how events should be sequenced and have it corrected.

At first he kept track of the calendar of his life by relating events to dates, saying: "On 24 August 1978 we went to . . ." "On 15 March 1980 we got. . . ." "On 11 November 1981 at 4 o'clock in the afternoon, you said. . . ." His memory for dates and times of events was faultless. There was never any need to keep a diary. Mark could be relied upon to accurately produce all information needed, even down to the date and time the builder last came to fix a tile on the roof! For years he acted as the family database.

The calendar was the second yardstick he was given in the onslaught on time, and again there were two calendars, one weekly and one daily. Every night he peeled off the day and discarded it into the wastepaper basket, and every Monday he turned the page and again discarded the week that was. The third and most effective marker he devised for himself, using nature's oldest time piece, the moon. He became obsessed with the phases of the moon. These offered a stable and predictable event in his timeless, confused world, rising and setting with unfailing regularity; unfolding their shapes, from the sickle to the oval, to the round, as they moved across the sky from east to west with eternal precision, only to refold and move in reverse order, always on course, always on time, finally to disappear as predicted and reappear anew. A seasonless progression of time that never faltered, with a phase for each day. As the mariners of old navigated by the stars, Mark navigated and charted his daily course by the moon. He needed no sextant to measure the angle of elevation as each phase appeared above the horizon; he knew exactly where to look; it was indelibly imprinted in his mind's eye. Even in the worst of weather, a single glimpse of the bright patch marking the position of the phase was enough to satisfy him that the moon was in the heavens and all was well with his world. He could then sleep and face the morrow with confidence and security. At this period of his life he had no awareness of how illogical his obsession was. In one of his poems "Obsessions" (below the last verse) he depicts, with hindsight, the anxiety and stress he felt until he could see it.

I have seen it now
I can go to bed
At last I can lay down
My tired head.

Over time, then, the concept of next week or last month crept into his consciousness and seeped through his senses, and as this sense of perception grew so did his speech. Another measurement scale necessary to help with this distortion of perception was the thermometer, because even in his late teenage years Mark still could not perceive the meaning of being either too hot or too cold. He would happily run out into the snow in short sleeves, and sit sweltering in an overcoat in the mid-day summer sun. In the depth of winter he swam in the cold North Atlantic sea, standing on a deserted windswept beach to towel and dress. He appeared to have no innate evaluation of the concept of warmness and coldness as if his internal thermostat had been damaged. It was not that he did not *feel* the cold or heat. Rather it was that when he *felt* cold or hot he did not *know* what was wrong with him. He did not make the connection; as if he could not relate feeling to cause. So ground rules had to be laid down, "No sea swimming below a certain temperature"; "No overcoats needed above a certain temperature"; "When the sun is shining dress down"; "When the snow is falling wrap up." Thermometers appeared both inside and outside the house. In time, he learned to look every morning at the gauge on the wall outside his bedroom window and to dress according to the figures he saw there.

Throughout his early years Mark was hyperactive but apart from obsessions/fixations his activities were unstructured, and when it came to the ordinary everyday activities of life he was without motivation. If left to his own devices he would either return to his obsessions or his activity became aimless. He had a curious inertia of purpose when it came to tackling any constructive activity. An inability almost, to initiate, apart from his obsessions, constructive action. This is similar to what is seen in Parkinsonism. None of the factors that motivate the average child were built into Mark's system. He never imitated the actions of another. He knew no necessity to conform; saw no reason to please those around him; felt no pressure to emulate his peers; had no drive, no desire to excel; no sense of urgency to achieve, spurred on by the passing of time and the thought of a bleak future lying ahead; no motivation to leave the cocoon of his own world and build a bridge to the unknown around him; no internal desire to set out from his oasis in the *eye of the storm* and fly through the turbulence to the world beyond. Because, unlike the average child, Mark had no mental wings. They had either never developed in utero or had atrophied soon afterward. So he had to be enticed across the isobars, step by slow step. A bridge of motivation was slung high up above the turbulence; the slats were made of food.

Fortunately he loved food. His greatest delight was baking, when he took part and sampled the results. Baking sessions then became the order of the day and could be guaranteed to overcome all inertia. Mark, in his chef's hat and with wooden spoon, was master of ceremonies. In time these sessions were used to get him to read. The cook went on strike until Mark would read a little of the recipe for the food to be baked that day. If Mark was not motivated (which rarely happened) then the "goodies" had to be shop-bought and they never tasted quite so good, nor could he enjoy the "miracle" of watching the raw materials being transformed into the finished product. Later the cook went on strike again until Mark would write part of the recipe. As he learned his reading and writing through food, so also he learned his spelling. Eventually words like *pavlova* and *pineapple-upside-down* tripped off his tongue. It all made for painless progress. Had Mark not been a food enthusiast, motivation would have been a very real problem indeed.

Mark loved stories. He sat motionless and enthralled when someone read to him, and of all the stories read, his great favorites were the Enid Blyton Famous Five series. All twenty-one books were read to him again and again until, thumbed, creased, battered, chewed, and dog-eared, they finally dis-integrated, but not before they had given him the beginnings of speech comprehension. When the reading session began, Mark took the book in his hand and, quoting the previous three or four pages verbatim from mem-ory, he picked up the reader's hand, pointed to where they had stopped the previous time, and used his formula of "Want ut Have ut." He then listened spellbound, eyes riveted to the page, until finally the exhausted reader fell asleep and that was it until the next time. How long the session lasted was entirely dependent on the stamina of the reader!

Throughout his early school years he spoke in Famous Five language (the particular style of speech spoken by the children in the Famous Five series) and when his class peers were delightedly exclaiming "Great, we're getting our holidays tomorrow!" Mark said "Cheers, tomorrow we're breaking up for the hols." Fortunately the school contained pupils from a number of different countries so it passed relatively unnoticed. In the junior school Mark, having a great sense of fun and of the ridiculous, got on well with a certain section of his classmates. When there was mischief to be done, like letting frogs loose during choir practice, he was a willing participant. He was also very popular during examinations because of his great rote memory. Before the dreaded exams the whole class gathered around and tapped into his memory for anything from the Nika Riots of 532 to the full text of *The Owl and the Pussycat* by Edward Lear or perhaps to decline a French or Latin verb. These he delivered verbatim, but there was no point in asking him questions on mathematics or science, as he was incapable of seeing relation-ships and had few powers of reasoning.

In time Mark became one of the leaders of the school model airplane club. Having poor manual skills and "soft" neurological signs (see glossary), he did not excel at model making. Rather his forte lay in the fact that he could recite at will the exact detailed specifications of every World War I and II aircraft, including wing span, speed, bomb load, armament, engine design, and horsepower. His passion with aircraft of this period and earlier became the dominant obsession of his life. Even today, books and films about aircraft are top favorites. He still takes an occasional peek into one of his complete collection of Biggles books written by Captain W.E. Johns, that great flying ace of World War I. Mark's boyhood heroes were "The Red Baron," Erich Von Richthofen of World War I fame, and Douglas Bader of World War II. In more recent times these have been replaced by those two modern heroes of Formula One Motor Racing, Michael and Ralf Schumacher. Mark moves on.

By the age of ten his communication was based on a combination of learned formula, Famous Five language, and a very little spontaneous speech. Then, as his time/space perception improved, he began to gather momentum. Comprehension and ability to translate thought into word grew slowly, and by the time he reached his midteenage years he could just about hold his own with his peer group and pass for the quiet, shy type with some idiosyncrasies. Having virtually no spontaneous ideas, his speech was mainly concrete and functional. Often there was a time lapse of days or even weeks between Mark receiving information and being able to relay it; as if the information had been temporarily lost and could not be retrieved. When asked about this his answer was always the same: "I didn't know it then but I do know it now."

His lack of insight into his own behavior and the behavior of others was truly disconcerting. He could report other people's behavior but had great difficulty commenting on it, seeming to have no faculty for computing either his own thoughts or the thoughts of others; as if he could not stand aloof from his own thoughts and think about them from outside; as if he could not ruminate or cogitate about them. The when, where, and how questions—"When is the film on?" "Where is the match on Saturday?" "How did you miss the train?"—caused no difficulty. But the why questions seemed to hover in a void: "Why do you have to be in school early tomorrow?" or "Why did Hugh give you the book?" Such questions never received a satisfactory answer; one that would give any real insight into the cause. He seemed incapable of making a judgment or indeed incapable even of a single abstract thought.

Never knowing when someone was making a joke at his expense, he took the most outrageous comments seriously. To remedy this situation the family set themselves up as a drama group and using role playing began to develop in him some sense of his own thoughts and insights into the thoughts and behaviors of others. The mass media of television proved useful for this. All his favorite programs were taped, and much discussion was held on how and why the characters interacted as they did. No opportunity was lost to tap into his own thoughts, trying to give him some sense of introspection and retrospection. At the start the progress was negligible, but as with all his advancements, little by little, drip by drip, the rough surface was molded and polished; the seeds of insight were planted and the beginnings of introspection took root. From then on it was just a matter of nurturing the growth. Now well into his twenties, he writes poetry, much of it dealing with his own thought processes. A number of his poems have been published in magazines and books. The following poem describes his turbulent, racing thoughts in terms of music. It is called "The Drone of the Pipes."

The Drone of the Pipes

Tuning up the drones the hum begins,
Matching sound to chanter
The vibration swells in the
Auditorium of my mind.
Adjusting the drones
The low buzz sinister and eerie.

The Uileann Pipes, musical chimes,
The regulators combining full bodied pitch.
Harmony
Creating a blend of delicacy.
The Bag Pipes join in, the wail strident,
They howl and shriek.

Both sets of pipes play the same tune
A reel "The Mountain Road"
Another "The West Wind" starts off slow
Accelerates to a brisk pace.
Other instruments join, on the second count,
Fiddle, Flute and the Bodhrán
Banjo romps to the racing tune.
The vibrant drones dominate the background.

The elated mind speeded up
Reminiscent of time
That races on
Happy, joyous, full of life, laughing, freed
Like a race horse about to run amok.
Going like the wind
Speeding,
A car on the motorway.

Both reels have stopped.
The drones once again audible
For a few seconds more;
Time and thought cease suddenly
The drones die.
Golden silence; mind tranquil;
The audience rises
Clapping thunderously in applause.
And the "encore" begins.

Insight indeed; the labor had borne fruit! There was however an element of "savant talent" in Mark's poetry. It would be more true to say that he disgorged poetry rather than to say he wrote it. Writing poetry involves preliminary drafting and structuring and subsequent revision. Mark never did this. His poetry seemed to come to mind en masse, as a block. It flowed as he wrote it down. Sometimes it flowed as he walked, and somebody else had to write it down or it was lost. Thereafter he never looked at it nor changed a syllable. Months went by without his ever writing a word, then some stimulus, perhaps something like a butterfly, triggered off the impetus and he wrote several poems in a day.

Throughout his growing years Mark rarely made eye contact when he was speaking or being spoken to. Fixing his gaze at a point on the shoulder of his companion, he looked right through him. Every effort was made to get him to make eye contact but he did not appear to know where to look, saying "But I *am* looking at you. I'm concentrating very hard." In his younger years one of his very perceptive teachers had picked up on this point. In filling in Mark's Christmas report this teacher wrote the following comment: "Mark's apparent inattention is, in fact, hard concentration." It had been noticed that on the rare occasions when Mark did make eye contact he always used his peripheral vision, thus using the rod cells of the retina, which do not have strong visual impact. These rod cells are distributed around the periphery of the retina and are the cells we all use for vision in low light intensity. The cone cells, by contrast, are located in the fovea of the eye. This is the point of keenest vision, where the cells are specialized for perceiving fine detail and also of course for color. In scanning and recording the minute details of his environment, Mark obviously made use of the fovic area. But what about faces? Could it be possible that Mark was processing facial recognition with his peripheral vision? It was time for reflection.

Memory harkened back to a young Mark who never seemed to recognize any of the characters in his favorite black and white television shows unless he could hear them speaking. The same young Mark who loved rubbing and sniffing hair and treated every visitor to the house to an enthusiastic display of hair rubbing and sniffing. The family had long been used to this treatment. This antisocial habit had been actively discouraged as he grew older, but although the rubbing stopped, he never lost his interest in hair. When meeting somebody for the first time, he took great notice of their hair while listening attentively to their voice. Was it possible that Mark was using hair color, and perhaps texture and smell, as well as voice, to recognize people? Could he have difficulty with perceiving faces? A question was tossed at him one day: "Mark what color eyes have you?" He did not know the answer. Looking quickly at the eyes of the speaker, using his peripheral vision, he said "Brown!"—it was the wrong color. Why did Mark not know the color of his own eyes? The short answer was because he never looked in the mirror. All his life he had avoided mirrors; any effort made to get him to look in one caused great distress. But it went deeper than that. Mark, at times, can see neither his own face in the mirror nor the faces of those around him. He can always see hair and clothes, but not faces. In the mirror he can see the shape and color of his hair and the shape and color of his clothes but most times there is nothing in between. The most disconcerting aspect of this perception is its variability, as faces seem to appear and disappear at will, so that when he looks in the mirror or at people he never knows if he is going to see a face or a space.

On probing further into this question it transpired that Mark, even though now well into his twenties, is processing facial recognition below the ten-year-old level. He has three levels of face perception: (1) no face visible; (2) piecemeal processing, being able to see eyes laughing, lips moving, or a forehead wrinkled in perplexity; and (3) being able to see a full normal configurational face. Shortly after this revelation it was discovered that Mark had no difficulty with seeing faces on color television. To use his own words, "On television a person's face can be viewed in the whole context without fragmentation." At this juncture a long-running video was made of family and friends, and Mark could then see himself properly for the first time and find out the real color of his eyes. When, years previously, videos of his favorite programs had been used to give him insights into the thoughts and behavior of others, none of the family had even the remotest idea that he had a problem with face perception. Further probing revealed that he has no difficulty with processing faces in photographs or magazines, provided they are in color. But faces in black and white photographs and photographs in sepia come and go like "faces in the flesh" and in white light. Conversely, the human face seen in colored light, for example, standing under a street lamp, is quite visible in contour. Another bit of the jigsaw puzzle now began to fall into place. The reason why the color on Mark's television was always set at maximum strength, giving a strong technicolor picture, was now becoming apparent. As a result of these new discoveries, mirror work and face perception exercises were undertaken with Mark. These included using the sense of touch, the tips of the fingers, to explore the outline of the face at times when it is not visible. Now when Mark looks in the mirror if he cannot see his face he will slowly trace the skin of his face area with the tips of his fingers, and this solid feeling of reality beneath his hands can help to bring it into focus. It has also become obvious that his degree of face perception is closely allied to anxiety levels; on days of high or acute anxiety levels, all faces are just a void. As expected, on calm days perception is better and finger exercises bring better results.

It has been pointed out that faces are, socially and biologically speaking, probably the most important structures surrounding an individual, and there is no doubt but that they are one of the principal ways of differentiating people from inanimate objects.[10] Small wonder then that Mark paid no at-

tention to people in his earlier years. It was the sound of the human voice
that first alerted him to the presence of his fellow beings. Over the last ten
years there has been a growing body of evidence in the literature to show
that some people with autism have a face perception deficit. This will come
up for further discussion later.

Mark also had a perception problem with his limbs. Most times he could
not feel exactly where they were unless he could actually see them. As a
young child struggling with shoe laces and zippers, his phrase of "Hands
won't do what they're told" became familiar, and when this happened, in
frustration he slapped his hands and bit them. This probably helped him to
feel where they were. Often, as a young toddler he bit the hand nearest to
him because he could not locate his own. In contrast to the average child
Mark never developed proper hand specialization; having no dominant hand,
he was neither right- nor left-handed. Instead he used his right hand for
work on the right side of his body and his left hand for work on the left.
The average child will not do this. He will specialize one hand for fine motor
work like writing and using tools.

Even when Mark bit himself he never felt pain and his hands never looked
bruised. At times he complained that his hands felt like "inert lumps of iron,"
and he liked the solid feeling of the watch straps on both his wrists. He
explained that this made it much easier for him to feel exactly where his
hands were. This calls to mind the work of Carl Delacato, which will be
reviewed later.[11] Much time was given to exercises designed to improve
Mark's ability to feel his hands with greater ease, and slowly over time this
feeling of inertness receded, and as he became more dextrous it disappeared.

In summertime it was not possible to get him to wear a short-sleeved shirt
or shorts. Eventually the reason for it came to light—if his arms and legs
were not covered in similar fashion to the remainder of his body, they gave
him the impression of being detached and floating. He found this very disconcerting, and it may well have been associated with his faulty sense of
depth perception and whatever way his exposed limbs reflected the light
differently. Possibly due to a reduced sense of proprioception (see glossary),
he could not feel his limbs with ease and consequently he relied heavily on
his vision to know where they were. When they were not dressed in similar
fashion to the rest of his body, they lacked the visual continuity he needed
to locate them.

Of all Mark's perception problems his faulty perception in depth took the
longest to remedy. Even in his late teens bridges were still a challenge. If
he looked down into the water he felt it rushing up to meet him and feared
being engulfed. He developed a great terror of wide rivers and at times
crossing over was well-nigh impossible for him when he was both young
and not so young. When climbing stairs, if he looked up, he felt the ceiling
coming down to meet him, if he looked down, he felt the floor rising up.
Fearing being mangled between the two, he often stood immobilized in the

middle, not able to move up or down. Then he had to slide down on his seat or be led down slowly by the hand. The strength of his reaction depended on such factors as the height of the stairs, the way the light shone on it, the angle, the color.

Around this time he heard about a special type of perspex colored filters, called Irlen Filters, being used successfully with scotopic sensitivity syndrome (see glossary), with dyslexia, and some other conditions, and also with people who have a distortion of depth perception. These filters are worn as glasses, and they work on the principle of altering the timing by which visual information is received and processed. They are tailored to the individual's needs.

It was decided to try them. Mark went for the test which revealed that he did have scotopic sensitivity. On wearing the filters his depth perception improved. Crossing wide rivers is now no longer such a great worry, and he will hop on an escalator with ease and comfort. However it has been found that anxiety levels play a part here also. The least improvement is seen on days of high anxiety levels. The Irlen Filters, however, brought only minimal improvement in face perception. At the times when faces were just a void, they made no impact (there were obviously other factors at work here), but they did bring about a slight improvement in piecemeal processing. Also, they helped to produce far more legible handwriting and the ability to read comfortably for long periods of time. Reading had always been difficult for Mark because he kept losing his place when the letters moved about the page and the text kept getting blurred.

In his early twenties Mark received a professional diagnosis of Asperger syndrome from a clinician who specializes in the Asperger field. This specialist stated that on the basis of Mark's past case history and records his original diagnosis would have been Autistic Disorder. He also explained that Mark, in common with many other young people, had moved along the autistic spectrum from the classic Kanner type autism to the more high-functioning Asperger type.

Shortly after this Mark underwent a cognitive assessment. His WAIS-R profile presented a Verbal Scale IQ (VIQ) of 98 and a Performance Scale IQ (PIQ) of 74. His Full Scale IQ was 86. The picture that emerged from the WAIS-R was that of a young man with visual-motor, perceptual, and spatial visualization difficulties. His strengths were in the area of language development, memory, richness of ideas, and fund of information. He had difficulty deciding between essential and nonessential details, and he might overattend to details in his environment and as a result miss relevant cues. This led to social misinterpretation and confusion. This also affected his capacity to anticipate, judge, and understand the possible antecedents and consequences of events or situations. He achieved an adequate comprehension score and a low picture arrangement score, which suggested that he could understand social situations in the abstract but once he was involved with them he was unable to decide what they might mean or to decide how to act. His ability to recall facts appeared to be influenced by habitual, overlearned responses. His short-term memory related to his interest in the task, the function or meaning of the task, and his motivation to succeed. His performance on arithmetic, vocabulary, and object assembly subtests showed that when he had a framework to superimpose on a set of problems he would succeed. If the rule was clear, concrete, and effective, Mark would use it.

The above pattern of significantly higher VIQ and lower PIQ has been found in some recent studies undertaken to compare the cognitive profiles of children with high-functioning autism (HFA) with children with a diagnosis of Asperger syndrome (AS). Only the AS children showed the significantly higher VIQ and lower PIQ pattern. In the HFA group these were not significantly different. This suggests a relationship between the AS individuals and a specific subgroup of learning disabilities called the nonverbal learning disabilities (NLD). This will be discussed in more detail later.

In addition to this cognitive assessment Mark also underwent a full range of metabolic testing to establish if he had any inborn errors of metabolism. On analysis there was no evidence of any metabolic disorder. It is estimated that the percentage of children with autism who prove to have an identifiable metabolic disorder is probably less than 5 percent and that at present most of the biochemical analyses are useful only as research tools in an ongoing effort to understand the biology of autism.[12] Mark also underwent a computer tomographic (CT) scan (see under brain imaging in glossary), but this did not show up any abnormalities. Throughout the 1970s and 1980s there was a perception that a CT scan should be performed as part of the assessment of children diagnosed with autism. However, it has now been realized that the CT abnormalities found in the brains of autistic individuals were associated only with the presence of coexisting disorders and not with the autism itself.[12] The clinical perception that structural brain imaging should be routinely performed in assessment in autism has now changed because research has shown that a series of CT and magnetic resonance imaging (MRI) (see under brain imaging in glossary) studies of autistic subjects, previously screened to exclude those with disorders other than autism, have confirmed the absence of brain abnormalities that would be characteristic of autism.[13] Finally, Mark underwent twenty-four-hour EEG (see glossary) testing to detect the possible presence of seizure activity. While this did show some abnormalities, the findings were inconclusive and no definite result could be drawn from them. On analysis of research to date it is considered that there is inadequate evidence at the present time to recommend EEG studies in all individuals with autism.[12]

CHAPTER 3

❧✦❧✦❧

JOHN K.

John K.'s case history is used to highlight the extreme sensitivity to sound (hyperacusis) found in some autistic people. John is a high-ability young man with a professional diagnosis of "subthreshold autism" or "atypical autism." He is solitary, a loner preoccupied with his own special interests and obsessions. He remains emotionally detached. His isolation was evident from a very early age when at ten or eleven months he went rigid when picked up, arms and legs stretched out bar tight, rejecting all human contact. In shopping malls and crowded places he quivered and trembled with tension. As a toddler he put up massive resistance to being held, never clinging or holding on. Instead he kept himself rigidly aloof, fighting like a little tiger to get free, screaming until he was put down again. He strenuously resisted every overture to touch, particularly light touch. The gentler the touch, the worse the reaction. Eventually it was decided to accept his rejection and stop trying. When out walking he twisted and pulled at the hand holding him while setting up loud demands to "Walk a'own." As he grew older a friendly punch in the arm was taken as a mortal insult because of the impact it had on his skin, and he attempted to hit back at anyone jostling him in a crowd. A light, affectionate touch on his face was met with "Don't hit me again."

From an early age he refused to wear certain clothes. His skin seemed to crawl, and at times it was possible to observe a ripple going through it. He constantly complained of the sensation of goose pimples all over his body. Obviously suffering from tactile overload, he often felt there was something touching his skin, and he shivered and itched for no apparent reason. "Mear-sie" was the word used to reject rough scratchy clothing, saying that rough clothing tormented him. Every effort was made to ease this situation by buying all clothes on the basis of comfort and keeping a wary eye on cosmetic products.

Of all his sensitivities, sound caused the greatest distress, and his reaction to it dominated the harassed household for half a lifetime because when the sensory overload became too great John headed straight for the nearest wall and banged his head. This harrowing sound reverberated around the house, the hammer blows ricocheting from wall to wall. All attention was riveted on where in the house John was at the time, and the nearest family member ran with the cushion trying to get between John and the wall. Often they arrived too late. Every conceivable strategy was tried to stop John's head banging but nothing worked. When he came to a certain pitch of sensory overload, it appeared to be the only course of action that brought relief. Eventually the walls in all the rooms in the house frequented by John were heavily lined with insulating styrofoam to cushion the impact.

He appeared to have no defense against the constant cacophony of sounds bombarding his eardrums. It greatly hampered his ability to function. Every sound, great and small, impinged. Lying awake at night, he tossed and turned, distracted by a wandering snail feeding inside his window or the hum of the electricity pulsating through the house wires. He heard the phone ring as the impulse travelled down the line, long before the first peal ever sounded in the house. Calling out "Phone," he then dashed madly to pick up the receiver almost knocking down whoever got in his way. In the course of time, the old-fashioned fire-alarm bell was replaced by one of the new muted electronic phones, and to everyone's surprise he stopped answering it. Apart from still calling out "Phone" before it even rang in the house, he lost all interest, and there was no longer any danger to life and limb. Apparently the sound of the bell had felt like a pneumatic drill going through his brain, and his instant reaction had been to stop it at all costs. Cognizance was then taken of the other loud bell in the house, the doorbell. John had also made answering the front door his top priority, often leaving the caller standing unannounced in the hallway. The doorbell was then transformed from a "laser-like-stab" (his words) to musical chimes, and he never answered the front door again. Having no great verbal facility for communicating his feelings, John instead used behavior strategies. The family learned very early on that every behavior tells a story.

He was musical and had perfect pitch. As a result he was abnormally susceptible to distortion of sound. This was very obvious when a helicopter passed overhead. He was visibly effected, not by the noise of the engine as might have been expected, but by the "whup, whup" of the displacement of air as the rotor blades revolved. No matter how high up the chopper was, he heard and felt it. This vibration caused him to lose concentration and lose touch with reality, often slipping into psychosis. These short periods of psychosis, although temporary, were intensely vivid.

The sound of a vacuum cleaner set off one of his strongest reactions, the high-pitched whine causing him to head for the nearest wall. Long after the vacuum cleaner had been switched off, John could still hear it in his mind, and in times of stress it returned to plague him, even though the vacuum cleaner was nowhere in sight. This internal sensory interference is called "white noise," and it is thought to greatly decrease the system's ability to deal with the world.[11] John could not cut out white noise, which came to him from a number of sources including helicopters, harsh strident voices, certain car engine notes, and similar vibrations. This white noise, coupled with the noise in his environment, led to great distractibility and at times made it impossible for him to concentrate on speech. When he reached this stage of overload, his face was ashen grey, particularly the center of his face, his nose, and upper lip. They stood out with an almost luminous pallor in sharp contrast to the rest. The greater the overload, the longer it took him to clear the backlog. After a day at school it took at least three hours of peace and quiet to clear the system. Whenever he was given more than one instruction at a time, he called out "Too much static coming in, system overloading!"

Throughout his young years his hearing was checked professionally a number of times, but his hyperacusis was never picked up on. Possibly the instruments used were not sensitive enough. So over the years the family just geared its lifestyle and activities to try to cope with it. Household appliances were never used when he was around. They were either put on hold for years or used when he was out of the house. The egg whisk took the place of the electric mixer, and after years of obsolescence the broom reappeared from the broom cupboard. The one exception was the dishwasher. John loved the swish of the water, just as he loved the swish of fast cars on a road or the sound of the breeze whistling through the trees.

Occasionally he has had the experience of synesthesia when his senses became scrambled and he saw sound in terms of light and felt taste in terms of texture. A certain frequency of low, eerie sound always produced circles of black and white light before his eyes, rather like the haloes of light experienced in some forms of migraine, and the taste of a certain type of cake containing sage and honey produced the image of mink that he could touch and rub with his hands. People with synesthesia have their senses hooked together. In their world one sensation involuntarily conjures up another, and when they hear certain sounds they see color at the same time. In one doctor's case the sound of her beeper always produced three brilliant red lightning bolts in front of her eyes, and the sound of a dog barking always produced white spikes. In another case, that of an architect, the taste of mint invariably produced tall columns of smooth ice-cold glass, which he could feel with his hands.[14] Synesthesia has been documented in the medical literature for over two hundred years, and in the general population it affects about ten people in every million. Very many of these are artists and musicians. While the most common form of synesthesia is sound/color, occurring when the sound and color channels become intertwined, sometimes all five senses clash together along with a feeling of movement. Synesthesia is thought to be a normal brain function in every one of us, but the actual working out of it appears to reach conscious awareness in only a handful of people. There is a strong link between synesthesia and photographic memory, and many synesthetes have strong powers of recall.[14]

Experiences very similar to synesthesia have been documented in people with autism.[15] In exploring the experience of autism through first-hand accounts, these authors report on a young man whose sensory channels get confused so that sometimes sound comes through as color. He also finds that sounds are often accompanied by vague sensations of movement or texture, or perhaps shape, color, or scent, and that sound stimuli can also interfere with other sensory processes like sight and taste. Synesthesia is thought to be located in the limbic system of the brain, and as a result stimulants like the caffeine in coffee and tea will reduce it, while alcohol, which damps down the cortex of the brain and turns up the limbic system, will make it more vivid.[14]

As John grew older his extreme sensitivity to sound did not diminish. Most of the coping was done by avoiding the situation where possible. The family, continuing to research new ways of coping, came across some literature describing the use of sound filters, worn as ear plugs, to treat people with hyperacusis. These were known as personalized ear protection (PEP) and were in fact linear sound filters. They attenuate or filter out both the higher and lower frequencies of sound. The criterion for design was based on the individual's audiogram. It was decided to try them. John had the standard audiology examination called an audiogram (see glossary). After this audiogram John was duly fitted for the sound filters, and the impressions were then sent abroad to be tailor-made to his needs.

On returning a few weeks later for the filters, John's normally booming, monotone voice was louder than usual, due to either excitement or nervous tension, as he entered the clinic. He stood quietly as the audiologist fitted the plugs neatly into his ears. Then the first big surprise came: "The noise in my head, it's gone; I can't hear the vacuum cleaner in my mind now," he said in a quiet voice that had dropped by at least two octaves. Later while having lunch in the canteen, he ate with total concentration speaking in a quiet normal voice, and when somebody dropped a tray full of dishes behind him, and all around him people jumped, he barely reacted. Turning around to see what had happened, he said quietly "Oh! somebody's dropped their dinner." In the past this incident would have been the cause of a major shockwave due to the sound sending a massive surge of adrenaline through his system. It would have provoked a strong reaction, possibly leading to some very embarrassing behavior as he acted out on the adrenaline rush.

Over the next six to eight months he wore the sound filters for an average of five hours a day, and gradually his ears appeared to become retrained to the sense of sound and became far less sensitive, even when he was not wearing the filters. Slowly but surely the head banging decreased and within a few months it stopped altogether. John never banged his head again. During this time also, his voice changed and gained some of the normal inflection and nuances of speech common to everybody. In explaining this he said "I always had so much noise in my head that I had to boom out on high power in order to hear the sound of my own speech above the din."

Over a year later the household appliances were back in use. He no longer needed to wear the filters as his hearing had become adapted to cope with the frequencies of sound that had caused such problems in the past. Now in times of stress and tension when the white noise returns to plague him, just wearing the filters for about half an hour will clear it. As time goes by he needs to use them less and less.

Little scientific research seems to have been undertaken into this problem of very acute hearing in autism. Most studies just refer to the fact that it exists. There is however one recent investigation that looked into it in some detail. Having investigated eleven autistic patients with hyperacusis, and eleven healthy controls, this study found that the cells in the medial olivocochlear system of the ear were altered in the autistic patients as compared to the controls. This alteration is believed to be correlated with hyperacusis. It is further suggested that the auditory attention deficit in autistic individuals may also involve this system. As yet there is no known treatment to improve the efficiency of these cells.[16] More recently other researchers have related hyperacusis to serotonin reduction in the forebrain.[17] Up to the present there has been virtually no help for autistic people who suffer from auditory processing problems because although sensory differences have been well documented clinically in autism, there is a scarcity of systematic research that could contribute to early diagnosis and individualized treatment for them. Now, however, that scene is beginning to change, and the call has gone out to the international research community emphasizing the need for both basic and applied research in this area.[18]

CHAPTER 4

BRYAN O'B.

Bryan O'B. was well into his teenage years when his life became severely complicated due to fluctuating blood sugar levels, strong allergic reactions, and depression. This presented itself in the form of intense irritability and agitation, coupled with a craving for sugar in all its forms. White bread, chocolate, sweets, cookies, and cakes were demolished by the handful. This in turn led to further agitation, and a spiral of downward behavior culminating in guilt and depression. Living with Bryan became something of a nightmare, like living with a keg of nitroglycerine, because one never knew when he was going to erupt.

After much trial and error to find the cause of this deteriorating behavior the path of alternative medicine was chosen, and Bryan was seen by a specialist in that field skilled in finding allergies and foods that are toxic to the system. The problem was very quickly pinned down and traced to its source, which was constantly fluctuating blood sugar levels due to the overconsumption of white sugar and refined foods, complicated by strong allergic reactions to certain other foods and an intolerance of gluten, the protein in wheat and in some other cereals. In addition, Bryan's immune system was obviously not functioning well because he was badly affected by Candida (yeast fungus), and he still carried the residues of former infections, including Salmonella, coupled with the residues of many of the childhood illnesses he had suffered from in his earlier years. These created a heavy burden on his immune system. We will see later that there is now an impressive body of evidence available showing the involvement of a faulty immune system in autism. Most, if not all, the studies undertaken on the immune system of autistic persons show immune dysfunction.

As a result of this consultation he was put on a diet free from all refined white sugar, white flour, yeast, caffeine, and gluten. This diet was woven around fruit and vegetables, fish, meat, and other sources of protein, natural sugars, for example, lactose, the sugar in milk, and high fiber gluten-free carbohydrates. These foods ensured the slow release of glucose sugar into the blood stream, thus stabilizing the level, which in turn prevented the constant fluctuations in blood glucose level he had lived with up until then. Certain other foods were added to this diet to improve and protect his immune system and to reduce the growth of the yeast fungus in addition to balancing the normal intestinal flora.[19] Homoeopathic medications were used to rid his body of residual infection.

Bryan adhered strictly to this diet for a period of eight months, and on the return visit to the specialist the results of his examination showed substantial physical improvement. But the greatest improvement of all was seen in his behavior. The irritability and agitation, which had been most obvious before meals, possibly due to low blood sugar level, were dramatically reduced, and as long as the meals were on time and the food plan strictly adhered to, his behavior returned to near normal.

Christmas came and with it the festive season. When surrounded by all the Christmas goodies, his will power failed, and succumbing to temptation, he fell a victim to the cakes and puddings and just about everything else in Santa's larder. Perhaps the resulting behavior is best glossed over. Let it suffice to say that the family learned a never-to-be-forgotten lesson: for Bryan overconsumption of white sugar, refined foods, and caffeine could be as explosive as gunpowder. It still remains a memorable Christmas for all the wrong reasons.

As long as Bryan kept to his food plan he remained well until a few years later, at the end of his first year in university, he began to suffer from a severe form of recurrent brief depression, preceded by a period of intense agitation and pacing. Prior to this he had not come to the attention of the psychiatric profession because up until then the family had been successful in managing his condition themselves and were loathe to burden him with the trauma of assessment and all the negativity of a psychiatric label unless there was help forthcoming. Bryan's parents themselves had never needed a professional diagnosis to realize that the condition that affected their son was autism. Now, however, they decided to seek professional advice because the scene had changed and this depression was severe enough to disrupt Bryan's studies and there *was* treatment for mood disorders.

The crippling, almost immobilizing, depressive phase of Bryan's illness lasted up to three days and came initially in a six-to-seven-week cycle. This very fast, rapid cycling mood pattern was very atypical, and as a result

Bryan's mood swings were wrongly diagnosed as being part of an autistic condition, whereas they were in reality a comorbid psychiatric disorder of very rapid cycling bipolar mood swings. As a result of this wrong diagnosis, he was treated with a standard antidepressant medication, and while on this medication his condition grew progressively worse because it resulted in swinging the moods into the manic phase of the illness. This made his condition much more serious and difficult to deal with. The highs he experienced were not the expected euphoric or elated highs, with their corresponding buzz of good feeling, but instead took the form of extreme restlessness with intense irritability and anger; a sensation of great uneasiness including severe pressure in his head. His speech was unstoppable as he frantically tried to outstrip his own racing thoughts. This type of elation is very distressing and is called a "dysphoric" elation. Much valuable time was wasted while different antidepressant medications were tried in an effort to bring the mood swings under control, and all the while Bryan's condition deteriorated. Eventually the family made contact with a clinician who was experienced in the treatment of autism and comorbid psychiatric disorders. Here Bryan received his correct diagnosis of rapid cycling bipolar mood swings, comorbid with high ability autism. Over time the mood swings were controlled with a standard mood stabilizer and a low dose of a neuroleptic medication (see under antipsychotic drugs in glossary), and without antidepressants, but Bryan never recovered sufficiently to be able to return to university and complete his studies. There are in the literature a number of well-documented cases of autistic children, some as young as six years of age, who developed the symptoms of bipolar mood disorder and were treated successfully along similar lines to those described for Bryan. In a number of these cases not only did the manic-like symptoms improve but also there was a marked improvement in the person's ability to function and cope and in their autistic condition as well.[20] The comorbid psychiatric disorders of autism will be discussed again later.

This addition of the secondary psychiatric disorder comorbid with his basic autism now made life very difficult for Bryan. There were so many situations that taxed him to the utmost in his ability to cope that panic was never far from the surface. Criticism was one factor he found very difficult to come to terms with. Perhaps because his ego was so fragile, his sense of identity so slender, any attack on it, even in the form of negative comments, was devastating and very damaging. Sometimes even ordinary advice was looked on as a form of criticism. A conversation, running along normal lines and going very smoothly, could suddenly erupt into anger when unintentionally a word or two of advice or constructive comment, crept in from the parent. In coping with Bryan's temperamental reactions a number of ground rules were laid down and strictly adhered to. The most important was "Never criticize, and couch all advice in humorous terms."

Perhaps his strong overreaction to criticism had something to do with his literal mind. So many people with autism interpret speech in its most literal sense. Every statement is taken as if it were the absolute truth and treated as such. It is not seen as possibly a generalization that can have many different interpretations, or that what is being said may often depend on the mood of the speaker. If one is a concrete, literal, thinker it can be difficult to interpret the overexaggeration of another's speech.

Bryan had a literal mind and was a visual thinker. His thought processes worked by association. Every thought and experience he had, he compared in his mind to an allied but totally different set of circumstances. For example, time was always seen in terms of a journey. He would visualize a bus on the road, and every marked event of the day was compared to a landmark along the way. The close of the day then was seen as the final destination. If the day passed quickly the journey was compared to a short route, and all the events related to actual towns, villages, hamlets, crossroads, and signposts on the route. This was his method of fixing them firmly in his mind. The events of the day could then be recalled by association. If the day seemed long and tedious, a longer route that he was familiar with was chosen, and again the same scenario played out. The following day the next journey began.

Generally speaking during the school year the journeys were long, with very many landmarks along the way. During the holidays they were short, the bus travelled at full speed, and the green fields and woodlands flashed by. In this way he developed powers of almost total recall. When he wanted access to any day of the year he just replayed the video in his mind. In the beginning it was difficult to make sense of Bryan's thought processes because they were associational rather than logical. One needed to be like Agatha Christie's great detective Hercule Poirot, and "Use the little grey cells, mon ami," to put the clues together and solve the mystery. Having done that, it was then easier to tune in to his wavelength and communicate more meaningfully with him, offering help when necessary. Because his thought processes worked visually and by association, he had a poor grasp of the principal of cause and effect, and as a result he often associated random facts. Such irrational thinking led to confusion and uncertainty, generating fear in what must have seemed a very unpredictable world, because in Bryan's mind the same incident, which could occur again and again, was rarely associated with the same antecedent. Each time he looked for a different cause for the same effect. He appeared to have few mental structures in place to form a bulwark against this. This innate impairment in the principle of causality led to what appeared to be an extraordinary absence of common sense. So what was to be done? Much effort was invested in learning examples of the principle of cause and effect—"if you do this, that will happen," "this will happen, if you do not do that," "what is the cause of this action?" "what is the effect of that happening?" It grew into a game that was played out on paper. Bryan became vitally interested and very innovative in thinking up new examples so that the drawing sheets were covered with little blue boxes labelled "go to cause" or "find effect," with red arrows darting to their targets. He grasped the principle relatively easily. But translating it into action "on the ground" was much more difficult. It soon became obvious that it was going to be a giant step for him to bridge the gap between the "knowing" on the one hand, and the "applying," when in everyday situations, on the other.

So the ultimate answer to all of this was to develop in him a sense of logic, and to move him away from thinking by association, to thinking in sequence by logic. In other words to give him another way of learning. The more he brought his intelligence to bear on his thought processes the easier this became. The process is ongoing.

Another serious drawback to thinking by association arose when he came up against a word with a number of different meanings. One such word was *fox*. When he first heard the word *fox*, it referred to an animal with fur. Shortly afterward some friends with the surname of *Fox* come to live in the neighborhood. One day he was offered a sweet called a *Fox* mint, and finally he learned that you could *fox* people. Because he connected up events in his mind using key words, the concept of the same word having four very different meanings upset his modus operandi, and because of this, at times, many of his comments were irrelevant to what was going on in the conversation around him. One wonders if there are other languages where this does not happen. This predicament was very evident in conversation when a specific topic was being discussed. A conversation that had begun about somebody getting a *fine* for speeding, would suddenly veer off into a discussion of the weather, and if tomorrow would be *fine* enough for a picnic, leaving everyone around the table totally nonplussed, wondering what was the connection. This was known in the family as "Bryan hijacking the conversation." However, if the discussion was traced back to its origin, the key word that caused the shift could always be found. The real confusion arose when there were too many shifts, and no topic could be followed to its logical conclusion. Then, if there were guests present, the situation took on all the nightmarish quality of the mad hatter's tea party in a scene from *The Adventures of Alice in Wonderland*.

Because Bryan was impulsive and loved to share his ideas in conversation, it took a long time to turn this situation around, and to prevail on him to follow the conversation rather than trying to lead it when guests were present. A target was then set. His brief was to listen and fit in with the subject under discussion, and then and only then, when he had a relevant comment to make, should he join in and make it. As a reward he was promised a time at the end of the evening when he could give free rein to his obsessional interests. Slowly it worked, and in listening to logical, sequential, thought processes, and waiting for his turn to join in, he learned much. He learned to discipline his mind and prevent it from following a trail of words. Instead he had to follow a single line of reasoning to its logical conclusion. From this he gradually began to develop the beginning of logical thought. He was learning to learn by another route.

Having little concept of the abstract, he had little ability to integrate it into his thinking. When, as a very young child, he first heard the metaphor "It's raining cats and dogs," he ran to the window to look out calling "Where cat, where dog?" Then a look of great disappointment spread across his face when all he saw was the rain pouring down. Gradually all the common proverbs, metaphors, and idioms were taught to him and their meanings explained. Then, should he came across them in conversation, he would know what they stood for and not be confused. This strategy worked well. One such metaphor was "I run on a very short fuse." Very early on in life he latched on to this and used it to explain his own temper tantrums. As he had a very low frustration tolerance level, this statement was particularly appropriate. But while Bryan could use proverbs and idioms and accept them in the conversation of others, there was always a question mark over whether he had any real appreciation of them. The family often laughed together over the "it's raining cats and dogs" story, until one day very many years later, Bryan himself turned the tables when he came home from school saying,

I must tell you a funny story I heard today. It's about two pilots flying a B25 over London during the war. They were delivering spare parts to a bomb factory. As they approached the city in a rainstorm both oil-pressure gauges dropped to zero and the engines ran rough. They began to lose height fast, and the captain decided to jettison the cargo. Peering into the murk through the swish of the wipers he said, "Heck! it's raining cats and dogs." Under his breath the copilot muttered "It sure is, and in a minute it'll be raining Datsun cogs!"

After this incident it was unanimously decided that Bryan's proverbial education was now complete.

In his early years in common with many children with autism, Bryan reversed his pronouns and referred to himself as "you" and never "I." He always used "I," "me," and "mine" to refer to the other person and you and yours to refer to himself. Much has been written about this pronominal reversal in autism, and some writers attribute it to a lack of the concept of identity, a lack of the appreciation of self, that is thought to exist in at least some people with autism. But in Bryan's case it was just another example of his associational thinking. Because if we look at pronominal reversal logically from the standpoint of associational thinking, it makes sense. If you are constantly called "you," and told that things are "yours," then you begin to associate the words "you" and "yours" with yourself. If the other person always refers to himself as "I," and says "that's mine" and "give me that," then "I," "mine," and "me" become associated with the other person.

One day Bryan came home from school in a dilemma. Christmas was approaching and he wanted to give a present to his teacher. He had just enough money to do that but was afraid his mother would be offended if she also did not get a present. So his dilemma was translated into "How would it be if *you* gave teacher a present because *you* haven't much money and *I* wouldn't get anything? Would *I* be sad for *you* to leave *me* out of it?"

Studying other languages, in this case Irish and French, gave Bryan a concept of the rules of grammar, and just as he had to learn the right pronouns to use in each case with regard to both these languages, so in time he learned the rules of English grammar and having learned them, began to apply them without any great difficulty. His approach to the English language was an intellectual rather than a natural one. It was akin to learning a foreign language when one does not think in that foreign language but learns the rules of it sufficiently well to be able to express oneself in it. Because of this, in his early years his speech at times was slow and halting as he grappled with the problem of translating associational speech into the logical, sequential speech of those around him. As with all foreign languages the more practice one has, the better one becomes, and eventually one becomes practiced enough to actually begin to think in that foreign language. So it was with Bryan. As he grew older he was more and more able to bring his intelligence to bear on his thought processes and translating the associational into the logical became easier. As always, progress is ongoing, and as with Mark R., it would appear that once the first breakthrough was made and the foundation laid, momentum is gathered through the years.

An example of Bryan's use of words in associational thinking of a different kind was evident when he came home very late one evening, having been to the barber to get his hair cut. The conversation went something like this.

Mother: "Bryan you're very late, what happened?"

Bryan: "They were very busy. I waited hours."

Mother: "That's a surprise because this is normally a quiet time. Maybe they were *short* staffed."

Bryan: "That must be it. The last time I was very quick. They were *long* staffed then."

Bryan talked constantly to himself throughout his youth and teenage years. The current thinking at that time was to actively discourage this practice, and with Bryan it was actively discouraged. Who is it that said "We are all victims of the age in which we live"? Now the pendulum has swung the other way, and it is being realized that it can be beneficial for people with autism to talk to themselves because it helps them to get in touch with their own thought processes and keep the communication lines open. Also it is a valuable practice in transferring thought into word and helps to break the feeling of isolation. In addition some autistic people cannot always tell exactly where their body boundaries are, and talking to themselves can improve their sense of orientation.

Bryan had a tenacious tendency to perseverate (see glossary) either in thought or word. This phenomenon of repetitive thoughts, questions, and arguments is a common one in autism and can be very wearing and difficult to deal with. Because Bryan's need for reassurance was so great, it was never sufficient to answer a question just once or twice. It had to be answered again and again, the salient points discussed, and the same arguments put forward to prove the point, not just a dozen or two dozen times, but ad infinitum. At times like this he had great difficulty breaking off from a certain train of thought, as if he was stuck in a groove and could not shift attention. It was always an indication of a high anxiety level and inner turmoil, often giving an exact opposite impression to the reality of what he was feeling. For example, it took the family a long time to realize that when Bryan perseverated about going on a journey, making minute plans and going over each one in detail time and again, thus giving everyone the impression that he was looking forward to it, the reality was he did not want to go because it was too anxiety-provoking. He himself did not seem to be aware of this; he needed to be brought face-to-face with it, and when he was the perseveration stopped immediately.

In these cases, staying calm and reasonable and answering each question logically rarely worked, so a coping strategy had to be worked out over time. Eventually it was found that if this cycle of repetition was interrupted at the beginning, by getting him to write down his thoughts, questions, and line of reasoning, and the answers he himself could come up with, then a much clearer picture emerged. It was then possible to pin down the real cause of his problem and hopefully solve it. He understood issues much better when the facts were written down and teased out. He needed the visual impact of the words to clarify his thoughts and feelings. He owned a small portable typewriter, having learned to type in his teenage years. The very act of typing it out on paper helped enormously to get to the root of the problem and to stop the tendency to perseverate.

To return again to the question of criticism, as Bryan grew older he was able to explain why he reacted so badly to any form of criticism. Because he was very self-critical and intolerant of his own mistakes, he believed that any criticism levelled at him from outside was true. This made him feel worthless and useless. Always he had tried to live up to what was expected of him, and having his defects emphasized meant failure. "It shattered his ego," to use his own words. In the face of it he could never get his thoughts together quickly enough to defend himself or put forward his viewpoint. A verbal defense was never possible. Then fear of failure crept in, and the stab of fear brought with it the inevitable surge of adrenaline and the inevitable angry reaction.

He attended mainstream schools and found criticism from teachers particularly difficult to handle. Working long hours, he toiled over the home-work at night and on weekends. When his work was criticized he felt his efforts were neither recognized nor appreciated. Most teachers probably do not realize how damaging criticism can be for some students, particularly those with a poor self-image. Even in the life of the average child the class-room can be a hostile enough environment at times. Because high-ability autistic people are more sensitive than others, they become more aware of how different they are, and they try all the harder to measure up to the normal standard. Consequently the school routine makes enormous demands on their resources.

As he entered his teenage years the gaps between himself and his peers began to loom large on Bryan's horizons. It brought with it an understand-able amount of anxiety. Integrating a more advanced autistic child or ado-lescent into mainstream school is a daunting task indeed and requires all the combined resources of the child, the parents, and the teachers. At adolescent level, in the average mixed-ability class of thirty or so students, the mettle of any teacher who tries to do justice to the abilities of each student will be tested. Allied to this mixture of abilities will be the presence in the class of a number of students who are emotionally disturbed, others with perhaps visual or hearing impairments, others again from disadvantaged back-grounds. Most teachers rise superbly to the occasion, and Bryan's were no exception.

To look more objectively at the classroom situation, the problems Bryan faced were two-fold, caused by, firstly, an uneven intellectual profile, and secondly, his system's inability to cope at the sensory and emotional level. He had the necessary intelligence to achieve at an academic level, but fell far short at the human resource level in dealing adequately with the day-to-day stresses and strains of the system. This was compounded by the close proximity of large numbers of people. At times schools are among the nois-iest places in the world. The fourth component in the equation was that scourge of all school systems—the school bully or bullies.

His uneven intellectual profile showed the expected strengths and weak-nesses. His lowest scores were in imaginative and abstract thinking and in both abstract and mechanical reasoning, while his strengths lay in an excel-lent memory, both visual and auditory, an accurate ear for languages, and a love of words. He always received full marks on the aural tests, but fared badly at comprehension. In history he relied on his great rote memory for facts. In geography his ability for visual recall (maps, contours, etc.) earned him good marks. In music he had no difficulty with the concepts of pitch, tone, harmony, and rhythm and could write the score for a piece of music at first try. Biology was one of his favorite subjects. From an early age he had learned the Latin name of every tree, shrub, and flower in his environ-ment. Words like "photosynthesis" and "transpiration" came readily to him when other students were grappling with these strange sounding names.

Later when studying the complex biochemical details of these processes, he had no difficulty reproducing them in diagram form, due to his excellent ability for visual recall, but he had no in-depth understanding of what they really meant. Mathematics and physics or any subject requiring the ability to reason logically and to see relationships caused him great difficulty. He was competent at basic arithmetic, having managed his own bank account from an early age, and he always went shopping with a pocket calculator at the ready, thus balancing a neat budget. Keeping an occasional eye on interest rates, he could calculate profit and loss with ease. But beyond this, the realm of higher mathematics—algebra, geometry, theorems—did not come within his purview. These subjects belonged to an alien world. He did reasonably well in translating French and Irish into English, but the comprehension section of any language paper was a nightmare and always earned him the worst marks. Over time he developed a complex about the task of making a precis or summary of any passage from literature. This was mainly due to his tendency to home in on the nonessential rather than the essential, and so missing the main point at issue, the end results rarely made sense. Essay writing was a joy, and he had no difficulty with essays requiring concrete imagination like "A Train Crash on a Busy Suburban Line" or "A Penalty Shoot-out at the World Cup," but his imagination failed entirely when it came to essays requiring abstract imagination like "The Color Blue" or "To Be or Not to Be." Recently one of his classmates was reminiscing about an essay for which he, the friend, had received a grade A in their final school year. It covered six large typewritten pages. The friend quoted passages from memory, and Bryan listened in amazement as the ideas flowed. The title of the essay was "Walls."

Just as Bryan loved words, he loved poetry. His love of it was based on the rhythm, theme, tone, mood, and imagery of the words. From an early age he had rolled words around on his tongue just to get the feel of them, using them at will, and from childhood had had a large, varied vocabulary. At that age he had no difficulty understanding the meaning and imagery of words, but when the words were put together into phrases and sentences, he then seemed to lose the drift and meaning of what was being said or read. As a young toddler he loved to make his own "word salads," that is, stringing words together in a seemingly meaningless jingle. This is often referred to as nonsense speech or "idioglossa." But if Bryan's words were listened to carefully, they often added up to a summary of what was going on around him. One such jingle has been preserved for immortality. It was "Bexbissel umbrella bag rock-aby -baby sho sho sho." This was a summary of a day when as a three-year-old, he was taken to visit a friend in order to loan her the bexbissel (carpet shampoo machine). On the way there was great excitement when the umbrella turned inside out with the wind. Then there was great consternation when his mother forgot her hand-bag. The baby in the friend's house cried all afternoon amid much rocking, and finally the cat got in and upset the milk over the table and had to be shooed out. Bryan's jingle had been a brief resume of the day's events.

Throughout the school years there was always ready help available for homework, and Bryan loved having a helper to work with. He really enjoyed academic work when there was someone working alongside him. Being then highly motivated, he would willingly tackle any new material. But if a helper was not available, he developed a mental block against tackling anything new or difficult. It seemed as if he needed the presence of another person nearby to motivate him. The only time he broke through this barrier was when he was vitally interested in doing something and getting the results and knew there was no help forthcoming. Then if his motivation was strong enough, he would do it surprisingly well. In the last analysis one got the impression that, within reason, and in spite of his intellectual shortcomings, Bryan could do anything he really wanted to do, provided he wanted to do it badly enough.

Because of his system's stress levels, the sustained effort required at school every day took its toll. Enjoying the learning experience greatly, he got enormous satisfaction in succeeding in class work. There were many pluses on the academic, educational side but many minuses on the emotional side. The concentration required for constant attention in class was taxing in the extreme. When the effort and overload overwhelmed him, he withdrew and went into shut-down. As he could not escape physically, like Mark behind the thick folds of his blanket, he escaped mentally. And he really escaped, feeling nothing, seeing nothing, hearing nothing, all his senses closing down. He often compared it to "a television station going off the air," and he had no control over it; he felt as if "somebody had just turned off the switch." Eventually a sense of coldness made him aware again of his surroundings and brought him back to reality. It was then very difficult to pick up the threads of what was going on around him. In times like this, the availability of a resource room and the presence of a resource person for time out before the pressure became too great would have been of immense benefit because it would have provided the opportunity to withdraw at the first signs of shutting down.

In common with many individuals with autism, Bryan showed clearly in his everyday school functioning all the signs of executive dysfunction (see glossary). He was not able to plan ahead nor had he the basic flexibility necessary to accept changes in routine or cope with the unexpected, for example, a train arriving late or an event having to be cancelled due to bad weather. He was utterly incapable of taking a philosophical attitude toward any change of plans. Change led to acute anxiety, showing up in increased perseveration and sometimes full-blown panic attacks. His lack of organizational skills defeated him again and again. The litany of errors is a long one: losing the timetable in spite of having a dozen copies made at the beginning of the school year; arriving at school with the wrong books for that particular day (eventually a double set was purchased, one for school and one for home); constantly forgetting calculator, pencil case, locker key, sports clothes, both from home to school and vice versa (again a double set of everything helped out here); notes concerning meetings, days off, early closing, never arriving home from school (on occasion he arrived at school when it was closed for the day). All this in spite of constant liaison with other parents and peers. It added up to an enormous amount of unnecessary stress, causing a great sense of uncertainty and eroding his confidence. Difficulty in organizing himself between classes, which often involved moving from one room to another, slowed him down considerably and led to being late for the next class and being reprimanded. He seemed to lurch through every day, constantly feeling, to use his own words, "that he was swimming against the tide."

However, it was not all negative. Because of his necessity for sameness and a love of routine, the consistent, daily predictability of a school timetable offered the perfect structural framework. Certain classes gave great scope for movement and self-expression, like music, art, and experimental science. These he enjoyed enormously. Games offered a chance to escape from the burden of concentration.

The fourth component in the school equation was the bully. There are bullies in all schools. Some act verbally, some physically. Sometimes they come in the clothing of lone wolves, other times like jackals they hunt in packs. In emotional and psychological terms, the damage they do is incalculable. The impact of it can last a lifetime. They jeer; they mock; they kick; they punch; they steal self-esteem; they isolate; they segregate; they intimidate; they haunt; they stalk; they lie in wait; they instill fear; they halt academic progress. Like the predators they are, they feed off the emotions of their prey and cause untold misery during the vulnerable years of formation. They roam the jungle of the school yard seeking whom they may devour. They pick on the weak; on those who for a number of reasons will not defend themselves and on those who stand out because they are different. In a society that requires conformity, to be different is to be a target. What is it in the human psyche that causes one human being to prey on another? For too long schools have tolerated the persecution of one child by another. Going back in history, that caste system in public schools called "fagging" was regarded as a toughening-up process for life. Fortunately World War II put an end to it. Thirty years ago, one was expected to fight it out or grin and bear it, leading to a survival of the fittest policy. Why has there been so little political will in schools to deal effectively with such tyranny? Perhaps because bullying is in fact very difficult to deal with. It is so insidious that often attempts to deal with it may just drive it underground to reappear somewhere else, perhaps beyond the school grounds. But it is vital that it be tackled at an early stage. Any complaints of bullying should be taken up instantly at the highest level in the school and the pressure kept up until action is taken. Fortunately the damage it causes has at last been recognized, and there are now official ground rules to deal with it.

Bryan, because he was different, had to deal with his share of bullies, and they did their share of damage. But he also had his share of great support and friendship from a number of peers. They had a great loyalty to him and he to them, and they helped enormously to smooth his passage. Fortunately in the senior school the staff were vigilant, and any form of bullying was dealt with firmly and swiftly, so it never interfered with academic progress. The reward for all the hard work came when he obtained a place in university.

The stories of Mark R., John K., and Bryan O'B. are not yet finished. What does the future hold? The real test will come when they try to join the work force and move out to live independently in the world. Experience in many countries has shown that the difficulties involved in holding down a job on a daily basis defeat so many high-ability adolescents and adults with autism. They rarely have trouble in third level colleges, provided they are academically competent. The structured independent life style of the college student suits them ideally. At college there is a great levelling off of the hierarchy of the school atmosphere, and at that age students are very accepting of each other and are much more tolerant of differences and idiosyncrasies. There is a great mix of types and personalities, and they all tend to find their own level. Also, one is allowed to work in one's own space and to one's own pace, to a certain degree.

Life in the normal work force is very different, and many high-ability people who are well qualified for a job are not able, because of their emotional vulnerability, to stand the stresses and strains of the daily task. There is huge stress involved for them in working, cheek-by-jowl, with large groups of people. The daily banter of the work force is beyond many who do not have an intrinsic appreciation of the subtle nuances of social interaction; the nonverbal cues, such as the nod, the wink, the lift of the eyebrows, the shrug of the shoulders, the gesture of the hand, and the myriad of other unspoken messages that pass between people communicating volumes without a single word being spoken, do not form part of their repertoire. They have no faculty for deciphering these nuances. The inability to tolerate criticism in any form, or sometimes indeed to even take direction, is a strong negative. The pressure of deadlines, the sensory overload, their own internal stress factors, their inflexibility and great difficulty in adjusting to change, all these make up a formidable list. Their intolerance of their own shortcomings (they expect so much of themselves that they are often defeated by their own very perfectionism) and their high frustration levels (their knowledge that they are different and can do nothing about it) further compound the issue. It is not surprising that so many well-qualified people, even some with Ph.D. degrees, are sitting at home unemployed.

The lucky ones are those who manage to find a special niche in the community as a result of some special talent. Those whose abilities lie with the arts have an advantage—musicians who can take their place with their academic peers, journalists who can free-lance, artists like Jessy Park who become self-employed. People with autism are talented in so many different facets of art. One young person recently observed shows great talent in calligraphy and other crafts and may have potential for future self-employment. Those with mathematical ability have found serious employment with banks and financial institutions, where they can work under special conditions within these companies. It is in trying to fit in with the ebb and flow of normal employment in the average work force that the problems of integration become apparent.

So, what then, lies ahead for Mark, John, and Bryan? Like all of us they share their hopes and dream their dreams. Will they find fulfillment in our world?

PART II

SOME PROFESSIONALS

To see a World in a Grain of Sand
And a Heaven in a Wild Flower,
Hold Infinity in the palm of your hand
And Eternity in an hour.

"Auguries of Innocence," William Blake (1757–1827)

CHAPTER 5

THE EARLY DIAGNOSTIC YEARS

The prestigious and highly acclaimed University of Vienna, in the early years of the twentieth century, with its strong Freudian concepts, was responsible for the academic education of the two professionals who would come to be central players in the arena of autism for much of its first quarter century. They were Leo Kanner and Hans Asperger. So the diagnosis of autism and the search for its causes were born against the backdrop of early twentieth-century psychodynamic theory (see glossary).

DR. LEO KANNER AND DR. HANS ASPERGER

Leo Kanner and Hans Asperger were both Austrian. They were born within ten years of each other, and even though both trained in medicine in Vienna, they never actually met. They came to live in different countries. In 1924 at the age of twenty-eight Kanner emigrated to America to the Johns Hopkins clinic in Baltimore, while Asperger, ten years his junior, stayed on in Vienna where he became professor of pediatrics at the University of Vienna in the years after the war.[21] It is an interesting example of synchronicity in time, but not in space, that they both described autism almost simultaneously. Kanner called his syndrome "early infantile autism," and his account of it was published in 1943.[4] In the same year Asperger submitted his doctoral thesis on his first cases to the University Pediatric Clinic in Vienna. His thesis was published the following year.[21] They had both used the same word—*autism*—and there is a remarkable similarity between both their accounts. The word *autism* was used originally to describe the thought disorder that is present in schizophrenia. Originally Kanner had thought that infantile autism, as he described it, was related to schizophrenia. Later he reconsidered this view.

There is much controversy and discussion as to whether Kanner's autism and Asperger's syndrome are the same condition differing only in degree, or are they, in fact, different entities drawn from different genetic backgrounds in different areas of the world? This will be discussed in greater detail later.

Although Kanner first attracted significant professional attention with his textbook *Child Psychiatry* in 1935, his greatest claim to fame was his work with autism. This has ensured him his place in psychiatric history. In his original paper entitled "Autistic Disturbances of Affective Contact" he described eleven cases, all of whose subjects were of above average intelligence.[4] His account of these eleven cases are classics in their field and almost defy improvement. His first case was a five-year-old boy described here in Kanner's own words:

At the age of one year "he could hum and sing many tunes accurately." Before he was two years old, he had "an unusual memory for faces and names, knew the names of a great number of houses" in his home town. "He was encouraged by the family in learning and reciting short poems, and even learned the Twenty-third Psalm and twenty five questions and answers of the Presbyterian Catechism." . . . His enunciation was clear. He became interested in pictures "and very soon knew an inordinate number of the pictures in a set of *Compton's Encyclopedia*." He knew the pictures of the presidents "and knew most of the pictures of his ancestors and kinfolks on both sides of the house." He quickly learned the whole alphabet "backward as well as forward" and to count to 100.[4]

In discussion Kanner lists the common characteristics of these eleven cases, which he considered formed a unique syndrome that had not been reported up to then: (1) The principle basic disorder is the child's lack of ability to relate to people and situations in the ordinary way, and it is apparent from the beginning of life. (2) The child exhibits an "extreme autistic aloneness" that disregards anything that comes to the child from outside. (3) When preparing to be picked up, the child never adjusts his body to adapt to the posture of the person holding him. (4) The child has an excellent rote memory but an inability to use language in any ordinary way. (5) With regard to language, there is a "parroting" of word combinations, sometimes uttered immediately and sometimes stored for later use (like in the case of Mark R. it can take many years to acquire the concept of "Yes"). (6) Word meanings can become inflexible and cannot be used in any connotation but the original one. (7) Children repeat personal pronouns just as they hear them. (8) Intrusion from loud noises and moving objects are reacted to with horror. (9) The desire to maintain sameness leads to anxiety and obsession-alism. (10) Finally, there is a repetition in both the child's actions and words that results in a great limitation of any spontaneous activity. Overall, as Kanner stressed again, there lay this profound aloneness.[4]

In his comments on the parents of these first eleven children, he noted that "all of our patients have come of highly intelligent parents." This led him to associate the occurrence of autism with the upper classes. On analysis he had found that of the fathers, four were psychiatrists, one a lawyer, one an engineer, one a plant pathologist, one a professor of forestry, one a chemist, one an advertising executive, and one a business executive. Of the mothers, nine were university graduates, one was a secretary, and the eleventh ran a theatrical booking office in New York City. Among the grandparents and relatives there were many physicians, scientists, writers, journalists, and students of art. All but three of the families were represented either in *Who's Who in America* or in *American Men of Science* or in both.[4] In seeking to evaluate this situation Kanner points to two facts that for him stood out prominently. The first was "a great deal of obsessiveness in the family background" and the second, the fact that in the group "there are very few really warmhearted fathers and mothers."

In the whole group, there are very few really warmhearted fathers and mothers. . . . Even some of the happiest marriages are rather cold and formal affairs. Three of the marriages were dismal failures. The question arises whether or to what extent this fact has contributed to the condition of the children. The children's aloneness from the beginning of life makes it difficult to attribute the whole picture exclusively to the type of the early parental relations with our patients.

We must, then, assume that these children have come into the world with innate inability to form the usual, biologically provided affective contact with people, just as other children come into the world with innate physical or intellectual handicaps. If this assumption is correct, a further study of our children may help to furnish concrete criteria regarding the still diffuse notions about the constitutional components of emotional reactivity. For here we seem to have pure-culture examples of *inborn autistic disturbances of affective contact* [his italics].[4]

Hans Asperger entitled his paper " 'Autistic Psychopathy' in Childhood" and it is reviewed here from the translation by Dr. Uta Frith.[22] In describing the clinical picture of autistic psychopathy, Asperger points out that even though there are considerable individual differences, the autistic personality is "highly distinctive." These individual differences lie in the areas of the individual degree of "contact disturbance," of intellectual ability, personality, and special interests. He considers that the condition is obvious from the second year of life, emphasizing that it is a natural entity that persists over time.

He then discusses in detail the characteristics of the condition, focusing on factors such as the peculiarities of eye gaze and drawing attention to the fact that autistic children "seem to perceive mainly with their peripheral field of vision." He comments next on the scarcity of both facial expressions and expressive gestures. In considering movement in general he holds that they may move constantly, but the movement is mainly stereotypic. With regard to language, he points out how unnatural it is; often caricature-like and directed to the space around the person spoken to rather than to the individual himself. In the area of autistic intelligence, he holds that mechanical learning is difficult for autistic children but that they are capable of producing "original ideas." Here he focuses on learning and schooling difficulties, indicating that their difficulties lie in the mechanical aspects of learning and in the area of inattentiveness; they tend to go their own way. He emphasizes that the "essential abnormality in autism is a disturbance of the lively relationship with the whole environment."

Moving to the area of social behavior, he further elaborates on the above point in the context of the fundamental disorder being "the limitation of their social relationships." He illustrates how these children have to actively learn social rules and skills that other children acquire intrinsically. The family unit, he holds, is where conflict can be observed and that this is where "autistic acts of malice" can occur. He considers that the entire personality of these children is decided by their limitation with regard to social relationships, stating that they are not psychotic but that they exhibit "a greater or lesser degree of psychopathy." He comments on their fundamental isolation and the real defect in their ability to understand other people: "The autist is only himself"; "He dwells among people as if a stranger"; "It is as if he were alone in the world."

He draws attention to the stereotypic behavior in the young child, which can take such forms as rocking, monotonous repetitive play with one object, for example, a shoelace, for hours on end, and lining toys up in "patterned rows." In contrasting their relationship to objects with that of the average child, he indicates that, unlike the average child, the autistic child does not have a normal relationship with objects. These can be ignored; for example, there may be little interest in toys, or objects can be fixated upon. The child's relationship can be limited to collecting objects not for the sake of using such possessions or playing with them, but merely to possess them. He also comments on the abnormalities in sensory perception; the hyperacusis and its opposite—hypoacusis; the extreme tactile sensitivity and inability to tolerate rough clothing; the strong reaction to taste and hypersensitivity of the throat.

Turning to the area of genetic factors, he indicates that over the course of ten years he and his colleagues have observed over two hundred children, all of whom showed autism to some degree. In cases where it was possible to get to know relevant family members, including parents, they noted the presence of "related incipient traits" in all cases. This led Asperger to bring up the question of genetic factors, and he discusses the "inherited disposition," the mode of inheritance of this condition. He considers that it was unlikely to be simple and would "undoubtedly" be polygenetic, and wonders about the possibility of its being a dominant or a recessive trait. Like Kanner, Asperger was struck by the high intellectual backgrounds of the ancestors of his patients, which included important academic and artistic families. Of the fathers in particular, many attained high office, even though they might have had obvious peculiarities.

Frith records that Asperger was convinced that autism "ran in families" and always held fast to his conviction that the condition had an organic or biological cause. In his hospital the children were treated within the Department of Pediatric Medicine and not within the Department of Psychiatric Medicine. She also comments that he did not allow the ideas of psychoanalytic theory, prevalent all around him at the time, to influence his thinking on autism and that he was sympathetic to parents, feeling that they often understood their children very well.[21]

To return again to Asperger's work, having opened his paper with four detailed case histories illustrating the salient features of the condition, he closes it with a discussion of the social value of the condition. He considers that able autistic people, particularly those of above average intelligence, can achieve significant success in their chosen lines of work and can rise to prominent positions because of their innate qualities, such as special interests, which compensate for deficits.[22]

As previously mentioned, autism was diagnosed and came to prominence against the background of twentieth-century psychodynamic thinking. Throughout the 1920s the etiology (see under aetiology in glossary) of mental illness was being looked into and possible causes discussed. Among the factors considered were parental attitudes, particularly those of mothers, and these were examined in an effort to determine whether parents could have caused mental illness in their children. This was the era of the theory of the schizophrenogenic mother. Unavoidably, many professionals working in the mental health field became caught up in this controversy.[23] Some participated on one side of this argument, others on the opposing side, and others again were ambivalent and fought on both sides. Inevitably the question of what causes autism was caught up into this maelstrom and the controversy ranged on into the 1960s and 1970s. Numerous theories and papers were produced putting forward the idea that the child had been normal at birth but had developed autism as a result of inadequate nurturing, particularly inadequate mothering.[23] The gap between the reality of autism and the image of autism widened as the perception began to grow that parents could indeed be the basic cause of mental disorders in their children. The stone was thrown into the pool and the ripples would spread ever outwards. As the theories floated to the surface, theories of cold, professional "refrigerator" parents[23]; theories of children who behaved like concentration camp victims because they feared their mothers, with mothers cast in the role of

SS guards[24]; theories that infantile autism is precipitated by parents whose wish it is that their child should not exist[25]; perception solidified and emerged disguised as fact.

It was a bleak and difficult time for parents, as they were made to feel guilty—made to feel that they were responsible for causing autism in their children.[8] No cognizance ever seems to have been taken of the healthy, outgoing, successful siblings of the autistic child; no marvelling at the dichotomy of parenting that could have produced on the one hand, a normal, stable, well-adjusted child, and on the other, a withdrawn sibling with autism.

This parental culpability theory, this psychogenic cause (having its origin in the mind rather than in the body), gained wide acceptance and greatly impeded the progress of knowledge, and the future course and cause of autism.

CHAPTER 6

SENSORY SENSATION

One of the first professionals to systematically challenge the theory that parents cause autism was Dr. Bernard Rimland, a professional psychologist and parent of a high-ability young man with the syndrome. His book *Infantile Autism: The Syndrome and Its Implications for a Neural Theory of Behavior* received the distinguished Century Psychology Series Award. This award is given for work considered to be a significant contribution to the field of psychology. His research was a landmark in its time.[26] Rimland is the founder and Director of The Autism Research Institute in San Diego, California.

DR. BERNARD RIMLAND

In the first section of his book Rimland sets out the psychogenic view of autism and points to the flaws and inconsistencies in the arguments of its supporters. He then puts forward his own observation of autism as a cognitive dysfunction, writing that "it is possible to trace its [early infantile autism] diversity of symptoms and manifestations to a single critical disability: *The child with early infantile autism is grossly impaired in a function basic to all cognition: the ability to relate new stimuli to remembered experience.* The vital connections between sensation and memory can be made only with difficulty." From this, he concludes, it will follow that the child will not be able to form concepts nor will he understand abstractions. While acknowledging that autistic children excel in tasks such as putting together the pieces in a jigsaw puzzle and similar tasks involving block design tests, he indicates that this ability is just an exercise in perceiving form. He adds: "Perception, the linking of meaning to sensation, is not required, except insofar as the child must understand what his task is." In reviewing the work of other researchers of this period, including Goldstein, Rimland illustrates that they also considered the impairment in autism to be one of forming concepts.[27] This impairment in what they termed "abstract attitude" would, they considered, be obvious in the sphere of language. It would show up in lack of comprehension and not being able to "understand or use language in its symbolic and conceptual meaning."

Goldstein (as reviewed in Sacks[8]) was interested in this overall, cohesive capacity of the mind. He called this "the abstract attitude of the mind." In his studies of brain damage he found that whenever there was extensive damage, above and beyond the damage to specific abilities in say, speech, sight, or some other specific function, this damage could cause impairment in abstract attitude. This he felt could be more damaging than any impairment to a specific ability like speech or sight.

Having discussed the work of Goldstein and others, Rimland then moves on to debate the question of where in the brain this organic impairment in autism could be found. He outlines his reasons for focusing on the network of nerve cells in the brainstem, called the reticular formation, as being this site. Thirty years later, with the advances in modern methods of research, there is now evidence from several studies to show that the brainstem in autistic children has dysfunctional areas.[28] In addition, the results from auditory brainstem evoked response studies have also indicated brainstem malfunctioning.

Moving on again to comment on how the reticular formation might be implicated in perception dysfunction, Rimland puts forward the idea that excessive response to stimuli could be a feature of impaired "response inhibition," whereby the child with autism is not able to discriminate between what to regard and disregard, while the average child will have a higher threshold of control in this area. The role of the reticular formation in the phenomenon of sensory deprivation is then discussed. He considers that many of the facets of autism are similar to those seen in people who suffer from sensory deprivation, drawing parallels between men who have been living in isolation in the polar regions for lengthy periods of time and the behaviors seen in autism; the unfocused gaze of the autistic child and how he ignores people; his detached "autistic aloneness"; his apathetic attitude and irritability; his withdrawal into a world of his own; his lack of communication.

He points again to this similarity of behavior seen in those who suffer from sensory deprivation and those who suffer from autism when he discusses the effects of sensory deprivation on the average young man, as observed by Hebb, who writes that observation has shown that when you remove the normal bodily contacts, sights, and sounds for a few short days from an otherwise healthy college student, he can become severely disturbed. So much so that he can hallucinate and suffer from depersonalization (see glossary) and derealization.[29]

As Rimland then points out, "it is not the lack of sensory stimulation *per se*" that matters but the "lack of *meaningful* sensory stimulation" that causes the psychological disturbance. Finally he asks the question "And what of the child whose sense organs are intact, but whose neural structure does not permit stimuli to register?" and answers it with "There appears to be adequate reason for believing the perceptual abilities of autistic children to be so severely impaired that sensory deprivation psychosis must be considered a real possibility."

This prize-winning book, to which Leo Kanner had written the foreword, struck at the heart of the parental culpability theory and is generally accredited with sounding its death knell.

DR. EDWARD M. ORNITZ

Throughout the late 1960s and 1970s then, there was a scientific swing away from looking at psychodynamic theories to explain autism. Proper scientific procedures were beginning to be adopted, and autism looked at objectively in the light of modern scientific evidence. There are many researchers associated with this period, including Dr. Edward M. Ornitz of the Department of Psychiatry and Brain Research Institute at the University of California in Los Angeles.

For over thirty years Ornitz has been involved in research into the condition of autism and has published a large body of scientific literature on the subject. In 1976, in conjunction with Dr. Edward Ritvo, also of the Department of Psychiatry, UCLA, he undertook a critical review in which they looked back over the history of autism research since Kanner first diagnosed the condition.[30] They surveyed those studies that were based on serious scientific efforts and avoided those that were based on theories and opinions. They came to the following twelve conclusions summarized here:

1. Autism is a specific syndrome and it can be clinically defined by behavior.
2. It is evident at birth or shortly afterward and is life long.
3. The symptoms of it indicate an underlying disorder that has an effect on the rate of development, on the regulation of perception, on language, on intellectual and cognitive abilities, and on the ability to relate to others.
4. Autism cannot be caused by any known psychological conditions in the environment of the child.

5. Diagnosis is based on early developmental history prior to three years of age. This must indicate malfunctioning in perception, language, rate of development, and ability to relate. Many individuals show disturbances in movement (e.g., hand flapping, toe walking).

6. Autism can occur on its own or comorbid with other disorders affecting the central nervous system.

7. It affects children from all over the world, from all races and creeds, and from all intellectual and social backgrounds.

8. There is no treatment available, based on fundamental causes, that will change the progression of the disorder.

9. Correct diagnostic procedures involve a full medical and neurological examination. They must take into account the fact that seizure disorders can develop as the child grows older.

10. Behavior therapy and special education programs will help the prognosis in most cases. These should be undertaken by trained specialists and parents. All programs should be periodically updated to take into account the clinical changes that will occur over time in most cases.

11. With regard to the outcome, in autism they held that the intellectual impairments in about two-thirds of individuals are severe enough, unfortunately, to warrant being classified as retarded throughout their lifetime.

12. Finally, they concluded that further basic research into the organic process underlying autism is necessary if a rational treatment program is to be developed.[30]

Also in this paper these researchers discuss in depth the disturbance of perception that occurs in autism. They comment that one of the striking and unique aspects of autism is the failure of adequate regulation of sensory input. In behavior terms this shows up as either too little response or too much, and these states can follow each other in the same child. When there is too little response to, for example, auditory stimuli, the child will not react to either speech or sounds, and he may have no startle response to sudden loud noises—no startle reflex. Similarly, the child may not react visually to a new person or an object in his surroundings. Also, as these authors indicate, in the first two years of life, there is frequently a lack of response to pain and touch. When an object is handed to a child, he may not grasp it and it falls away. In addition, he may show no reaction to cuts, bruises, and injections. Conversely, there may be exaggerated overreactions to all the same stimuli, as when such children develop an exaggerated overreaction to certain fabrics and certain rough textured foods. Ornitz and Ritvo discuss how these children can be generally ambivalent in their response to stimulation. For example, the child who spins and twirls himself seeking out vestibular stimulation at one time may reject entirely any rough and tumble play on another occasion.

Even though the existence of sensory perception problems in autistic children has been documented as far back as Kanner's original diagnosis and subsequently a substantial number of papers published on the subject in the 1960s, 1970s, and 1980s, yet overall this question of disturbance of perception in autism has largely been ignored. This situation is only now beginning to be remedied. Over the last twenty years the emphasis has been mainly on the disturbance in communication and language and in relating to people and objects.

About ten years after the above paper appeared, Ornitz wrote a major review of the scientific literature on sensory processing difficulties in autism.[31] In the beginning of this paper he sets out two hypotheses. The first emphasizes the disturbances of language and communication in autism and assumes an underlying cognitive defect presumably originating in the cortex of the brain. The second emphasizes the disturbances of sensory regulation and motility and takes cognizance of the role of the brainstem. He then goes on to discuss in detail the scientific and medical evidence for both hypotheses. He reviews the findings of his own research and the research of others in the field. Finally, he concludes that there is neurophysiological evidence for both hypotheses, explaining that in the older autistic person the language and cognitive defects will be more obvious, while in the younger child the disturbance of sensory perception and motility will loom larger. He continues:

The autistic syndrome consists of three major clusters of behavioural disturbances: relating to people and objects; language and communication; and sensory modulation and motility. These symptom subclusters might occur independently, or any one might influence one or more of the others. Assuming some interrelationships, it is difficult to imagine how the disturbances of relating and of language might evoke those of sensory modulation and motility. On the other hand, a number of clinical investigations, reviews, and theoretical proposals have stressed that social awareness, motivation, and use of language in autistics seem to be dominated by disordered perceptual processes. . . . Thus disturbances of relating, language, and communication can be considered consequences of inconstancy of perception due to faulty modulation of sensory input. The autistic child cannot relate to or imitate that which he cannot reliably perceive. Cognitive defects could similarly be explained in terms of distorted sensory input; the autistic child cannot make *sense* out of *sensation*.[31]

Throughout the 1970s, 1980s, and indeed into the 1990s, the focus in autism has been on primary cortical processing and not on secondary sensory processing. At the end of his analytical paper Ornitz puts forward the view that the reverse may well be the case, stating, "This conclusion is consistent with much of the experimental evidence reviewed in this paper as well as the clinical observations suggesting that the disturbances of social relating, communication, and language are secondary to a disorder of sensory modulation."[31]

DR. CARL H. DELACATO

The practical application of the scientific work of Ornitz, Ritvo, and others came to the fore in the clinical practice of Dr. Carl H. Delacato. Delacato's work on autism is based on his theory that children with autism are not psychotic: they are brain injured.

In *The Ultimate Stranger* Delacato gives an account of his work with children with autism over a number of years during which he co-opted parents as cotherapists.[11] His book is devoted almost entirely to the question of impaired sensory perception in autism, and in it he tells the story of how he came to make "sense out of sensoryisms" and puts forward his theory. He takes very careful cognizance of the strange behaviors of the autistic children referred to him for diagnosis and help, comparing their behaviors to those of children with other disabilities including visual and auditory impairments. These strange behaviors took the form of constant movement such as rocking, spinning, twirling; self-injurious actions of slapping, head banging, and hand biting; tuning out and going deaf; screaming for no apparent reason; suddenly clapping their hands over their ears; and many more. Over time he began to see these "sensoryisms" in terms of impaired sensory input. Following on this he concludes that in some strange way the children themselves were working out their own coping strategies and treatments in an effort to co-exist with their sensory difficulties. He divides the sensory dysfunction into three categories.

Hyper: He considers that this signified that *too much* of the sensory stimulus was affecting one or more of the five senses.

Hypo: This, he holds, was the reverse. In this case *too little* of the sensory stimulus was being registered in one or more of the five senses.

White Noise: In this situation he suggests that the inefficiency of the processing mechanism gave rise to permanent internal interference, which kept "jamming the system." This white noise, he felt, could occur in any of the five senses.

Many of these children had been referred to Delacato because of their severe behavioral problems, and he found that in his experience the greatest behavioral problems were seen in those children who were hyper to sound and touch and who had white noise in sound and touch. Moving on to discuss in turn each of the individual five senses, in terms of these three categories, he gives guidelines on how to make sense out of the child's reaction to the impairment and how to treat it.

Hearing

The hallmarks of the hyperacusis child are stated to be an ashen-grey facial pallor (see John K.) and a tendency to act deaf and withdraw from the sounds around him. He states that it is easy to be misled by these children because they can make so much noise themselves. However, he holds, this is their defense mechanism because in this way they can block out external sounds and substitute their own level of sound, which they can control. The therapy recommended for this group is quietness at all levels: avoid crowded situations, do not shout, avoid, above all, sudden loud noises. He treated his hyperacusis patients with valved earplugs capable of closing down at a given noise level. He reports success with this treatment, and that in its wake behavior improved.

He recommends the reverse of this treatment for the child who had too little of the sound stimulus getting through to his auditory system. In his experience these children loved loud sounds, and his advice is to give them more sound stimulation. With regard to white noise in the auditory system, he considers that the symptoms of this will be a constant cacophony of sound coming from within the body processes, for example, the heartbeat. This he holds, will heavily impinge on sounds coming from outside.

He quoted the case of Ann who wore a helmet because she constantly banged her head.

Let's assume Ann heard a constant and painful ringing noise in her head. What would she do to change the noise? If this auditory white noise were loud enough, it drowned out all sounds coming from the outside and could be very painful coming from the inside. When she banged her head, the noise stopped for a bit. . . .

Each of these activities made the sound that she heard inside her head different. We gave her an electronic stethoscope so that she could spend a great deal of time listening to each part of her body at rest and when quiet. She began to learn about her body noises, and she began to listen to us as we whispered to her. As her head banging decreased, she became able to survive.[11]

Vision

The twirling or spinning child is thought to be the hyper vision child. These actions, he believes, bring on optical illusions, and this child can be obsessed with bright objects such as the moon and stars but will shy away from reflecting surfaces. Reading can come easily to him, and he can have remarkable visual recall. Sunglasses are essential for this child, and he must avoid overbright light indoors and outdoors. Delacato holds that the key symptom of the child who sees too little is rocking and also a fascination with light sources such as the sun, which is dangerous to the eyes. This child can be fearful of dark places. Mark R. would be symptomatic of what is considered to be the white noise vision child, as he is the one who looks through people as if they did not exist. This child would appear to be looking inwardly much of the time. For him Delacato recommends constantly focusing his attention on the outside world, and he outlines treatment therapies and gives guidelines on how to achieve this.

Touch

Touch or tactility is different from the other senses because the organs of touch are in the skin, which covers the entire body. The skin contains the receptors for touch, pain, pressure, and temperature. Proprioception refers to the sensations coming from the body during movement and when at rest. The hand is the most tactile part of the body. The hypertactile child will likely be oversensitive to touch; he will have too much of the stimulus. The most obvious sign will be the rejection of touch. These are the children, like John K., who as babies go rigid when picked up. As toddlers they fight to get free when held. They can be tormented by rough textured clothing. Delacato points out that they can be so overwhelmed by touch that their bodies feel tense and strained.

In contrast, he regards the hypotactile child as the one who does not feel pain, like Mark R. He can be hurt and not cry. These, he considers, are the self-mutilating children. Delacato describes them in Susan, when he writes

> Susan . . . was hypo in tactility. Not enough of the tactile message from the skin arrived at her brain. Her biting of her hands was her attempt at normalising the channel from her hand to her brain.
> Susan no longer bites. She no longer needs to bite. We have normalised for her the channel between her hand and her brain. . . .
> Susan doesn't bite her hands any longer, for one simple reason. If she bit her hand now, "It would hurt" she says proudly.[11]

The hitting and slapping child is thought to be the victim of white noise tactility, and Delacato describes how this kind of behavior can come in cycles, adding that this child will be calm for periods of time and will then develop a tactile outburst of slapping, and finally become calm again until the next outburst. *The Ultimate Stranger* ends with a number of case histories illustrating the different degrees of impairments in the five senses and the treatment strategies devised for the children involved.

In his theory Delacato was one of the first therapists to make a connection between some problem behaviors and distorted perception in the five senses; the first to make "sense out of sensoryisms."

DR. A. JEAN AYRES

Into this climate of research into sensory processing problems and its practical application comes the work of Dr. A. Jean Ayres. Her original text book entitled *Sensory Integration and the Child* provides enlightening insights into the world of the senses, and she is credited with being the first researcher in the field to identify problems of sensory integrative dysfunction. What follows summarizes and gives insights into her theory.[5]

Ayres defines the basic work of sensory integration as being one of organization so that the body functions as a harmonious whole. To achieve this all stimuli from outside must pass (sensory route) efficiently into the central nervous system (CNS) for processing and back out again (motor route) for action. If one has good sensory integration all this takes place effortlessly. Ayres compares this to the analogy of lines of traffic moving swiftly along major highways approaching and leaving a big city. Conversely, if one has poor sensory integration there will be traffic jams in the system when some information will get lost and never arrive or arrive too late, so the CNS will not get the necessary information to work efficiently. This is defined as sensory integrative disorder.

Drawing on the basic observations of Dr. Jean Piaget, Ayres focuses on the early years of life as being of great significance in developing sensory integration. It is now, she holds, that the "body percept" (see glossary), the internal "sensory picture" of the body, is being imprinted in the brain, as the young child explores his environment, absorbing sensory information. This internal perception of his own body, now patterned into his brain, will be used, it is thought, as a reference source to direct his future movements. At this stage of his life, she considers, a child's primary focus is in orienting his body to sensation. The more skillfully this is achieved, the better the prognosis for higher cognitive functioning.

As previously explained, proprioception refers to the sensations coming from the body during movement and when at rest. During movement, proprioceptors send out a constant stream of impulses giving information about the position of the body in relation to space at any given moment in time, and as Ayres observes, this keeps the body image updated and consequently the brain can coordinate muscular activity. Many children who, like Mark R., have impaired proprioception and cannot feel their limbs, have to rely heavily on their sense of vision to locate them.

This possible failure of proprioception, this feeling of not being able to locate where your body parts are, has been described before under Mark R. Up to the age of about twenty, Mark sometimes lost touch with his outer body. When this happened he felt his body was floating and disconnected, and he had to map out again and again to find it and to locate his arms, legs, hands, and feet. This loss of a physical body ego led to depersonalization or derealization. Experiences of this type are very familiar to medical staff working with amputees. They report that one of the biggest challenges facing therapists is the identity crisis that these amputees experience; their loss of a sense of self; their deep disturbance of body image, their want of being, of existence. Interestingly enough, the constant use of mirrors to reestablish identity is one of the first lines of treatment.

A physical body ego has been described by Freud as being the basis of a sense of self. He held that the ego was first and foremost a body ego. Lacking, at times, this feeling of a body self-image, Mark doubted his own identity, his own reality. Who was he? Where was he? What was he? He felt trapped, suspended in time, immobilized, encapsulated. Physically and mentally frozen, he felt terror floating to the surface as he searched for his bodily outline and extremities. This state, however, was usually transient, and it passed, leading to profound relief. Yet on very rare occasions it did last a number of hours. Since his early twenties Mark has reported that he is rarely tormented by "this feeling of floating off into limbo" (his words). There are in the autism literature references to experiences similar to Mark's.

More recently, Mark in his mid-twenties, having received regular professional Ki Massage, has reported improvement in his overall ability to feel his limbs. He also reports feeling more grounded and to having a deeper development of body ego and consequently of the ego of self, and, for the first time in his life, the ability to walk with his eyes closed and to find his way around a dark room.

In neurology, cases of failure of proprioception do occur but they are rare, or rather they were rare until recently. Now apparently large numbers of patients are turning up everywhere with severe sensory neuronopathies (see glossary).[32] As the author of that information states, most of them are health faddists, who are on megavitamin doses and have been taking enormous quantities of vitamin B6 (pyridoxine) (see glossary). As a result there are now some hundreds of "disembodied" persons but most of these can hope to get better when they discontinue taking Pyridoxine.[32]

To return again to the work of Dr. Ayres, she explains that we also have another sensory system called the vestibular system constantly giving bio-feedback to the brain on the position of the body in relation to the force of gravity. When the vestibular system is dysfunctional, as seen in Mark R., a child will walk off the end of a wall. She also points to other areas where vestibular impairment can impact on social behavior, such as faulty judgment in gauging how close to stand to another person and difficulty in locating people in a crowd. Moving on to discuss the impact of the vestibular system on the physiology of the child, she notes that an underactive vestibular system, because it lacks the ability to modulate, will contribute to hyperactivity and distractibility. In addition, hand and brain specialization can be affected, as seen in Mark R. She holds that a child so affected will use his right hand for work on the right side of his body and his left hand for work on the left, thus not developing hand specialization, but instead developing similar skills in both hands. When Mark was pruning roses if the rose was growing on his right side he pruned with the right hand; when the rose was growing on his left side he simply passed the clippers to his left hand; if the third rose was growing on his right, back went the clippers again to the right hand. This considerably slowed down his working ability. Much training was put into getting him to use both hands in unison, as normally everything was done with a single hand, and when he was using his right hand his left was in his pocket and vice versa. By contrast, the average child will develop one hand for fine motor work, such as writing or using tools. This, Ayres holds, will in turn affect speech development in the cerebral hemispheres.

In referring again to the work of Piaget, Ayres writes that he suggested that the brain has to have a tangible, concrete knowledge of the body, the environment, and its physical forces before it is in a position to deal with abstract concepts. The more securely this concrete foundation is laid down, the more substantial will be the basis for abstract thought. In the light of this theory it is easy to see how children with autism can be so disadvantaged in their development during the early years. While they are mired in repetitive, ritualistic routines, the monotony of their activities stands out in stark contrast to the normal exploratory play of their peers. A correlation has now been found between this underexploration of the environment seen in autism and an anatomic abnormality of the cerebellum (see glossary) of the brain. This will come up for discussion later. Ayres puts forward the idea that any child who suffers from distorted sensory perception will be impaired in his ability to form a proper "body percept."

Moving on again, this time to the area of motor planning (praxis), she explains what is involved in praxis (see under apraxia in glossary). For motor planning to proceed with ease, the vestibular, tactile, and proprioceptor senses must coordinate smoothly, but these senses are dependent on information stored in the brain. Obviously if this information is not readily available, there will be impairment in the system. Ayres writes that a deficiency in motor planning can lead to aphasia, which is a disorder in generating speech and also in understanding what others say. There are a number of references throughout the literature about the difficulties autistic children appear to have in initiating constructive action, similar to what is seen in Parkinsonism. This finding has led to speculation that their difficulty with communication might be one of praxis (performing) rather than cognition (knowing). A striking example of how this inability to initiate action can hinder a patient with Parkinsonism is dramatically described by Dr. Oliver Sacks in his medical classic *Awakenings*.[32A] He tells of a patient who describes herself as suddenly coming to a full stop in the corridor, seeming to be deprived of all ability to move or indeed of life. She would remain motionless like this unless or until either the power of touch or of music came to her aid. Even the lightest possible touch would enable her to move again and keep moving as long as the other person was with her. But when they stopped she stopped also, feeling lifeless as before. Sacks comments that these experiences are very common in cases of Parkinsonism (see glossary) and are generally dismissed in terms of being reflexes due to contact. But he considers that in her own estimation this particular patient's experiences went far deeper than that.[32A]

What then, can be done to improve sensory integration in children with autism? In reporting on her work in this area, Ayres has found that on the standard tests for sensory integrative function autistic children were found to score on a par with children who have poor motor planning skills. Their ability to locate tactile stimuli can be so impaired that they may not know where their hands and feet are unless they are visible. She has found that this situation can often be improved by touch pressure treatment. The sensory processing abnormalities most commonly seen in her experience when working with autistic children were (1) the children either overreacted or underreacted to stimuli; (2) vestibular and tactile sensations were not being correctly processed, therefore their ability to perceive space and their own relationship to space was impaired; and (3) their motivation system was dysfunctional. As Dr. Ayres expresses it, their "I want to do it" system was impaired, and although they were active children, their activity was aimless and repetitive, and they were not self-motivating beyond their routines. However, she writes, when they were given sufficient motivation they could then "turn on the I want to do it system." With regard to therapy she found that some children have gained from it while others have shown little or no improvement.

In summing up she tells us that she considers the ability to organize percepts and to respond to percepts to be fundamental to human behavior. Consequently, if a person is not able to properly perceive his "physical environment" or accomplish tasks within this environment, he will be without the foundation for "organizing more complex material."

In 1972 Sensory Integration International, a nonprofit organization, was set up to further the work of Dr. Ayres. Its aim is to provide and support educational training programs, information, and evaluation and treatment services to the general public as well as to healthcare and educational communities.

How much emphasis has the scientific community placed on sensory integration therapy as an intervention in autism? In a recent overview of existing empirical studies researching the effectiveness of it, Dawson and Watling, of the Center of Human Development and Disability at the University of Washington, report that there has been relatively little systematic, controlled research in this area; so little in fact that conclusions cannot be drawn. They review four studies, three of which had fewer than six people taking part. In addition there were no control/comparison groups set up for these studies. The fourth study involved eighteen children (6 to 12 years old), and this study found no changes in vocal behavior, which was the criterion used to measure difference. This intervention was, however, of very short duration (two 30-minute sessions). This team holds that conclusions cannot be drawn from so few studies. In discussion they point to the fact that very little is known about which subgroups and age groups are most likely to derive benefit from sensory integration therapy, and they call for research to: (1) establish the essential features of the sensory and motor abnormalities in autism, as well as chart their course and prevalence; (2) establish to what extent these sensory distortions and motor dysfunctions are associated with other behaviors and/or diagnostic characteristics (this information would be useful in pinpointing subgroups); (3) design controlled studies to determine which type of treatment interventions would be most effective and which age groups and individuals would benefit most from intervention. Pointing to the fact that there is evidence to suggest that regions of the brain involved in sensory arousal and motor functions (cerebellum, brainstem, and frontal lobes) are dysfunctional in autism, they add that almost all aspects of social, cognitive, and academic functioning will be affected by "sensory sensitivities and motor difficulties."[33]

CHAPTER 7

⬥⬥⬥⬥⬥

WHAT RESEARCH HAS
REVEALED

Kanner's work in the field of autism became widely known internationally but because of the war and conditions in Europe after the war, Asperger's work did not reach the same international audience. This was also partly due to the fact that his original paper was published in German. Apart from some discussions of his work in the 1960s and 1970s by a number of authors, it was Dr. Lorna Wing who reintroduced his findings to the English-speaking world.[34] Subsequently, Frith published an English translation of Asperger's original 1944 thesis.[22]

DR. LORNA WING

Dr. Wing, of the National Autistic Society Centre for Social and Communication Disorders in Bromley, Kent, is a parent/professional and a founding member of the National Autistic Society of the United Kingdom. In her paper, "Asperger's Syndrome: A Clinical Account," she points out that Asperger used the words "Autistic Psychopathy," the title of his thesis, in the sense of an abnormality of personality. Confusion arose because psychopathy is normally equated with sociopathic behavior. Hence her reason for using the neutral term "Asperger's syndrome." Among other factors, the clinical characteristics, developmental path of the condition, differential diagnosis, and care management of Asperger syndrome are discussed in the paper, and the material is based on Asperger's own account and on thirty-four individuals that she personally diagnosed.

On summarizing Asperger's description of his cases, she comments on a number of points:

Perhaps the most obvious characteristic is impairment of two-way social interaction. This is not due primarily to a desire to withdraw from social contact. The problem arises from a lack of ability to understand and use the rules governing social behaviour. These rules are unwritten and unstated, complex, constantly changing, and affect speech, gesture, posture, movement, eye contact, choice of clothing, proximity to others, and many other aspects of behaviour.[34]

While illustrating that those with the syndrome typically have strengths as well as impairments, she cites the excellent rote memory, the musical accomplishments, and mastery of board games such as chess. With regard to "special interests"—that is, the tendency of people with the syndrome to home in on one or two special subjects (like Mark R. with World War I and II aircraft) and research out every conceivable fact down to the last detail about those specific subjects—Wing adds the rider that they "have little grasp of the meaning of the facts they learn."

Adding some modification to Asperger's account, she comments on the areas of communication and imagination, noting that in the first year or two of life a child with the syndrome may show a great lack of will to communicate at any level, either in action, expression, or speech. There can be a conspicuous lack of interest or delight in the presence of other people. With regard to the ability to indulge in "imaginative pretend play," she considers it to be either absent or considerably impaired. She disagrees with Asperger's observations on speech, which he refers to "as an especially intimate relationship with language" and "highly sophisticated linguistic skills." Her own assessment of this speech is that:

Despite the eventual good use of grammar and a large vocabulary, careful observation over a long enough period of time discloses that the content of speech is impoverished and much of it is copied inappropriately from other people or books. ... The language used gives the impression of being learned by rote. The meanings of long and obscure words may be known, but not those of words used every day.[34]

She also disagrees with Asperger's assessment of people with the condition in the area of "originality and creativity in their chosen field," stating that "it would be more true to say that their thought processes are confined to a narrow, pedantic, literal, but logical, chain of reasoning." On the subject of intelligence she notes that Asperger did not make available evidence of tests to substantiate his belief in the high intelligence of his subjects. One-fifth of her sample fell into the category of below average intelligence. Because the cases described by Wing all had been referred to her due to additional problems of adjustment or comorbid psychiatric disorders, she considers her sample is "probably biased towards those with more severe handicaps." A considerable proportion of her own cases had comorbid psychiatric disorders.

In the final section on management and education, she acknowledges that this will be decided by the degree of impairment and general standard of the individual child and the school in question. Some people have progressed well in mainstream schools, while others have been more suited to special schools. The decision will revolve around how able the child is. School bullying can be a serious problem for many, and the staff will need to be vigilant to deal with it. She suggests that as children grow older and develop more insight they realize they are different and consequently they can become extremely sensitive to criticism and can fall prey to anxiety and stress. In these cases counselling by an experienced person can be helpful, but it will have to be kept simple to adapt to the individual's ability to understand. Wing recommends that it take the form of listening to anxieties and tensions and giving reassurance.

This clinical account of Asperger's syndrome ends with a number of case histories to illustrate the conditions described. These include the case of a young man who exhibited the characteristics of Asperger's syndrome in conjunction with mental retardation and the case history of a boy who, like Mark R., had classic autism as a child and who moved along the spectrum until he exhibited all the characteristics of Asperger's syndrome.

When writing many years later Wing said of this present paper under review that the purpose of it was to put forward the hypothesis that the "so-called syndrome was a variant of autism," even though the author gave the arguments for and against this viewpoint.[35]

We have seen that the diagnosis of autism is based on behavior, the three cardinal features being autistic aloneness; repetitive, stereotyped behavior; and failure of communication or abnormal communication. Could these symptoms found together in autism be merely a coincidence or do they in fact constitute a syndrome? To answer this question, Wing, in conjunction with Dr. Judith Gould, undertook a major epidemiological and classification study in the Camberwell area of London.[36] The study was aimed at children under fifteen years of age. In all, close to a thousand children were screened and 132 of them were selected. The first criterion for selection was the presence of any one of the following three behaviors irrespective of intelligence level:

a. Impairment of ability or no ability to interact socially, especially with their peer group.
b. Absence of or dysfunctional verbal and nonverbal language.
c. The presence of repetitive, stereotyped behavior.

The second criterion was that the intellectual ability to function should be in the severely retarded range. The selection of the children was based on their having one or both of the above criteria. In this way two groups of children were identified: (1) A socially impaired group of which over half were severely retarded, and (2) a comparison group of "sociable severely mentally retarded" children.

An analysis of the results showed that impairments of "reciprocal social interaction" occurred in approximately one in every five hundred children. In addition, approximately one in every two thousand had shown a history of "typical autism." This latter figure was similar to that obtained by other researchers of that era. Also their findings showed that "All the children with social impairments had repetitive stereotyped behavior and almost all had absence or abnormalities of language and symbolic activities. Thus the study showed a marked tendency for these problems to occur together." The impairments then were not just three separate impairments occurring together by coincidence. They did in fact constitute a "triad of impairments."

Also in this study the authors categorized the children on the basis of their ability to interact socially into:

1. *Social aloofness.* Children classed under this heading showed very severe impairment of social interaction. Some remained withdrawn in all situations.
2. *Passive interaction.* This described the behavior of those who did not make social contact themselves but when other children pulled them in to join their games, they accepted social interaction.
3. *Active, but odd interaction.* These were the children who did make social approaches of their own accord, but their behavior was inappropriate because it mainly revolved around their own preoccupations.

More recently, in a letter to the *Lancet*, Wing elaborates further on the above three groups.[6] She considers that the children in group three, active but odd, tend to fit Asperger's clinical description of his syndrome. She also adds a fourth group that she calls "the loners," stating that

The most subtle form of the triad, described by Sula Wolff, is found in people of average, high, or outstanding ability, including fluent speech, who tend to prefer to be alone, lack empathy, and be concerned with their own interests regardless of peer-group pressures. Their schooldays are often stressful and difficult because they will not conform to the demands of teachers or of fellow pupils. Most are happier as adults and may follow successful careers, sometimes of high academic distinction. Some learn the rules of social interaction by rote, while others remain solitary by choice.[6]

DR. CHRISTOPHER GILLBERG

Dr. Christopher Gillberg is professor of child and adolescent psychiatry and head of the Child Neuropsychiatry Clinic at the University of Göteborg in Sweden. In conjunction with Dr. Mary Coleman of the department of pediatrics at Georgetown University School of Medicine in Washington, DC, he has coauthored *The Biology of the Autistic Syndromes*, which is now in its third edition.[23A]

Gillberg has done much work on the neurobiological underpinnings of the autistic spectrum disorders. He and his colleagues have published the results of a study of twenty children (aged 3 to 21), all with full-scale IQs above 65. Three of these were classed as having typical Asperger syndrome, the remainder being classified as fairly typical examples of "pure" Kanner autism. All children underwent a full clinical and neurobiological assessment including CAT scan; auditory brainstem response; EEG; chromosomal cultures; cerebrospinal fluid (see glossary), blood, and urine examinations; and a thorough physical examination. An analysis of the results showed that three-quarters had definite abnormalities on at least one of these examinations. The authors go on to point out that the remaining five subjects who did not, may well show abnormalities in the future when more sophisticated assessment techniques become available. They conclude by stating that perhaps in the near future the condition of autism will gain acceptance as being evidence of neurological dysfunction.[37]

Two years later Gillberg published his findings of another study undertaken to find some answers to the question as to whether Asperger syndrome existed as a separate condition with its own distinction from "mild variants" of autism, and as to whether it represented "a personality variant or was it a disorder" and could clear distinctions be made between these two.[38]

In this investigation he compared a group of twenty-three children fulfilling the criteria for Asperger syndrome (AS) with an equal number of children classified as having infantile autism (IA). Both groups were matched for age and IQ. Less than one in ten were mentally retarded, and almost a fifth were of above average intelligence. The boy:girl ratio for the AS group was 10 to 1; and for the IA group it was 3.6 to 1. All the children underwent a thorough clinical and case history assessment. The following neurobiological investigations were also carried out on twenty of the IA group and twelve of the AS group: (1) a chromosomal culture in a folic acid–depleted medium; (2) an ABR, auditory brainstem response; (3) a brain CAT scan; and (4) an EEG in the waking state. An analysis of the findings revealed that almost two-thirds of the AS children showed up with abnormal results on CAT scans, ABR testing, and EEG recordings, chromosomal cultures, or cerebrospinal fluid (CSF) analysis. Or else they had a major diagnosis indicating brain abnormality, for example, epilepsy or cerebral palsy. In the infantile autism group, almost four out of every five had abnormal results.

In discussing these findings Gillberg asks whether the Asperger syndrome children are different from the children with Kanner autism and concludes that they are and they are not. He holds that they are different in that they are not so impaired as the basic Kanner "prototype" children, but on the other hand, when considering neurobiological background conditions, they are not all that different. He then puts forward some assumptions regarding clumsiness in children with AS, saying that they differ from children with IA in having relatively poor motor skills. Even though motor skills were not a diagnostic criterion for this particular study, the vast majority of the AS group had such problems.

At the end of his paper he comes to the conclusion that on balance, the evidence would suggest that Asperger syndrome represents a "mild variation of autism." He feels that in clinical practice the term could be useful because a diagnosis of autism can be regarded as one of the saddest diagnoses a doctor can have to inform parents of, and that when a child is not so severely impaired a diagnosis of AS might be more acceptable.

When addressing the subject of outcome in autism and autistic-like conditions, Gillberg reviewed a number of surveys and follow-up studies, commenting that there is little systematic, empirical, documented evidence to show what, in fact, the outcome in autism is.[39] This is because so few studies had been undertaken. The first of these was published by Lotter when he reviewed all published cases of outcome in autism up to the mid-1970s.[40] He discarded all but eight on the grounds of faulty diagnosis, lack of proper follow-up procedures, and some other factors. These eight studies included 474 children. Gillberg gives a six-point summary of Lotter's findings:

1. The outcome was quite variable. Many had very poor social and academic progress while others did very well.

2. In giving a breakdown of the figures it transpired that two-thirds were in the poor outcome category but one-third was not.

3. The mortality rate for the age group was higher than normal (1.5%). In the average population it is about one-third of that.

4. There was a high rate of epilepsy. It is now known that the overall rate of epilepsy in autism is about one-third of all cases.

5. A few studies reported significant changes in adolescence. Some deteriorated but some improved considerably.

6. A small proportion, less than one in ten, held jobs or went to college in early adult life. This was irrespective of treatment given.

Gillberg moves on to a consideration of the most recent studies of outcome in typical autism cases. This time he divides the findings into three groups:

1. Those who do well and those who make significant progress. He points out that virtually all studies report a small proportion of children who appear to do well

or very well by adolescence or early adult life; commenting that "most experienced authors in the field have come across quite a number of children who appear to 'grow out of autism.' " In discussing this fact he states that the cure will often be attributed to the treatment given to the child, but the fact remains that many such children receive no treatment. He considers that "It seems much more likely that some, as yet unidentified, neurobiological phenomenon accounts for the 'growing out of autism.' "

2. The many who remain extremely handicapped. In discussing this group he gives figures from his own follow-up study of a combined group of adolescents and young adults with autism and autistic-like conditions. Of these almost two-thirds did poorly or very poorly in their late teens and early adult life. Overall 4 percent were almost indistinguishable from normal, and another 11 percent had made exceptional progress. Epilepsy occurred in slightly over one-third of all cases.

3. Those who have severe adolescent problems. With regard to this group, he comments that perhaps the most surprising finding of the study was that more than half of all cases showed either a temporary or a permanent aggravation of symptoms during a follow-up study in adolescence.

He summarizes:

Outcome in autism is quite variable (and in many cases clearly dependent on underlying causes). Slightly less than 10% do very well in adult life, hold jobs, and even have families in some cases. This proportion, of course, varies according to criteria used for diagnosing autism. Those children who have a tested performance IQ exceeding 70 and have some communicative speech around the age of five years and who have already at that age begun to show considerable improvement are the ones most likely to have a very favourable outcome in adult life, regardless of treatment given. Some 60% of the whole group of children with typical autism will grow up to be completely dependent on other adults in all aspects of life.[39]

DR. UTA FRITH

Dr. Uta Frith is professor at the Institute of Cognitive Neuroscience at University College in London. Her field is cognitive psychology (see glossary).

In discussing the possible basic underlying cognitive dysfunction in autism in *Autism: Explaining the Enigma*, she puts forward her theory of "impaired central coherence."[7A] She points first to the question of the uneven performance of autistic children on intelligence tests, stating that "*The pole of worst performance* lies on those subtests that demand a high degree of communicative competence"; and that "*The pole of best performance* lies on those subtests of which Block Design is the most typical." The Block Design test requires the child to copy an abstract pattern with little cubes within a given time limit. All autistic children do well on this type of test. Next she traces the path of success on Block Design tests to "an ability *not to take account of context*." In fact autistic children do badly on IQ tests where context is important, and they do well on those tests where a wider context is missing. This is opposite of what is seen in normal children.

Frith then produces evidence to show that autistic children score above average for their age on a second test, the Embedded Figures test. This is a test where smaller figures hidden in a larger design must be identified. This test requires the ability to "disregard context." She first asks the question, "Why is it normally so strangely effortful to detach the hidden figure from its embedding context?" She answers it with "It is as if there were a strong force that pulls information together. It certainly feels like a force, because in order to disembed the hidden figures, one has to resist a natural tendency to embed. It is as if detachment had to be fought for and as if coherence was the stronger of the two."

She then explains the question of "coherence of information," putting forward a simple basic model of the mind in terms of peripheral input and output processes and central thought processes. The input devices transform sensations into perceptions. The output devices carry out action. In between are the central thought processes that interpret, compare, and store information. They also initiate action. Frith focuses the search for the cognitive dysfunction in autism on these central thought processes, hypothesizing that here there must be a central, cohesive force that pulls together large and small amounts of information. She proposes that in autism this central cohesive force is weak and lacking in control and that this results in "an incoherent world of fragmented experience." She then produces evidence in support of her theory and concludes:

> The red thread running through all the results is the high performance of autistic children on tasks requiring isolation of stimuli, favouring detachment, and their low performance on tasks requiring connection of stimuli, favouring coherence. In contrast, for young normal children, retarded children, and also unschooled older children from a different cultural background, the balance goes entirely in the opposite direction. Therefore, we assume that a central cohesive force is a natural (and useful) characteristic of the cognitive system. But we also assume that it is significantly impaired in Autism.[7A]

Frith then discusses the question of theory of mind and autism. What is a theory of mind? She describes it as the ability to "predict relationships between external states of affairs and internal states of mind" and calls it the ability to mentalize. To test the hypothesis that autistic children lack a theory of mind, she describes the Sally-Anne experiment. For this purpose two dolls are used, one called Sally, the other called Anne. Sally has a basket and Anne has a box. Sally puts a marble into her basket. Then she goes out. While Sally is away Anne takes the marble out of the basket and puts it into her box. Then Sally comes back. At that point the question is asked "Where will Sally look for the marble?"

When this experiment was tried out with autistic, normal, and mentally retarded children, the results were revealing. Most of the nonautistic children gave the correct answer by pointing to the basket. In contrast the vast majority of the autistic children got it wrong. They pointed to the box. Most of the autistic children did not seem to be able to infer that if Sally had not seen the marble being transferred to the box, she would naturally assume that it was still in the basket. They could not mentalize Sally's own belief about the marble. When carrying out other experiments designed along similar lines, Frith and her colleagues got similar results.

The origins of theory of mind are then discussed and the connection between developing a theory of mind and the ability to pretend. Asking what has to happen for this to happen, she points out how the mind of the normal infant is equipped from birth with the knowledge of such fundamental concepts as "time, space and causality." This allows the child to form representations about people and objects and enables the child to "learn specifics about his world." Representations, in turn, "bring the world into the mind." She refers to the work of Dr. Allen Leslie who puts forward the idea that in the second year of life the ability to pretend begins to develop, and out of this grows the ability to mentalize. Therefore she indicates "pretence can be seen as a precursor of a theory of mind." She draws attention to the fact that there is a conspicuous absence of pretend play in children with autism, and that reality-oriented play is present in autistic children but rarely, if ever, the make-believe play found in the average preschool child.

Finally, Frith makes the connection between Wing's triad of impairments and a theory of mind, stating "Better than any other theory so far it can explain the three symptoms that constitutes Wing's triad of impairments and which are seen in all autistic children. Wing's triad refers to impaired social relationships, impaired communication, and impaired make-believe play."

Research into theory of mind, ToM, is ongoing. Over the last decade a number of instruments have been devised to assess theory of mind in children with autism, and specific programs exist to develop theory of mind skills in these children. These have proven successful in that the children who received training were able to pass ToM tasks. However the evidence is that (as in the case of Mark R.), while they could understand such situations in the abstract, this did not always translate into success in the real world. Ozonoff and Miller set out to teach more able autistic children theory of mind concepts, but even though they could now pass such tasks on paper, there was little improvement in the real life area of social skills.[41] The results of other studies conducted along similar lines showed corresponding findings. It would appear that even high-functioning autistic children or children with AS, when in actual social situations, may not be able to use this knowledge. It has been found that performance on theory of mind tasks was correlated with IQ, and this suggests that cognitive impairment may be a factor influencing this ability.[42] Attempts have been made to use ToM tasks to separate high-functioning autism (HFA) from Asperger syndrome (AS), but these studies have yielded conflicting and inconclusive results. This may reflect the lack of consensus on the definition of AS.

DR. DIGBY TANTAM

Dr. Digby Tantam is clinical professor of psychotherapy at the University of Sheffield in the United Kingdom, and he also has published the outcome in adulthood of people with Asperger syndrome.[43] In this survey he interviewed forty-six subjects. Their mean age was 24.4 years and the sex ratio was six males to one female. He found that in this sample two-thirds showed impairment in social ability, while almost all were found to have significant impairment in the area of nonverbal expression. In addition almost all of this group showed limited and "asocial special interests." On the question of outcome, his findings showed that over half of his sample were living in residential care, slightly less were living with parents, and just a few were living independently. Some of this sample were married. Less than 10 percent of the group were currently employed, and 4 percent were in higher education. In discussing his survey in detail, Tantam gives case histories to illustrate the salient features.

On the topic of complications of Asperger syndrome, he records that of eighty-five adults whom he examined clinically, over one-third had a superimposed psychiatric disorder. In common with Wing and Tantam a number of other researchers have reported this higher than expected risk of mental illness among the Asperger syndrome population. Tantam's own figures report an incidence of mania in almost 10 percent of his sample and schizophrenia in a further 3.5 percent. The single most common disorder was depression, occurring in one in every seven cases.

In dealing with the question of clumsiness in Asperger syndrome, he reports that almost all of the above individuals examined were judged to be clumsy, and he suggests that the motor difficulty here may lie in learning movement rather than performing movement. This would lead to the situation whereby movements that require little learning would not be clumsy, while those that require much learning, like social behavior, would be clumsy. Discussing the problem an Asperger person would have, as a result of his clumsiness in coordinating gaze and movement, he reflects that this area could result in a lack of ability to follow the behavior of others and consequently to grasp the essentials involved in social behaviors.

On the question of intelligence, his research showed that there was considerable variation in IQ scores between the individuals involved. The overall average verbal IQ was slightly over 90, and the performance IQ a little below 90. In one individual the PIQ was greatly in excess of the VIQ, whereas in another the PIQ was thirty points below the VIQ. Overall, 12 percent of his sample were mentally handicapped. Here he points out that, as other workers have documented, the condition of Asperger syndrome does not exclude mental handicap.

Tantam then documents his own hypothesis concerning Asperger syndrome. This hypothesis suggests that "Asperger syndrome results from a failure of congenital gaze reflexes, which ensure that the normal infant attends to social signals preferentially and locks the normal infant into the ebb and flow of social interaction. . . . According to this hypothesis, the lack of inbuilt gaze responses results in the person with Asperger syndrome being unable to acquire the fundamentals of social competence."

In the light of the growing evidence that people with Asperger syndrome have difficulty with both recognizing faces and recognizing emotions, Tantam undertook an investigation of sixteen adults with AS while using seven adults without AS as a control group. Still photographs and video recordings were used. His results showed that the AS group were significantly worse at interpreting "still photographs of posed emotions" than the control group. They were also worse at most of the tests using the video recordings, and significantly worse at the tests involving faces or sounds alone.

Subsequently Tantam was again involved in a study of this aspect of autism and Asperger syndrome.[44] This team began by summing up the research into face perception over the previous twenty years and put forward the idea that one way of accounting for peculiarities in facial perception is to argue that children with autism perceive faces in terms of their component properties alone, rather than viewing the face as a whole.

In this study they set out to test three hypotheses with regard to face processing in autism: (1) Was it specific only to the problem of perceiving emotional expression? (2) Is it true that at least some autistic children have an impairment that is specific to face processing? (3) Is there a general perceptual deficit in autism? For this study they recruited a number of able autistic children (IQ of 75 or above), most of whom had a diagnosis of Asperger syndrome, and a number of low ability autistic children (IQ below 75). Both groups were matched with suitable controls. This study was divided into two parts. The first part tested the children's ability to recognize, in photographs, the emotions of sadness, anger, and surprise and also tested their ability on stimuli that had nothing to do with face processing, for example, shape, color, and design.

The second part of the study was designed to investigate what strategies the autistic children used to process face perception when compared with controls, and having found the answer to that, to investigate whether this was due to a deficit that applied only to emotion or perhaps only to face perception, or was it in fact part of a more fundamental perceptual problem. Photographs of faces were again used. A statistical analysis of the results showed that the high ability autistic and Asperger syndrome children performed worse across all tests, both facial and nonfacial, in comparison to the control group. There was no support for the idea that the deficiency applied only to recognizing emotions or only to recognizing faces—to quote, "There is no evidence of a selective disorder specifically relating to the recognition of facial expression of emotions. The results lend themselves to an interpretation in terms of a general perceptual disorder, whereby children with autism may be unable to make use of configural information in faces, which leads to reduced expertise in all aspects of face perception."[44]

With regard to the low ability children, the results showed no significant differences on any of the tests between the autistic children and the mentally retarded children used as controls for this group. Also there was no evidence of either an emotion-specific deficit, a face-specific deficit, or of a general perceptual deficit in the low ability autistic children. In their discussion this team stated that "It is possible that general mental retardation was responsible for this absence of difference in performance, with all children performing badly on the tests." However, they add that the mental age of both these groups of children corresponded to that of normal four- to five-year-olds, and they were selected only if they were capable of understanding the instructions.

In their final summing up these authors point to literature that suggests

that the transition from reliance on isolated features to the use of more relational configural information is not something specific to face perception, but is a general process that occurs as one develops expertise with a particular class of perceptual stimuli. Our results suggest that this transition fails to occur for individuals with autism, who continue to rely on piecemeal processing of visual stimuli at an age when other children would have progressed to configural processing.[44]

In conclusion they suggest that for some autistic children "training might be necessary in face perception generally, and not just in the area of emotional expressions."

CHAPTER 8

INTERVENTION, EDUCATION AND BEYOND

In the course of studying autism in the early 1970s, researchers discovered that children with autism have difficulty in responding to more than one stimulus at a time. When the responses of three groups of children—children with autism, mentally retarded children, and children without a handicap—were compared on the basis of their reaction to the stimulus of sound, sight, and touch, the responses made by the children without disability involved all three stimuli. By contrast, the mentally retarded children made their response on the basis of two stimuli, while the children with autism had learned the response on the basis of one stimulus only.[45] Over the last twenty years many other researchers have carried out experiments along the same lines and have obtained similar results. In contrast, by age seven the average child can respond to instructions containing four components with 100 percent accuracy.[46] There is evidence from the literature, which contains papers from a number of researchers in this field, that a disturbance in responding to more than one stimulus at a time may be associated with abnormal development in such areas as speech, language, and social behavior. Since this fact was noted a number of programs have been devised to teach children with autism how to respond to a stimulus containing more than one component. This approach is called "multiple-cue training," and it has been proven successful. A very comprehensive account and detailed review of the literature on this subject is given in the work of Dr. John

Charles Burke of the Kennedy Institute and Johns Hopkins University School of Medicine.[46]

DR. O. IVAR LOVAAS

Dr. O. Ivar Lovaas of the Psychology Department at the University of California in Los Angeles was one of the first therapists to implement a behavior modification program in very young children with autism. In 1981 he and his colleagues published a book entitled *Teaching Developmentally Disabled Children*, which later became known as *The Me Book*.[47] In it they set out a step-by-step guide for parents on how to teach their developmentally disabled child. This is a very intensive program. All work is carried out on a one-to-one basis and expanded into all the situations in which the child lives—the home, the school, and the community. In their guiding advice to parents these authors point out that there is much hard work involved and they recommend that a teaching team of workers be recruited to help with the program in order to prevent burn-out on the part of the parents.

Inherent in their teaching philosophy is the belief that while the average environment is the best setting for teaching the average individual since this has been molded over time by the average person, by contrast, individuals outside this average range require a special environment for learning. The reason for this, they hold, is that this latter group does not seem capable of learning well in the normal environment which has not been molded to their specific needs. However, they consider, this special environment should be as close as possible to the natural one because this will facilitate the hoped for transition over time of the child back to the normal environment. One of their principal aims in the education of people with developmental disabilities is to achieve as good a level of functioning as possible in the normal conditions of life.

What is the success rate of the Lovaas program? In 1987 Lovaas published a paper in the *Journal of Consulting and Clinical Psychology*, detailing his program and giving the results of a long-term follow-up study of behavior modification treatment in two groups of similarly constituted young children with autism with no marked differences between them on all test scores.[48] The program spanned fifteen years in all. Each group contained nineteen subjects. At intake the level of intelligence was the same for both groups. Two children in each group obtained scores within the normal span of intelligence; seven were in the moderately retarded span; and ten were in the severely retarded span. One group was called the intensive treatment experimental group, and they received in the range of forty hours of one-on-one treatment per week for two years or more. The other was the minimal treatment Control Group, and they received less than ten hours of one-on-one treatment per week for two or more years. This group also received additional treatment; for example, inclusion in small special education classes. There was also a second control group, but the results from this group are not reported here. One of the conditions of recruitment for this study was that the child's age be less than forty months if no speech was present and less than forty-six months if the child had echolalic speech. Parents were recruited as part of the treatment unit, and they received intensive training so that the child was worked with for almost all of his waking hours every day of the year.

In the first year of the program the goal of the treatment was to reduce self-stimulating and aggressive behavior, to teach the ability to carry out simple instructions, to teach imitation, to teach how to play with toys, and to get these behaviors extended into family life.

In the second year of treatment the focus was on teaching expressive and abstract language and to foster interaction with peers and also to get these behaviors undertaken outside the school and integrated into normal life. In this way the children would be prepared for coping in a preschool environment.

The third year concentrated on the teaching of appropriate emotions; tasks like reading, writing, and arithmetic; and also on learning how to learn by observing how others learn.

What were the results? In the experimental group nine of the children (47%) passed with success through normal first grade in a public school and achieved an average to superior result on IQ tests (range 94–120). Eight children (42%) passed first grade in aphasic classes and achieved an average IQ score of 70 (range 56–95). Two children (10%) were placed in classes for autistic/retarded children. Both these children were profoundly retarded. Overall, this experimental group gained on average 30 IQ points over the children in the Control Group.

The Control Group did not do well. Of this group of nineteen none of the children recovered well enough to receive normal first grade placement. Eight (42%) were in aphasic classes, and the remaining 11 (58%) were in classes for the autistic/retarded.

This project was begun in 1970, and as of 1986 the experimental group was reported to have maintained their progress. Only two individuals changed status; one was moved from an aphasic to a normal classroom, and the other was moved from an aphasic to an autistic/retarded classroom.[48]

In a recent discussion of current interventions in autism, educationalist Polly Yarnall, M.Ed., comments on the increasing knowledge now available about autism in the areas of neurology and genetics and considers that this information is not yet having a significant effect in defining what would be the best educational interventions for any given child, and that this new research gives rise to new considerations that need to be incorporated into behavioral and educational interventions.[49] She analyzes in brief a number of interventions in current practice asking such questions as: Do all inter-

ventions deal with the problem of impaired executive function? Which programs are best at addressing the visual approach to learning found in most
children with autism? With regard to the difficulty experienced by so many
individuals in the area of endeavoring to process auditory and visual stimuli
at the same time, what interventions would best address this issue?

In summarizing the advantages and concerns regarding the Lovaas approach as a current intervention in autism, Yarnall lists the advantages as
being: a recognition of the need for one-on-one instruction; the use of
repetition in reinforcing learned responses; the ability to engage the child's
attention for increased lengths of time; and its effectiveness in some children
in evoking speech. She describes it as a "jump start" for certain children and
considers that the best results will be obtained for those children with higher
IQs and in the "mild-to-moderate range" of autism.

In listing the concerns with the approach she points to the program being
strongly put forward as THE approach for autism despite the absence of
"any comparative research" in support of this claim. In addition she lists that
the curriculum does not allow for differences in subtypes of autism and that
it puts emphasis on training in being compliant and being dependent on
prompting. She also considers that the neurological deficits underlying autism, for example, the ability to shift attention and areas of executive functioning may be ignored in view of the strong emphasis on a behavioral
approach. In conclusion she sums up that the program may place too much
stress on the child and/or the family and that the high cost (reportedly av-
eraging in the range of $50,000 per annum for each child) will prevent equal-
ity of access.[49]

The number of programs providing intensive early intervention treatment
in autism is increasing. In a recent study of early intervention in autism, six
such programs, including that of Lovaas and his colleagues, were reviewed
by Rogers.[50] In four of these programs applied behavior analysis (ABA) was
the type of treatment listed, and the hours of tuition per week varied from
fifteen, to fifteen to twenty-five, to twenty-seven, to forty (Lovaas). First,
Rogers points out that none of these studies used the most strict experimental methodologies which would have involved random assignment of the
children to different groups, in addition to selecting appraisers who were
blind to all facets of the research. However, she nonetheless holds, there was
much common ground between the results recorded by the studies. All had
reported marked speeding up of "developmental rates," giving rise to marked
IQ gains, as well as considerable improvement in language. There was also
a reduction in the symptoms of autism as well as better social behavior. She
concludes that the findings point to the fact that some classes of intensive
intervention undertaken early in life would seem to be able to reduce the
devastating effects of autism. She also concludes that the evidence points to
younger children between two and four being able to reap more benefit from
a given program than do older children. She puts forward the idea that

in autism, it may be possible to environmentally mold development at a certain vital period in early life. She points to two important necessary areas of future research which need to be undertaken so that programs of this nature can be made available to much larger numbers of children with autism. These are (1) to identify, in these programs what the vital factors are which bring about sound, positive improvements, and (2) to compare and contrast different sub-groups in autism on the basis of, for example, IQ, and on the basis of verbal capacity, in order to establish how they benefit from individual areas of each program. She emphasizes that all these questions need to be answered using strict scientific protocols.[50]

More recently, in December 1999, the United States Surgeon General David Satcher, M.D., in releasing the first-ever report on mental health, included an overview of autism. In it, under the section on treatment, he points to the importance of early intervention, stating:

Because autism is a severe, chronic developmental disorder, which results in significant lifelong disability, the goal of treatment is to promote the child's social and language development and minimize behaviors that interfere with the child's functioning and learning. Intensive, sustained special education programs and behavior therapy early in life can increase the ability of the child with autism to acquire language and ability to learn. Special education programs in highly structured environments appear to help the child acquire self-care, social, and job skills. Only in the past decade have studies shown positive outcomes for very young children with autism. Given the severity of the impairment, high intensity of service needs, and costs (both human and financial), there has been an ongoing search for effective treatment. Thirty years of research demonstrated the efficacy of applied behavioral methods in reducing inappropriate behavior and in increasing communication, learning, and appropriate social behavior.[51]

In view of all of the above, How young then is young? Many experienced clinicians and observers agree that many parents of a child with autism become aware very early on, even in the first few months of life, that there is something seriously wrong with their child. Lack of eye contact is often the single most common abnormality reported by parents, while abnormal responses to sensory stimuli are a close second. The problem then for parents becomes one of trying to get a diagnosis and trying to get it as early as possible so that the best program can be initiated to help their child.

Checklist for Autism in Toddlers (CHAT) has been designed as a means of diagnosing autism in infancy. It was used to obtain data on the incidence of autism among 16,000 children in Southeast England. These children were screened by their medical doctor or health visitor during their routine eighteen-month-old developmental checkup. Earlier research had suggested that children who failed three items on the CHAT were at risk of having autism. In the present study twelve children out of the sixteen thousand consistently failed the following three items on the CHAT:

1. Protodeclarative pointing (PDP); this means pointing at an object, not to get it, but to direct another person's attention to it, to share an interest in it. The normal nine-to-fourteen-month-old infant will do this.

2. Gaze monitoring (GM); that is, turning to look in the same direction as an adult is looking. Again, the normal nine-to-fourteen-month-old infant will show this behavior.

3. Pretend play (PP); this form of play makes its earliest appearance in the normal infant, in simple form, at about fourteen months.[52]

When the researchers examined these twelve children, they diagnosed ten of them as having autism. When these ten children with autism were examined again at three-and-a-half years of age, their diagnosis remained the same. Also, the two remaining children who did not receive a diagnosis of autism at eighteen months, received a diagnosis of developmental delay. The researchers concluded that "consistent failure of the three key items from the CHAT at eighteen months of age carries an 83.3 percent risk of autism; and this pattern of risk indicator is specific to autism when compared to other forms of developmental delay."[52] These authors stress that at this stage expert diagnosis should be sought.

An investigation is now being set up in order to find out how many children with autism were missed by the test. Subsequent research indicates that the CHAT was less sensitive to milder symptoms of autism, as children later diagnosed with PDDNOS, Asperger, or atypical autism did not routinely fail the CHAT at eighteen months.[12] This research also quotes studies using home videos, which correctly identified infants with autism at twelve months of age on the basis of the following four behaviors: eye contact, orienting to name being called, pointing, and showing. Other research suggests that diagnosis at eight to twelve months is now feasible and that consideration of behaviors not previously thought to be diagnostic, such as motor behaviors, may lower the threshold for identification even more.[18]

There is in the literature a report of two siblings, now in their teenage years, whose functioning deteriorated in the second year of life until they met criteria for autistic disorder. They are reported to have recovered completely after being treated with a form of intensive behavioral and language therapy based on the work of Lovaas (1981).[53] Their mother has written the story of their treatment and recovery in a book entitled *Let Me Hear Your Voice* under the pen name of Catherine Maurice.[54] These two children were diagnosed as having autism around the age of eighteen months by noted psychologists, psychiatrists, and neurologists in New York City. So there is no possibility of having had a mistaken diagnosis of autism. Three of these professionals have gone on record to state that there are now no signs of autism in these two children.[53]

Another book, *Autism: From Tragedy to Triumph*, by Carol Johnson and Julia Crowder, tells the story of Drew.[55] Drew himself has written the afterword to the book. It is a biographical essay written by Drew for a second-year psychology class. Drew was in fact one of the intensive treatment experimental group patients on the Young Autism Project set up by Dr. Lovaas.

DR. KIYO KITAHARA

Another pioneer in the field of education in autism was Dr. Kiyo Kitahara, a Japanese educationalist who in the early 1970s set up a private school in Tokyo for autistic children in order to educate them alongside their peer group without disabilities. Daily Life Therapy is the name she gave to her educational model. This model appears to be based on Eastern philosophy, which takes into account the relationship between body, mind, and spirit, and combines with it the Japanese focus on group education.[56]

In 1987 a Daily Life Therapy program was established at the Boston Higashi School but in contrast to the integrated program in Tokyo, the autistic children at the Boston Higashi are educated in a segregated environment. The Daily Life Therapy embraces a whole philosophy of education dealing with emotional development and social well being, as well as learning in the ordinary traditional sense. It is not just a curriculum for autistic children. Kitahara (as reviewed by Dr. Kathleen Quill and colleagues[56]) described Daily Life Therapy as consisting of three main features: to establish a "rhythm of life"; to stabilize "the child's weak emotions" through physical training, to remove the child's "spirit of dependence" through interaction in group education; and to nourish the development of the intellect by physical repetition. Much emphasis is placed on learning through imitation.

In the classroom the average pupil to teacher ratio is eight to one. Most of the activities for the day center around music, movement, and art. These are the main subjects on the curriculum. The philosophy behind this model is in sharp contrast to our Western special educational culture, which centers around the needs of the individual child. It is reminiscent of the great schools of ancient Greece, where the curriculum consisted of the three disciplines of music, movement, and mathematics, and this was combined with a group focus. These were designed to produce within the individual harmony, balance, discipline, the ability to abstract, to see relationships, and to focus one's inner rhythm. This was the educational philosophy which, over two thousand years ago, produced the Golden Age of Greek culture, a culture which changed the world and brought with it one of the greatest civilizations in the history of mankind. It also produced some of the greatest philosophers and scientists of all time, including Socrates, Plato, and Aristotle.

Insights into the Daily Life Therapy program are given by Quill et al. in the following extract.

Art, music, and movement lessons are highly structured. Instruction involves a high degree of behavioural patterning and repetition, for example, copying a display picture, imitating a drumbeat, or imitating a set of motor exercises. On a daily basis, children at the Boston Higashi School perform their musical and movement skills during school assemblies and for school visitors. The children's art work is displayed throughout the school. In this way, Daily Life Therapy is designed to focus on the children's strengths, in the hope of developing avenues for self-expression and building self-esteem.[56]

Quill et al. then discusses the physical exercise program and in this context draws attention to the work of Hardy.[57]

Daily Life Therapy incorporates the use of vigorous physical exercise as a central feature of the curriculum. The programme of intense physical exercise, dominated by running, appears to function as a means to decrease the children's undesirable behaviours by the natural release of beta-endorphins, and therefore, facilitates the children's ability to attend and learn [Hardy 1987 cite]. During the first months in the program, children ran outside for 20 minutes, 2–3 times a day. Children who are resistant to running are physically guided through the running course by an adult. An additional daily gym period includes gymnastics, aerobic exercises, and martial arts. The children engage in outside play for another hour, which involves soccer, basketball, biking, and climbing on play equipment. For the preschool children, the rigor of the exercise programme is modified. Long walks are substituted for running and regular playground equipment is used for outside play. Their gym activities include roller skating, biking, and sprinting, along with movement games requiring motor imitation.[56]

Anecdotal evidence from parents on the progress made by their children attending the Higashi School reports substantial improvement in the areas of challenging behaviors, ritualistic behaviors, self-care skills, and the ability to join in group activity. As Quill and her colleagues (who themselves observed marked decrease in challenging behaviors among many children at the school) comment, there is a possibility that in the case of children with autism some forms of learning such as behavior control, social skills, and the ability to imitate can best be acquired in a large group setting, whereas other skills, by contrast, may require individual attention. They also suggest that by concentrating on individualized programs, which aim to address the autistic child's "functional skills," their acquisition of social skills may be compromised. Finally, they comment on the increasing interest developing with regard to the relationship between problem behavior and physical exercise.[56]

In 1977 handicapped children in the United States gained access to education as their legal right for the first time. Eleven years prior to that, an educational intervention program was set up as a pilot project at the School of Medicine of the University of North Carolina. This was called the TEACCH program (Treatment and Education of Autistic and related Communication-handicapped CHildren). By 1972 Division TEACCH had been expanded into a state-wide program; more recently, in 1989, the organization initiated a collaborative supported employment scheme.

The basic TEACCH model is an interactive one involving parents, teachers, and professionals. The services include assessment and diagnosis, advice to parents on their role, a treatment plan tailored to the individual, and a consultative service to professionals and other organizations involved with autism.[58] The scope of the program extends from age five right through the junior school years to vocational training and supported employment. The focus in the first part of this section is on this latter area of vocational options and employment.

DR. MARY E. VAN BOURGONDIEN AND
DR. AMY V. WOODS

In discussing the TEACCH program in the context of "Vocational Possibilities for High-Functioning Adults with Autism," Dr. Mary E. Van Bourgondien and Dr. Amy V. Woods, at Division TEACCH in the Department of Psychiatry at the University of North Carolina, reveal the core concepts and philosophy behind the model.[59] They explain the four functional components on which it is based: (1) a collaborative focus on the part of all concerned; (2) a holistic approach as opposed to a specialist-oriented approach on the part of the professionals involved; (3) a person-centered assessment of the client's skills and deficits; and (4) what is defined as "a two-factor approach to treatment."

They confirm that central to the theme of the model is a close collaboration between parents and all professionals involved with all aspects of the child's and adult's life. They share knowledge, they share problems, they support each other, and they work together in the community for the life enhancement of the individual with autism. Because of this ongoing consultation and collaboration, the chances of a successful outcome are greatly improved.

The second concept of care requires that the professional who works with people with autism takes on the role of a "generalist," thus taking responsibility for the treatment of the whole person rather than just specialized care. As the above authors indicate, this will enable everybody working with the person with autism to cope with the full range of problems encountered. Because of the great variation in skills and abilities met with in autism even within the one person, the concept of an individual approach to assessment for training and placement is an essential third part of this program. They write that a specific program was designed in order to define the requirements of both adults and adolescents. This focuses on six particular areas of functioning: (1) "vocational skills"; (2) "vocational behaviors"; (3) "functional communication"; (4) "interpersonal behaviors"; (5) "independent functioning"; and (6) "leisure skills." The assessment here is based on existing skills and emerging skills and employs a "pass-emerge-fail" method of marking. By this method the person's overall abilities and deficits can be directly compared with the demands of the school or work setting. There is continuous on-the-job evaluation to monitor progress, and every effort is made to tailor the job to each individual's preferential strengths and interests. Finally, in the "two-factor approach to treatment" these authors concede that the best possible results will be obtained by improving both the abilities and adaptability of the persons concerned and also by taking cognizance of their weaker points and structuring the environment to counteract these qualities. This practice will ensure that the individual has every possible opportunity to cope well in the environment and be successful.[59]

An overview of the TEACCH supported employment program gives an account of the three models used.[58] With the reported high retention rate of almost 90 percent, this program is obviously successful and shows that, given the right working conditions, appropriate training, and sustained assistance, supported employment is a serious option for individuals with autism. Among the three models used are the individual placement model, where the job coach works with the person in finding the job, provides on-the-job training, and then withdraws but of course is always available if needed. In the dispersed enclave model a job coach is allocated to a group of people with autism who are employed by one particular business concern. These workers require day-to-day back-up from the job coach. The example given of the work done by the mobile crew model is in the area of house cleaning services. Here the job coach is at the work site on a daily basis with a few people who might have behavioral difficulties or difficulties staying on task. The mobile crew model has been found to be an excellent training ground, and from the experience gained there, trainees have been able to move to the enclave model. The authors of this report attribute the success of the program to its emphasis on long-term support services that are not simply limited to the work site but also extend into areas of social, vocational, and residential aspects of life.[58]

In commenting on the advantages of the TEACCH approach as an intervention in autism, Yarnall lists such factors as the dynamism of the model; the fact that it incorporates research from many fields of knowledge; the fact that it does not remain static; its ability to anticipate and support "inclusive strategies"; its compatibility with other therapies such as the Picture Exchange Communication System (PECS); its individualized approach and assessment; the way it can identify "emerging skills," giving the best possible forum for success; and its ability to modify the program to lessen stress on the individual or the family.

In commenting on the concerns some people have with the approach, she lists their belief that TEACCH, rather than fighting autism, "gives in" to it (a concern she disputes in her notes); also the fact that some people see it as an approach that segregates children with autism. In addition, she lists the fact that not enough stress is placed on "communication and social development" and that the practice of having independent work centers may lead to isolation. However, her notes point out that these are erroneous assumptions.[49]

MR. BARRY NEIL KAUFMAN AND
MRS. SAMAHRIA KAUFMAN

Barry Neil Kaufman and Samahria Kaufman are the parents of Raun, who was born with autism and was treated with an intensive early intervention program called "The Son-Rise Program." This program was devised by his parents when he was seventeen months old. On reaching his third birthday he was functioning above and beyond the level of his peer group. He is the subject of a book called *Son-Rise: The Miracle Continues*.[60] A film also called *Son-Rise* has been made about his treatment between seventeen months and four years.

Raun is now a young man with a high IQ, a university graduate, and a high achiever in both the academic and the social sphere. The Option Institute and The Autism Treatment Center of America run by his parents offer training and instruction to other parents in the method that they devised for their own son. The philosophy behind the Option Process is summed up in the title of another book written by Barry Kaufman, *To Love is to Be Happy With*.[61] By adopting this philosophy the parents make a conscious decision to love their child and his autism, to accept him as he is, and freely choose the option of being happy with him. This decision will then free them up to cast aside all negativity about his disability. From then on they can put their full energies into working with him for change. This attitude of acceptance on the part of the parents in turn gives the child the best possible environment for progress. The essence of the Son-Rise program is that we freely choose our options. We choose to be happy with a situation or to be sad and disappointed with it. As Barry Neil Kaufman describes it, "*The Option Process is not so much a tool or formula technique as it is an attitude and a developing process of seeing*. There is only one truth, although there are many paths leading to it."[61]

The Kaufmans were believers and teachers of the Option Process before Raun was born. They began their work with him making no judgments; setting down no conditions; having no expectations. Acceptance was the first part of the therapy. The next step was to observe him and his behavior closely. They then joined him in his "isms." Whatever he did, they did alongside him. On the basis of their observations they hypothesized three areas of apparent dysfunction. "First, his ability to perceive and digest data from people and events appeared severely inhibited. Second, he did not seem capable of using whatever information he could absorb in a manner meaningful to others. And third, he had designed compelling internal systems to stimulate himself . . . all of which drew him further inside."[60]

Having established this base, they then formulated a three-pronged program, the first part of which revolved around always demonstrating an attitude of non-judgment and acceptance to their son. They then set out to make Raun aware of the world around him and to make it increasingly attractive in the hope that he would want to join it. Sound and music of all kinds, from Beethoven to jazz, played a part in this phase of the program. Emphasis was also placed on establishing eye contact. In addition, Raun was put on a natural diet of whole foods, fish, high-protein vegetables, and all sugars, additives, and preservatives were eliminated from his diet.

The third phase then, "would involve developing a teaching program for him that simplified every activity and every event into small and digestible parts. We would help him dissect his external environment into comprehensible portions so that he could build new pathways and construct new roads where old ones might have been damaged or broken. For us, autism was a brain or neurological disorder that short-circuited the process of perceptions and the utilization of memory."[60] Also great attention was paid to encouraging and inspiring Raun to connect with the people around him through further eye contact and interactive play. As he developed more of a capacity to interact, play with, and be involved with the people in his life he then learned age-appropriate social, academic, and motor skills. Like the Lovaas program, this was a very intensive one, and all work was carried out on a one-to-one basis. Helpers were recruited and trained by Raun's parents to take over some of the therapy sessions so that eventually, between parents, siblings, and helpers, Raun was worked with on an ongoing basis. The great breakthrough came when he developed speech. This occurred within six months of the beginning of the program.

The Son-Rise Program at The Option Institute offers family training courses to parents with children with special needs. In these programs parents receive support and help in dealing with the strange behaviors of their child and insight and training in how to work with the child for change. Among other concerns challenging behavior is addressed, and strategies for coping with it are developed and learned. Parents are also given the opportunity to stand back from their situation, to view it objectively, and to talk through their own concerns. Anecdotal evidence from parents who have been on the training program and video-tape material is very positive about the benefits that both they and their child have received from training at the Son-Rise Program at the Autism Treatment Center of America. Programs are also run for professionals.[60]

DR. PAUL NORDOFF AND DR. CLIVE ROBBINS

Music is not generally thought of as a therapy for autism. Not just in an inactive, acquiescing, listening sense, but as a vigorous, energetic interaction with themes and rhythms under the guidance of a trained therapist. Under these conditions music has been described as a concrete experience of communication not dependent on abstract thought but allowing for interaction with others even in the absence of speech. It has the power to charge and change emotions and moods. These are some of the reasons why music therapy in this sense has been successful in helping autistic children to overcome their isolation and respond to those around them. Many children with autism, like Mark R., seem to find it easier to sing their first speech. Music is unparalleled in that it can approach the autistic condition from its core.[62]

Dr. Paul Nordoff and Dr. Clive Robbins were two of the pioneers in using music therapy to help children with different types of disabilities including autism. In the late 1950s and throughout the 1960s they travelled to a number of countries in Europe and parts of the United States working with children. The successful techniques they evolved were subsequently published in *Therapy in Music for Handicapped Children*. Today this work is still considered a standard reference text.[62]

They used the drums as their instrument of choice to introduce the children to music. Their aim was to encourage each individual child to express his inner turmoil and emotions through the beating of the drum in rhythm with the keyboard improvisations of the therapist who sat beside him at the piano. They felt that in this situation music should not be used as a tranquillizer, so they avoided quiet, soothing melodies and chose instead music that was often "wild and dissonant," in this way actively setting out to get in touch with the inner rhythm of the children and to discover how music-making affected them. They found that the children differed greatly in their approach to the drum. Some reacted spontaneously and expressed their feelings freely, while others beat mechanically and without expression. Their ultimate aim as therapists became one of trying to establish the level of pathology that lay behind each child's ability to communicate as revealed in his drum beating. They then worked with this, using the child's own activity at the drum to lead him into the "experiences of mobility and organisation latent in the world of music."

The account of Rosita will illustrate their work. Rosita was a withdrawn, sad, moody, six-year-old whose speech was echolalic and sparse. She was erratic and unpredictable and had an obsession with shoelaces and pieces of string, spending her time tying them into odd figures and shapes. In typical autism fashion, she reversed her pronouns and called herself by her Christian name of Rosita. She was fundamentally a musical child, but for the first few months of her therapy at each of the two weekly twenty-minute sessions she did not get involved musically. Instead she just beat the drum in a dreamlike fashion and then sat back and sucked her thumb. But as the weeks went by, slowly but surely, she got involved and began to play with great gusto, entering fully into all the improvisations. In time she herself led the improvisations, beating loudly and with tremendous vitality, thus playing a musical game with Dr. Nordoff. As he takes up the story:

Most of Rosita's music was very stimulating; a kind of dissonant "carnival" waltz alternated with an idiom used with very few children—jazz. This musical material was subject to all kinds of developments and variations to keep Rosita fully awake and active. The turning point of the work came in a session in February. She was very eager that day and I was able to lead the improvisation, and Rosita with it, into a tremendously energetic *crescendo*. She began to exclaim rhythmically with the music and then to sing, intently but quietly, "Rosita can beat it, yes she can!"—the words of her jazzy song.

This was a breakthrough into *song*. After this the drum-beating diminished; it had served its purpose. We have found this to be a therapeutic milestone with many children. As their drum-beating becomes ever more expressive of musical emotional involvement, they are propelled into new regions of expressive freedom. They simply cannot resist what is happening to them; they just have to sing![62]

Toward the end of this period of her music therapy they report a very significant improvement in her vocabulary. In addition, she began spontaneously to use the first person pronouns, and her behavior at home improved considerably. She also became much more responsive and communicative, and they were able to develop many songs for her.

Another pupil whose progress they describe was six-year-old David, who had impressive calendar skills. His reaction to music alerted them to the possibility of using music therapy as an aid in differential diagnosis. David had poor visual-motor coordination, but they soon discovered by listening to his performance on the drum that he had excellent audio-motor coordination. Similarly, while David did poorly in psychological tests, they discovered that musically his intelligence and perception were exceptional, and he showed "stable qualities of ego-function." Because of his poor visual-motor coordination, it had been impossible to teach him how to tie his shoes, and, as they point out, the normal approach to this is one of visual-spatial control. However, David had no difficulty in tying his shoes when the therapist put the whole process to music in the form of a song. He was then able to coordinate it very successfully on a time basis. The positive report from his music therapy was instrumental in gaining him a placement in a situation with good educational and psychotherapy facilities, and three years later he had progressed sufficiently to be able to attend junior high school at a level of one grade above his age.

One of their youngest pupils was three-and-a-half-year-old Russell, who was without speech. He suffered from intense anxiety and severe temper tantrums and spent long hours just sitting, rhythmically rocking back and forth, "half humming, half grunting." As the therapist accompanied Russell's rocking with Gregorian chantlike music, his sounds gradually changed to musiclike notes in the key of the improvisations but always to the rhythm of his rocking. Over time his musical notes broke free from this rhythm and ultimately they surpassed it. Then the rocking diminished as the rhythm of the rocking was incorporated into his beating on the drum. His therapists found that he was then free to move on to a new stage of development and after a period of time to consolidate his new "ego-organization," he was beating happily and with pleasure and determination on the drum, cymbal, and xylophone.[62]

The authors end this section of their book with future guidelines for empirical research in this area. Dr. Nordoff died in the mid-1970s, but his work is continued by Clive Robins and his wife, Carol, who are directors of the Nordoff Music Therapy Clinic at New York University.

CHAPTER 9

NEW DIRECTIONS

Because autism is defined as a behavioral disorder, over the last fifty years as we have seen, treatment for people with the condition has fluctuated in response to changes among professionals with regard to how such behavior should be viewed and dealt with. Over the last two decades the emphasis has been mainly on the cognitive aspect, and the approach has been a behavioral one, generating a number of specialized educational programs. In certain cases these programs have been very successful, and in many cases they have brought about an improvement in the quality of life for the people concerned. Now, in addition to special education programs, a number of professionals are beginning to look at autism from the point of view of dietary intervention in order to improve the ability of the child to learn.

DR. ANN-MARI KNIVSBERG AND
DR. KARL LUDVIG REICHELT

In the early 1990s a dietary approach to autism based on the results from urine analysis samples was proposed.[63] This resulted from the findings of abnormal urine patterns and increased levels of peptides (partly broken down proteins) from gluten and casein in the twenty-four-hour urine samples from some children with autism. Gluten is the protein found in wheat and other grains, and casein is the protein found in milk and milk products. It is thought that learning may be greatly limited by high levels of peptides in the body, especially by partly digested milk products. Once the diet is free from gluten and casein, the theory is that learning ability would increase, and children could then benefit more from teaching programs.

In order to test this hypothesis Dr. Ann-Mari Knivsberg of the Centre for Reading Research in Stavanger, Norway, and Dr. Karl Reichelt, of the Department of Paediatric Research at the University of Oslo, in conjunction with others, investigated a number of young people with autism.[64] This team chose fifteen individuals ages six to twenty-two years, and they were followed up for a period of four years. Seven were girls and eight were boys. They all had an increased level of peptides and pathological urine patterns in their twenty-four-hour urine sample and had been recommended for dietary intervention. At the start of the study all products containing gluten and casein were removed from the diet. The children and young adults were tested professionally in the following four standard areas: psychotic behavior; social, linguistic, cognitive, and motor abilities; psycholinguistic abilities; and nonverbal cognitive tests. These tests were applied before the diet, after one year, and again after four years. Teachers, as well as parents, cooperated with the professionals in this study. Substantial improvements were reported by these authors in all individuals who adhered to the diet.

From the parents' point of view, all of the children had made progress during the first year; some of course had shown greater improvement than others. They reported improvements in the area of communication, including less echolalia, less perseverative speech, a greater eagerness to communicate, a more adequate response when spoken to, and a greater understanding of the spoken word. The parents also reported an improvement in the ability to socialize, which showed itself in the way their children could now express their feelings, in how their resistance to physical contact had reduced, and in how they showed more interest in other children. Many of those who had had emotional outbursts and irrational fears became more manageable as these symptoms subsided, and there was a decrease in stereotyped behavior. They became less rigid in their behavior patterns and more flexible in adapting to change. Parents also reported a significant change in their attitude toward learning. It was much more positive.

These observations were backed up by evidence from the results obtained in the professional tests. In addition, when tested after one year, the urine patterns and peptide levels of each individual were found to be normal. A significant relationship was correlated between the reduction of peptide levels and the increase in skills and abilities. There was systematic progress in social, cognitive, and communication skills, which occurred as normalization of the urine pattern and peptide levels took place. The most significant changes occurred in the first year of follow-up. After that, there tended to be a levelling off of effect. Informal observations indicated that both their hypersensitivity and their high threshold for pain reduced while on the diet.

Some of the children underwent more change than others, but all changes were in the same direction.

Three children broke the diet, and they are reported to have suffered a significant regression. They had a "marked reduction" on all their raw scores when tested in the standard areas. This reduction coincided with the time during which they returned to their original diet containing quantities of wheat and milk.

A control group was not set up for this study, so it could be argued that a placebo effect might have played a certain role in the significant changes noted. The authors themselves point out that it is difficult to see how a placebo effect (see glossary) could account for such systematic progress in communication skills, as well as social and cognitive development, which coincided with the normalization of the urine samples. They also write that they found it hard to comprehend how a placebo effect could account for the children's decrease in sound sensitivity and tactility, as well as a reduction in emotional outbursts and awkward body movements.[64]

The positive results from this study would certainly warrant further research in this area.

Gillberg and Coleman, in a recent overview of diet responsive autism, ask the question as to whether diet responsive autism exists.[23A] They point to one study that found abnormal permeability of the intestine in nine out of twenty-one patients with autism, in comparison to none in the control group of forty. They also point to evidence from two different research studies of increased levels of antibodies to some components in milk, particularly casein, in a number of autistic children as compared to controls. They report that these findings gave rise to an open trial of a milk-free diet carried out at the University of Rome that showed very positive results. After the trial of eight weeks, distinct improvement was recorded in the behavioral symptoms of some of the autistic patients. Gillberg and Coleman consider that all of these results raise more questions than answers, and they point to the necessity for further "crossover studies."

They also draw attention to the fact that even though physicians generally have recommended to parents that at present the concept of diet responsive autism has not been proven, yet some parents have removed dairy products from their child's diet. They consider this to be a "worrisome" development because a significant number of autistic children have been found to have abnormally low levels of calcium in their urine. They further consider that this low level of calcium may be associated with an abnormality in electroencephalogram (EEG) results, as well as with seizures, and ocular self-mutilation. Dairy products are, of course, a major source of calcium in the diet.[23A]

In referring recently to gut permeability and autism, Dr. Theodore Page of the Department of Neurosciences at the University of California states that the most frequently expressed significance of it is the possibility of toxic substances passing through the gut wall into the bloodstream. As already mentioned, abnormal urine patterns and increased levels of peptides have been found in the urine of some autistic patients. Page considers that these unusual peptides may originate from a leaky gut and that they may be neuroactive. He points to the Knivsberg et al. study as showing that a decrease in autistic symptoms was associated with a reduction of these peptides in urine. However, as Page goes on to indicate, there have been no studies reporting a correlation between increased gut permeability and unusual peptides in urine. In view of this he holds it is difficult to establish whether this is just an "accidental finding" or whether increased intestinal permeability is an "important pathological mechanism in autism."[65]

DR. ISABELLE RAPIN AND DR. ROBERT KATZMAN

As we start into the twenty-first century the tools of neuroscience and molecular genetics are now sufficiently refined to break new ground. These tools are only just beginning to be applied to autism. In the light of modern research where does autism go from here? To sum up the past and get a glimpse into the future we go to the work of Dr. Isabelle Rapin and Dr. Robert Katzman.

Both Dr. Rapin, in the Department of Neurology at Albert Einstein College of Medicine in New York, and Dr. Katzman, in the Department of Neurosciences at the University of California, are workers in the field of neurobiology in autism. In a recent overview of where autism stands today, they paint a very clear picture of research on the move, poised to push out the barriers and extend the frontiers to enter new terrain, and as they write, "The time seems ripe for an all-out attack on autism."[66] Drawing a comparison between the successful pace of research into Alzheimer's disease and the slow pace of research into autism, they show how it is reflected in the work of the scientific community. "This is reflected in the scientific reports on autism, as compared with those on Alzheimer's disease (AD); in 1980, by happenstance, there were 113 articles (based on a key word Medline research) on autism and 113 articles on AD. In 1996, the number of articles on autism was 251, whereas the number on AD had grown to 2,382."

This paper, entitled "Neurobiology of Autism," lays bare the past and probes the future. Its authors discuss first the clinical and diagnostic picture and focus on its strengths and weaknesses, commenting that agreement on diagnosis regarding the salient features is high but that little is known about its pathological basis. They indicate that few adults receive a diagnosis of autism because the diagnosis of autism is based on accurate early childhood case history. Adults who present with autism are likely to receive a diagnosis of simple schizophrenia, inadequate personality, perhaps mental retardation, or epilepsy. As for mildly affected individuals, they may not be counted at all, even though their autism may have followed a typical childhood course and they may still need medical care.

They describe the sensory perception aberrations that occur in autism but say that the neurological basis of them is unknown, adding that "There has been no systematic attempt to study sensory thresholds in any modality [see glossary] in autism and only the most preliminary electrophysiological studies have been reported."

They highlight the question of overlap or comorbidity with other "behaviorally defined development disorders" such as mental deficiency, obsessive compulsive disorder, schizoid personality, manic depressive illness, to name a few, pointing out that diagnosis is dimensional similar to Alzheimer's disease.

Homing in on the span of the autistic spectrum, they raise the much discussed question of whether to lump or split. At present all cases of autism and autistic-like conditions are grouped together as a spectrum disorder. Should one count, they ask, only "nuclear" or typical cases under the diagnosis of autism, or should the "autistic like" cases also be included? And what of the cases resting on the fringes of the spectrum? The high-functioning ones that shade into the eccentric but odd normal population, and those affected with severe mental retardation? There are arguments on both sides of the lump or split divide.

With regard to the prevalence of autism, Rapin and Katzman comment that the incidence is much higher than is commonly supposed. They maintain that the *most* conservative estimate of the autistic population in the United States reaches 100,000. If the conservative estimate is used, the figure reaches 350,000. If based on the broadest estimate, it will be close to one million. All of which they say adds up to a staggering public cost.

Moving on to neuroimaging and the pathology of autism, they reveal that fewer than thirty-five brains of autistic people had been examined to date, and that none of these had been treated with the most modern state-of-the-art techniques. This is in sharp contrast to Alzheimer's disease, where hundreds of brains from well studied individuals have been examined. This brings up a point that has been much emphasized in the literature recently, which is that researchers working on brain structures in autism have been frustrated in their efforts due to scarcity of tissue. In order to address this issue, over the last few months the Autism Society of America (ASA) in a joint venture with the National Alliance of Autism Research (NAAR) have agreed to establish an Autism Tissue Center. This will create a database of individuals who have pledged to donate their brain tissue for research purposes upon their death. This material will then be made available to accredited researchers through a network of brain banks. This is a very important, progressive step forward in assisting research into the pathology of autism.

In summing up the state of research into chemical pathology, Rapin and Katzman state that "Current biochemical evidence is at best speculative, weak, and contradictory." They do, however, point to one of the more reliable findings, which is that an elevated level of the neurotransmitter serotonin has been consistently found in the blood of about a quarter of children with autism. Added to this is a new finding recently reported that suggests a link between a deviant serotonin transporter gene and autism.[67]

Finally, they review the genetic profile of autism and the complex question of how genes interact with the environment. Genetic studies are already under way in a number of laboratories. So far it appears that the pattern of inheritance varies among families but a link with the paternal line may be especially common in Asperger syndrome.

Over the last twenty years the question of autistic regression has been well documented in the literature, but the causes of it are unknown. In commenting on this phenomenon Rapin and Katzman state that about one-third of the parents of autistic children report that their infant or toddler underwent a regression. On average this regression occurred somewhere between eighteen months and two years. In some cases it came suddenly, in others it occurred over a period of weeks or months. In many cases development was entirely normal before it happened. In surmising about the cause of this regression Rapin and Katzman indicate that in a number of cases this regression has been known to have been preceded by an environmental stress, such as a harmless illness, a slight physical trauma, or the kind of normal stress that the average child will take in stride, such as the birth of a younger child. They propose that perhaps "A better surmise may be that the immature brain, given a genetic predisposition, may be susceptible to a variety of nonspecific environmental stresses that precipitate the regression."

Confirming that a minority of these regression cases is associated with epilepsy, they then discuss the role of epilepsy in language and autistic regression, writing that "Defining the pathophysiological role of epilepsy in autistic regression requires a concerted effort, including prolonged recordings of sleep EEGs close in time to the regression and longitudinal documentation of the behaviour and language of children who regress with or without evidence of epilepsy. If epilepsy is the culprit in even a fraction of cases of regression, its prompt treatment might achieve a first preventive treatment for autism."[66]

They end their overview of the status quo in autism today, more than half a century after Kanner and Asperger, with

Thanks in part to *Rainman*, the public is becoming aware that autism is not as rare as was once thought and that it is a serious developmental disorder of the brain rather than a bizarre and fluky behavioral aberration. . . . Genetic studies in multiplex [where more than one is affected] families, now underway, will not elucidate the neurological basis of autism without concurrent, sophisticated pathological, neurochemical, imaging, and electrophysiological studies. The ultimate goal is to understand the pathophysiology of autism well enough to devise specific pharmacological intervention and prevention.[66]

PART III

SOME QUESTIONS

Doth God extract day-labour, light denied?
I fondly ask:—But Patience, to prevent

That murmur, soon replies; God doth not need
Either man's work, or His own gifts: who best
Bear His mild yoke, they serve Him best: His state

Is kingly; thousands at His bidding speed
And post o'er land and ocean without rest:—
They also serve who only stand and wait.

"On His Blindness," John Milton (1608–1674)

CHAPTER 10

❦❦❦

ARE AUTISM AND ASPERGER SYNDROME (AS) DIFFERENT LABELS OR DIFFERENT DISABILITIES?

This chapter discusses the differences and similarities between high-functioning autism (HFA) and Asperger syndrome (AS) and probes the question as to whether they are the same condition differing only in degree or are they in fact, completely different entities and syndromes. When asked the same question, Dr. Eric Schopler of the Department of Psychiatry at the University of North Carolina answered it by saying that if these two diagnostic categories are compared according to the definition written in DSM-IV, the principle difference to be found between them is that autistic disorder is defined by an impairment in communication that usually involves developmental delay, whereas in Asperger syndrome no marked delay in language development is involved. This, he holds, while it may be a distinction that is clinically significant, is "not significant when AS is compared with HFA." He outlines the fact that a number of researchers have attempted to show that a distinction can be made between AS and HFA when the following characteristics are taken into consideration: "more clumsiness, pedantic speech, a higher full-scale IQ, or more impaired executive functioning."[68] But he argues that if a disability is to have a classification of its own it "should have a distinct causal mechanism, a particular course, or intervention." Indicating that this has not happened, he goes on to discuss the situation and points out that the view taken of autism in the United States may be quite different from that taken in Europe. He observes that Hans Asperger was an Austrian pediatrician, and his involvement with the German

Youth Movement may have given him access to a different type of patient, different, that is, from those referred to Leo Kanner. He suggests that in the United States the popular understanding of autism is based on the film *Rainman*.

Schopler does, however, also consider that the positive side of the AS diagnosis may be for professionals, as it will stimulate ongoing research to see if there is a meaningful distinction between AS and HFA. He concludes by maintaining that the decision to use the AS label was taken too early; that is, before a "meaningful clinical distinction had been found and demonstrated."

When writing again on this same topic two years later in the concluding chapter to *Asperger Syndrome or High-Functioning Autism?* Schopler maintains that the net effect of using the AS label before its proper time has been a negative one, and that is has served to slacken the momentum of what advancement had been accomplished to date in autism in the areas of understanding and treatment. He further considers that "premature use of the AS label serves as a seriously flawed model for how psychiatric diagnostic categories are formed."[69]

As previously mentioned it was Dr. Lorna Wing who reintroduced Asperger's work into the literature in 1981. Wing discusses this particular issue of HFA versus AS.[70] She raises the question as to whether the term AS "is of any value," putting forward "two main reasons for the limited usefulness of the label Asperger's syndrome in current clinical practice," as follows

The first . . . is that the diagnosis of autism is, in the minds of many lay people, synonymous with total absence of speech, social isolation, no eye contact, hyperactivity, agility and absorption in bodily stereotypies. There is a lack of understanding of the wide range of severity and the widely differing manifestation of the basic impairments. For this reason, parents without special experience tend to overlook or reject the idea of autism for their socially gauche, naive, talkative, clumsy child, or adult, who is intensely interested in the times of tides around the coast of Great Britain, the need for the abolition of British Summer Time, or the names and relationships of all characters who have ever appeared in a television soap opera, such as "Coronation Street." The suggestion that their child may have an interesting condition called Asperger's syndrome is much more acceptable.[70]

Wing's second reason is that many professionals who do not have special experience with autism think of it as a condition of childhood and, in making a clinical diagnosis in adults, do not consider autism as a possibility. As a result of using the AS label, attention has been drawn to the fact that an autistic person of normal intelligence can, in fact, be referred to a clinician for the first time as an adult. Also, awareness has been increasing that such a person may have a complicating psychiatric illness superimposed on his basic autism. This in turn will complicate treatment and management.

Therefore she maintains that in this connection an awareness of the Asperger condition is useful.[70]

More recently, when writing again on the HFA/AS controversy, Wing states that the developmental disorders are a particularly difficult area of diagnosis because the abnormalities of behavior involved result from irregularities of brain function. These in turn are caused by biochemical and/or anatomical malfunctioning, which in turn arises from the basic underlying fundamental cause.[35] This picture is further complicated by personality, changes with age, environmental conditions, and individual brain patterns. She considers that trying to recognize behavioral patterns within this "bewildering complexity is akin to classifying clouds." Pointing out that while it is possible to choose individuals who will typically represent Kanner's autism and others who will typically represent Asperger syndrome, the fact is that the greatest differences between the two are to be found when the "testable" verbal IQ of the child who has autism is low and the verbal IQ of the child with Asperger syndrome is high. The more similar the IQ results, the more similar will be the "clinical picture." She also stresses that it is the level of ability of the child that will ultimately decide the outcome and not the clinical diagnosis. When it comes to the needs of the individual child, she maintains that to be informed about how they function in the areas of social skills and verbal and nonverbal skills is far more useful than whatever diagnosis they may have been given.

In summing up she writes that in her view HFA and AS are not distinct conditions and that there are no grounds for believing that Asperger or Kanner or indeed anyone else has "as yet succeeded in identifying a separate syndrome." She holds that from the clinical point of view the most useful approach is that when an autistic spectrum disorder is present to diagnose it and make further subdivisions based on the level of ability in verbal and nonverbal skills and on the ability to interact socially.

Dr. Christopher Gillberg and his colleague Dr. Stephen Ehlers also addressed the HFA/AS issue when they reviewed the literature on both conditions.[71] They began by pointing out that to date there is no real clarification as to whether AS and HFA are separate conditions, but for the purposes of their discussion they try to keep them separate in order to better identify similarities and differences. There are at present no definite diagnostic guidelines for HFA. A summary of the few comparative studies that have been carried out suggested to them that it is IQ level that separates AS from HFA. These studies point to the higher verbal and also higher full-scale IQ in AS and to the lower full-scale IQ in HFA. However, it could, they hold, be a question of better verbal skills in AS than in HFA. In addition, they consider it possible that family history may play a greater role in AS. They also consider it likely that motor clumsiness may be more often associated with AS but not with HFA, adding that there is no general agreement on this, as different studies have given conflicting results.

In discussing outcome in HFA and AS, they hold that very little is known about the outcome and that to date no study has systematically investigated outcome in AS. They also reveal that there are data that show that approximately half of the total population of AS individuals, despite the problems being obvious during their teenage years, do not come to the notice of professionals until adult life, when it is likely that they will receive a range of different diagnoses. They draw attention to a study by Dr. Peter Szatmari that described the outcome of a group of sixteen HFA individuals (IQ range 68 to 110) at a mean age of twenty-six years. He found that one-quarter were considered "recovered." The remaining three-quarters, however, did not do well in terms of social outcome or occupational achievement. The presence of psychiatric symptoms in this group was also notable. In this study there was a correlation between nonverbal problem-solving skills and outcome. The better the nonverbal problem-solving skills, the better the outcome.

By way of conclusion they state that it is not clear as to what extent AS and HFA "represent separate or overlapping (or, indeed, sometimes identical) conditions," adding that some people with AS can have severe problems in adulthood and require psychiatric help. Following on this they stress the need for training adult psychiatrists in this whole area of autism so that they will be more able to recognize both AS and HFA in the patients presenting to them. At present very many of these patients are being presented with a "plethora of diagnoses," which range from schizoid/schizotypal personality disorder to paranoid disorder or even atypical schizophrenia or atypical depression.[71]

What then, are the criteria for diagnosing Asperger's syndrome? In 1994 Asperger's Disorder (Asperger's syndrome) appeared for the first time in the fourth edition of the *Diagnostic and Statistical Manual of Mental Disorders* (DSM-IV), produced by the American Psychiatric Association (APA).[72] In this edition Asperger's Disorder is classified as one of five different disorders under the category of Pervasive Developmental Disorders. These five are: (1) Autistic Disorder; (2) Rett's Disorder; (3) Childhood Disintegrative Disorder; (4) Asperger's Disorder; and (5) Pervasive Developmental Disorder Not Otherwise Specified–PDDNOS. *The ICD-10 Classification of Mental and Behavioural Disorders*, produced by the World Health Organization, also includes Asperger's syndrome as a category within the PDD classification.[72A]

In DSM-IV the criteria for the diagnosis of Asperger's Disorder contain much of the language used in the diagnostic criteria for Autistic Disorder, but an individual with Asperger's disorder must not have a "clinically significant general delay in language." Also, to qualify for the diagnosis of Asperger's disorder, there must be "no clinically significant delay in cognitive development."

The following are the diagnostic criteria for Asperger's disorder according to DSM-IV.[72]

299.80 ASPERGER'S DISORDER

A. Qualitative impairment in social interaction, as manifested by at least two of the following:

   (1) marked impairment in the use of multiple nonverbal behaviors such as eye-to-eye gaze, facial expression, body postures, and gestures to regulate social interaction

   (2) failure to develop peer relationships appropriate to developmental level

   (3) a lack of spontaneous seeking to share enjoyment, interests, or achievements with other people (e.g., by a lack of showing, bringing, or pointing out objects of interest to other people)

   (4) lack of social or emotional reciprocity

B. Restricted repetitive and stereotyped patterns of behaviour, interests, and activities, as manifested by at least one of the following:

   (1) encompassing preoccupation with one or more stereotyped and restricted patterns of interest that is abnormal either in intensity or focus

   (2) apparently inflexible adherence to specific, non-functional routines or rituals

   (3) stereotyped and repetitive motor mannerisms (e.g., hand or finger flapping or twisting, or complex whole-body movements)

   (4) persistent preoccupation with parts of objects

C. The disturbance causes clinically significant impairment in social, occupational, or other important areas of functioning.

D. There is no clinically significant general delay in language (e.g., single words used by age 2 years, communicative phrases used by age 3 years).

E. There is no clinically significant delay in cognitive development or in the development of age-appropriate self-help skills, adaptive behaviour (other than in social interaction), and curiosity about the environment in childhood.

F. Criteria are not met for another specific Pervasive Developmental Disorder or Schizophrenia. (Reprinted with permission from the *Diagnostic and Statistical Manual of Mental Disorders, Fourth Edition.* Copyright 1994 American Psychiatric Association).[72]

In commenting recently on the above criteria for the diagnosis of Asperger syndrome, Dr. Peter Szatmari of the Department of Psychiatry at McMaster University in Ontario indicates that the criteria in DSM-IV and ICD-10, although almost identical, are different from those in the literature, and may be excessively restrictive.[73] He reviews data in support of this and suggests that the present diagnostic criteria for Asperger syndrome may not be the "right" ones. He also affirms that the necessary family genetic studies that would prove that AS was a distinct disorder different from autism have yet to be carried out.

Remarking on current evidence, he suggests that the AS diagnosis could be seen in the light of a "prognostic indicator," which would separate out a group of children within the autistic spectrum who will evolve along a certain line of development and that if other children within the spectrum were to develop useful, productive language they also could join this developmental pathway but at a later stage. Questioning as to whether a "prognostic indicator" such as AS should be given disorder status, he considers this to be rather more a question of "policy and clinical judgment" than strict "scientific evidence." He concludes that the real core of the problem revolves around the notion of what constitutes a "disorder" in child psychiatry. Finally, he considers that while a diagnosis of Asperger syndrome "may provide a powerful interpretation of a child's unusual behaviour," nonetheless a label should not be seen in terms of being an explanation, and undue status should not be attached to it.[73]

The difficulty with these categories of diagnosis at a practical level is that parents cannot avail themselves of the appropriate services because they do not have the right labels. Some parents whose children received a diagnosis of AS or PDD have found that they were barred from appropriate educational facilities, social services, and insurance companies because for all of these services one must have the correct diagnostic label. Consequently, they were excluded from services designed for people with autism that could have been helpful. In many countries this arises from a State policy of attaching funding to placements or beds rather than to individuals; a place or a bed is funded but not a person. The judgment made on educational, medical, or residential programs for any child or adult must be based on individual needs alone and not on whatever diagnostic label the person has been given. Funding should be personal, and a range of options available to children and adults, in this way making the services person-centered.

To return to the differences between AS and HFA, apart from the Gillberg study already quoted, there are a number of other studies that compare the two conditions directly. The first compared eighteen AS, twenty-five HFA, and forty-two outpatient control children on a number of cognitive, social, communication, and psychiatric tests.[74] The main finding of this report was that, in essence, no solid difference was found between the AS and HFA children. In discussing their findings, these authors suggest that even though they did find some clinical difference between the two groups with regard to communication, social responsiveness, and a narrow area of activities, these were not severe enough to indicate the presence of a distinct disorder. They suggest that their results point to the fact that AS might be best thought of in terms of being a mild form of high-functioning autism.

There was also a suggestion from their data that the AS group had more psychiatric symptoms, excluding bizarre preoccupations, than the HFA group. They report that it was the presence of these comorbid psychiatric disorders that prevented the AS group from being recognized as suffering from PDD.

The second study compared twenty-six AS, seventeen HFA, and thirty-six outpatient control subjects.[75] This study was designed to address the following two issues:

1. Is there a difference in the cognitive profile of children with autism and children with AS?
2. Is it in language or abstract problem solving that the core cognitive deficit is to be found?

An analysis of the results showed that the AS and HFA group were impaired on all tests in comparison with the outpatient control group but were not really different from each other. The differences found were comparatively small, and the authors feel that they probably reflect degrees of severity rather than a separate origin or cause. They also feel that these results provide sufficient grounds for combining the high-functioning autism and Asperger syndrome groups into the category of pervasive developmental disorders. With regard to the second issue they found that when the HFA and AS children with IQs above 85 were compared with the outpatient control group, they showed marked deficiencies in all three of the following areas: (1) language comprehension; (2) motor coordination; and (3) facial recognition.

Dr. Ami Klin and Dr. Fred Volkmar of the Child Study Center at Yale University School of Medicine carried out a review of the above study,[75] a second study that found minimal differences between the two groups,[76] and their own study[77]—all of which had compared the neurocognitive profiles of AS with HFA.[78] They ask how the differences between studies can be reconciled and answer that it appears likely that the differences are related to diagnosis because the definition of AS has varied with the different studies, and there has been a corresponding variation in results. They argue for "the need to adopt explicit, and whenever possible, consensual, definitions of the condition to facilitate both comparability of research and clinical service." In their own study they found significant differences between groups of AS and HFA individuals whose diagnosis had been strictly defined. This study had arisen as a result of a fact that had come to light in the DSM-IV field trial; that is, a marked difference in patterns of verbal IQ (VIQ) versus performance IQ (PIQ) in both these groups. For this study they based their criteria on ICD-10 criteria. (They point out that the definitions of AS in DSM-IV and ICD-10 are similar but not identical.) To be included in their AS group, the individual had to meet ICD-10 criteria and also had to exhibit two extra features; namely, motor clumsiness and circumscribed interest. They consider that the definition of AS that they used may well have been closer to what Hans Asperger himself adopted. The nineteen HFA and twenty-one AS individuals chosen did not differ in terms of age, sex, or full-scale IQ. What were their findings? They found that the AS group exhibited a pattern of significantly higher VIQ and lower PIQ in comparison with the

HFA group (this was shown earlier in the WAIS-R profile of Mark R.). The VIQs and PIQs were not significantly different in the HFA group. They also compared both groups to the profile of assets and deficits found in individuals with nonverbal learning disabilities (NLD) (see glossary) and found that there was significant similarity between the NLD and AS (21 cases), whereas only one of the nineteen HFA cases showed this similarity. They sum up then by noting that their study showed a distinct correlation between AS and NLD but not between HFA and NLD and that this would constitute a neurocognitive distinction between the two groups.[78]

When writing more recently on the high-functioning autism versus Asperger syndrome controversy, Volkmar states that over time some very divergent views of Asperger disorder have arisen. It can be equated with "subthreshold autism," with "high-functioning autism," or with a condition that has important differences from autism. Controversy has also arisen because there are a number of other conditions that share features with Asperger syndrome, such as schizoid personality disorder and semantic-pragmatic disorder. He notes that the criteria for the diagnosis of Asperger disorder in DSM-IV "were clearly somewhat preliminary and may be improved (or totally discarded!) in future editions of the diagnostic manual."[79] He considers it worth stating that Hans Asperger himself thought the disorder to be distinctive and made careful diagnosis of the condition, but today the term "has come to be used very loosely and inconsistently." While holding that the "final word is not in on Asperger syndrome" his own view is that where intervention is involved, there are important implications, especially if a strict definition of AS is taken, because as seen above, the outline of assets and deficits may be different in AS and HFA. He concludes that in the last analysis the solid worth of whether or not to include it as a distinct category separate from autism will depend on "solid research which validates important differences in terms of clinical features of the disorder, natural history, family history, associated problems in the child, and so forth."

Why has so much controversy surrounded Asperger's syndrome, while Kanner's autism, described at the same time, achieved immediate acceptance? Schopler addresses this issue in detail and traces the controversy to what he considers to be its roots.[69] These he plants firmly in the original papers of Kanner and Asperger. While stating that Kanner's approach to defining his syndrome was based on "behavioral observation, empirical research, and rational intervention strategies," he adds that Kanner's case descriptions were "not only clinically lucid, they were also behaviorally observable" and that the "syndrome could be conceptualised into defining features, still used in diagnostic manuals today." In his 1944 paper Asperger, on the other hand, "Instead of developing diagnostic criteria, he cited a host of different characteristics."

While explaining that Asperger was primarily a clinician and educationalist, Schopler points out that he described his cases as he experienced them. In contrasting the writings of Kanner and Asperger, he comments: "His [Kanner's] robust diagnostic category has arguably inspired more empirical research and scientific understanding of a mental disorder than any other psychiatric label. . . . Asperger's own publications did not inspire research, replication, or scientific interest prior to 1980. Instead he laid the fertile groundwork for the diagnostic confusion that has grown since 1980 and is still blooming in this volume."[69]

Schopler then discusses the title of Asperger's original paper "Autistic Psychopathy in Childhood" indicating that in the detailed account that Asperger (1944) gave of his own cases it was clear that he was using the words in their currently accepted meaning and that he considered this behavior of such importance that he included it in the title. In this paper Asperger also made reference to the characteristics of autism similar to Kanner's autism. In view of this Schopler concludes that the principle characteristic distinguishing Kanner's autism from Asperger's autism could be held to be the presence of "psychopathy." Schopler also points to another factor which compounded this issue of confusion, arguing that, because unlike Kanner, Hans Asperger had not described a syndrome that could be identified and replicated, he left the field open to other researchers to put forward their own views of what constituted the syndrome. Other investigators who formulated views of the essential features were Szatmari and Gillberg. Subsequently, Schopler adds, a committee consensus approach to the formulation of the AS diagnostic criteria for DSM-IV and ICD-10 (WHO, 1993), helped toward a resolution of the confusion. The ICD-10 criteria are, however, designated research criteria, and this serves to distinguish them from DSM-IV criteria. It would seem that this was allowed for the purpose of taking into consideration some distinctions that did not seem "clinically meaningful" to those involved in drawing up the DSM-IV criteria.

Finally in his summing up Schopler refers to the research undertaken to differentiate between AS and HFA and points out that to date it has not resulted in establishing the identity of "a valid clinical subgroup." He adds "AS appears to be a product of culture, with a life independent of empirical [see glossary] evidence."[69]

More recently the team of research academics, who produced the Practice Parameters for autism, in commenting on the validity of Asperger's Disorder as a diagnostic entity separate from high-functioning autism, state that it "remains controversial," and that it is unclear as to whether or not it will stay separate from autism as a valid syndrome in its own right.[12] While indicating that the criteria in DSM-IV for "impairments in social interaction" and "restrictive and repetitive" behaviors in AS are identical to those listed under AD, they point to the different criteria for language. In AD it includes impairment in both nonverbal and verbal communication, while in AS there must be no evidence of "clinically significant" language delay. But as these authors add, when looked at objectively the language in AS is clearly neither "typical" nor "normal."

Moving on to the question of differential diagnosis, they discuss the similarities and overlap in AS with Semantic-Pragmatic Language Disorder (see glossary) and with the Syndrome of Nonverbal Learning Disabilities. They affirm that a diagnosis of a language disorder or of a learning disability is not an "appropriate substitute" for a diagnosis of autism because it takes no cognizance of "social deficits and restrictive repetitive interests." Finally, they point to research into Hans Asperger's original four cases, retrospectively carried out in the last few years, which reported that these cases actually do meet the current DSM-IV criteria for AD.[12] This would of course automatically preclude a diagnosis of AS.

CHAPTER 11

~~~~~

WHAT CAUSES AUTISM?

The problem of what causes autism is not yet solved. There are pointers, markers, and indicators but there is as yet no definite general consensus among professionals. In April 1995 the United States Congress, under the auspices of the National Institutes of Health (NIH), convened an Autism State of the Science Conference at the NIH in Bethesda. This was in response to the realization that autism, which was once thought to be a rare disorder, is now found to be one of the most common of the developmental disorders with a staggering cost to individuals with autism and their families in terms of social and emotional stress and to the state in terms of financial outlay. Autism was seen to be an urgent public health concern that deserved the best that could be provided in services and research.[80] Parents of affected children, being aware of the new findings in other developmental disorders, for example, fragile X syndrome and insulin-dependent diabetes mellitus, lobbied intensively to get the conference off the ground. As a result, the conference involved working groups of some of the most distinguished professionals in the field, from around the world, and parents' organizations played a major part in its initiation. The Autism Society of America (ASA) was the main instigator of this project. There is now a partnership established between the ASA and the NIH. They are committed to pushing forward the cause of autism, and to this end the NIH allocated $27 million spread over five years to fund autism research.[66] This figure has more recently been substantially increased. In addition, the NIH has already established and funded a network of autism research centers. At the opening session of this State of the Science Conference, the NIH stressed that it was assuming no consensus regarding the causes or potential cures for autism. "This is a problem that is not yet solved" and therefore it would be necessary to consider the widest possible series of explanations.[80]

One year later the conference had reported back to: (1) assess the state of the science in the autism spectrum disorders; (2) to identify gaps in knowledge; and (3) to make recommendations regarding promising areas of future research. In no area is this more necessary than in the area of brain research, allied to which are the areas of genetic studies and neurochemistry.

BRAIN RESEARCH

In reviewing the literature on autism generally, one cannot but be struck forcibly by the very large number of studies drawing conclusions based on just one individual case or else on a nonrepresentative sample of two or three cases, all of which has helped greatly to increase the confusion surrounding the research. Added to this is a lack of standardization of sampling techniques. Nowhere is this more applicable than in the area of brain research. There are many gaps in the knowledge of brain function in autism, and much of the research has posed more questions than supplied medical answers. So many different parts of the brain have been reported with abnormalities, and differences in findings are inconclusive. Now, however, some members of the team working on the State of the Science Conference have set themselves to address this issue and have come up with some specific answers.[81]

The first point they emphasize is that the vast majority of magnetic resonance imaging (MRI) scans in autism do not show obvious structural abnormalities and are interpreted as "normal." Of those that are not "normal" the main two areas in which structural abnormalities have been found are the cerebellum (see glossary) and the cerebral hemispheres. With regard to the cerebral hemispheres some researchers have reported too much brain tissue, others reported a normal amount, while others recorded a loss of brain tissue. How are all these to be reconciled? In her brief report to the State of the Science Conference, Dr. Pauline A. Filipek of the Department of Pediatrics at the University of California points to the cause of the confusion and conflicting results as being due to the "vastly differing protocols" used for the MRI scans, as well as the lack of uniformly matched controls with respect to age, gender, IQ, and some other factors. Having asked the questions "Who is studied? Who is the comparison group? How are they scanned? What is being measured and how is it measured?" she then proceeds to lay down guidelines for future work in this area. These include using larger samples; limiting samples to specific ages; using normal controls who are matched for age, IQ, and gender to the autistic patients; and using comparable MRI scanning protocols. This will standardize sampling techniques and make for more uniform results, which can be compared directly.[81]

Also contributing to the State of the Science Conference was Dr. Margaret Bauman.[82] Dr. Bauman with her associates at Harvard University are at the forefront of brain research in autism. Their research has found consistent changes in two distinct areas of the brain, namely the limbic system (see glossary) in the forebrain and the cerebellum and cerebellar circuits in the hind brain. Their detailed analysis of the limbic system has shown that the nerve cells (neurons) (see glossary) are smaller than average, but there is an increase in the number of them. In the cerebellum they found a reduction in the number of Purkinge cells and consider that "the preservation of neurons in the principal inferior olive in the presence of a significant reduction in the number of Purkinge cells of the cerebellar hemispheres" suggests that these abnormalities arise before birth and probably occur before thirty weeks' gestation. They also found that brain weight in most of the autistic patients who were less than twelve years of age was heavier than anticipated, whereas brain weight in most of the adult patients was less than anticipated. From their work there is a small amount of data available for Asperger syndrome. This shows that in AS there are very similar abnormalities confined to the same two areas, that is, the limbic system and the cerebellar circuits, but the degree of abnormality is very much more limited. Bauman states that "these findings suggest that abnormalities of the limbic system may be common to autism, high-functioning autism, and AS and that the phenotypic expression of each of these disorders [that is how they show themselves in the normal functioning of the individual] may depend upon the location and degree of abnormality within this circuitry."[82]

In discussing the implications of their findings in these brain studies elsewhere, Dr. Thomas Kemper and Bauman state that the "pattern of abnormally small, closely packed neurons in the limbic system in the autistic brains resembles that of an earlier stage of development and is therefore likely to represent a curtailment of normal development."[83] Other studies also have shown that these abnormal types of cells have fewer dendritic branches and make fewer connections than normal cells. This team draws attention to the fact that some of the symptoms of autism can be understood in the light of these findings because the circuits in which they occur are known to be involved with memory and emotion. They indicate that research has shown that there is evidence for two memory systems in the brain, namely habit memory and representational memory. Representational memory provides us with meaning in our lives, involves all sensory sensation, and takes into consideration the learning and recognizing of the significance of facts and events. It is accessible to conscious recollection. There is evidence that representational memory in humans may be "acquired at some time after birth." The average child between the age of four and seven will still not have reached adult level. This, they consider, could account for why autism manifests itself during infancy and childhood.

On the other hand, they indicate habit memory "is involved in skills learning, and automatic connections between a stimulus and a response." Habit learning is not accessible to conscious recollection. It is gained by repeated exposure to the same stimulus until a task is perfected. This memory system seems to develop in early infancy. In discussing their findings these authors point out that the brain tissue responsible for the carrying out of habit memory would appear to be intact in individuals with autism, and they add, "Consistent with the preservation of this rigidly specified memory system is the frequent preoccupation with repetitive and stereotypic behaviour seen in many autistic individuals." They also consider that habit memory could be implicated in the autistic child's sometimes "catastrophic reaction to change in the environment," and give an interesting insight into this bizarre phenomenon:

> With continued exposure to constant stimuli, such as in the appearance of the specific features of a room, the autistic individual may be able to learn its appearance with habit memory. A change of position of a piece of furniture in the room, however, may render the previously familiar room unrecognisable and therefore foreign. In addition, because habit memory is not accessible to verbal expression, the memory of the details of the room cannot be expressed verbally. The observer understands that the details are known only from the reaction to change.[83]

These researchers also found changes in some cells of the brainstem in a few of their cases, but this was not a consistent feature of all cases. In view of this they cannot be sure of its significance for autism. They did, however, carry out a very thorough search of the reticulate core of the brainstem and failed to find any recognizable changes to indicate abnormality.

While abnormalities in the limbic system would have been anticipated in autism, given the nature of the disorder (that is, impairment in social ability, lack of motivation, lack of interest in learning, very labile moods, or the opposite—blunted affect), the findings of abnormalities in the cerebellar tissues were a surprising feature of the research. This is because the cerebellum seemed an unlikely site for damage in what is considered a cognitive disorder like autism. But the results of this new research in autism, coupled with other research into neuropsychological studies in children, have given a new dimension to the role of the cerebellum in language, the ability to shift attention, and other higher cognitive functions.[66]

GENETIC STUDIES

There is evidence from studies carried out over the last twenty years pointing to the strong influence of genetic factors in autism. For example, following the birth of an autistic child, there is a fifty-fold increased risk of having another autistic child (1 in 10 to 1 in 20, as compared with 1 in 500 in the general population).[12] Added to this is the evidence from the results of studies of identical twins. Identical twins develop from the same fertilized ovum (egg cell) and therefore they share the same genetic material. One of the first identical twin (monozygotic) studies was undertaken over twenty years ago.[84] The results showed that among eleven pairs of twins examined, over one-third was concordant for autism. To be concordant means that both twins either do have autism or that both twins do not have autism. In a more recent study, a further seventeen pairs of identical twins were assessed and over two-thirds were concordant.[85] In both studies unidentical twins (dizygotic) were also included, and the concordant rate for the unidentical twins for autism was nil. Dizygotic or fraternal twins develop from two different fertilized egg cells and therefore do not share the same genetic material. Although these studies and others (89% concordance rate for autism for identical twins)[86] show a strong genetic connection it is not 100 percent so that environmental factors play a part as well, and there must be some gene-environment reaction taking place. What could be the nature of this gene-environment reaction? One of the first facets of this to be looked at was birth complications.

It has been thought for some time that complications at birth might have been one of these environmental factors, but overall the results are conflicting and inconclusive. A number of the older studies have shown an association between obstetric complications (OCs), and autism, but this has not been borne out in the more modern studies, including the study by Cryan et al.[87] In this study the birth records of forty-nine children diagnosed with autism were examined at four maternity hospitals in Dublin. As a control group the data from the previous same sex, live birth at the hospital was also recorded. This team found no evidence to suggest that people affected by autism had an increased rate of obstetric complications when compared with the control group: "These data do not support the view that OCs increase the risk for later autism." More recent research is pointing to the fact that obstetric complications could be the *result* of abnormal development in the uterus, rather than a contributory cause to the development of autism.[85] Another recent study also produces evidence of obstetrical complications being "due to a problem fetus, and not the reverse." In this series of eight cases, all of whom had chromosomal abnormalities, three children were found who had been born by Caesarean section because of a large head circumference.[88]

Reports indicate that approximately one quarter of individuals with autism have a head circumference above the 97th percentile. This is also true of postmortem brain weights. It would also seem that the large head size is not necessarily present when the child is born but can appear later as a result of increased brain growth in the early to mid-childhood years of development.[12]

Another factor being looked into as a possible trigger in the gene-environment reaction is a defective immune system. A number of studies have shown irregularities in the immune system in autism. These abnormalities include findings that, in some cases, the body is responding abnormally to its own brain tissue (autoimmunity) (see glossary). Weizman and his team were among the first to report this autoimmunity in autism.[89] They suggested that a so-far-undetectable brain injury associated with autoimmunity may play a role in the basic underlying disorder. Other researchers have found circulating antibodies directed against brain serotonin receptors.[90] Others again have identified serum antibodies to myelin basic protein in children with autism.[91] Dr. Reid Warren was one of the most prominent workers in this field. With his associates he found several immune system abnormalities in their sample of autistic patients.[92,93] These include a reduction in natural killer cells and a decreased number of T cells. Natural killer cells afford protection against malignancy and viral infections, while T cells have a powerful ability to deal with all foreign substances entering the body. In their more recent research this team reported that a major subgroup of autistic individuals that they tested had a null allele (alleles are the alternative forms of a gene, and a null allele is one that does not do its job because it produces no protein) (see under genetics in glossary) of the C4B gene on chromosome 6.[94] The C4B null allele has been found to be associated with increased viral and bacterial infections, including bacterial meningitis. More recently still, they report that when testing forty autistic individuals they found that nearly half of them had one of the three factors associated with a decrease in immunoglobulin A (IgA).[95] In summing up they direct attention to the fact that

An impressive volume of evidence has accumulated over the past few years suggesting that the pathophysiology of autism involves immune dysfunction. Most, if not all immunologic studies in autism, have found modified general immune function of one type or another depending on the age of the autistic subjects studied. . . . With respect to autism an inherited deficiency of the immune system may prevent the patient from clearing a pathogen in a timely and normal fashion, placing the patient at higher risk for the pathogen to interfere with brain development and/or triggering an autoimmune response resulting in the symptoms of autism.[95]

One of the studies reviewed included the results of treatment of some children with autism who were found to have marked irregularities of their immune system when compared to age-matched controls.[96] In this preliminary study these authors treated ten children with a six-month's course of intravenous immunoglobulin (IVIG). Immunoglobulins are a group of special proteins secreted by cells of the B lymphocyte cell line; they act as antibodies and are used to treat immune deficiencies. The treatment was given at four-week intervals. The observed degrees of improvement after treatment, which were based on clinical observation alone as systematic assessments had not been carried out, were given "arbitrary symbols" of + (minimal) to +++ (marked) to ++++ (striking). It is recorded that half of the sample were observed to be in the mild category, with four in the marked category, and one in the striking category. These improvements were mainly in the areas of calmness, better eye contact, and social behavior. Two patients were recorded as showing marked improvement in speech.

A more recent open pilot study found no statistically significant changes in their group of five autistic children after they had completed six months of IVIG clinical treatment. Prior to and during the treatment behavioral assessments were carried out by an experienced evaluator using standard measures of assessment. Immunologic testing had not been performed on these children prior to treatment, and their case histories had not shown an increased frequency of infections or seizure disorder.[97] Neither of the above studies were double-blind, placebo-controlled studies.

In a recent overview of IVIG treatment in autism, Plioplys discusses both of the above studies.[98] He considers that the first study quoted[96] gives results that were not within realistic limits, and that the second study[97] gives a better picture of a more realistic outcome. He refers to his own study, which involved ten children, all of whom had immune abnormalities. Of these, after treatment five had no clinical change, mild improvements were seen in four, but one child became fully normal during the treatment program. He states that this child's very significant response to IVIG points to the fact that there is a subgroup of children with autism who can be treated effectively if their disorder proves to be due to autoimmune factors. He issues a warning with regard to this treatment, stating that a prior immunologic work-up is necessary because it is essential to exclude the possibility of "selective IgA deficiency." Treating such a person with IVIG might lead to a severe anaphylactic reaction. Plioplys also points to the importance of investigating the possibility of epileptogenic abnormalities in children with autism because, he holds, these can go unrecognized and can be the cause of autistic symptoms, while if recognized they are treatable with anticonvulsant medication.[98]

Into this area of immune dysfunction and causes of autism comes a question that is being asked more and more often nowadays; namely, Are measles infections or measles immunizations linked to autism?

When recently asked this question Dr. Eric Fombonne of the University of London stated that it is important for professionals in the field to remain "skeptical" about claims of causes that are not backed up by solid scientific criteria. He points to the area of autism where firmly held convictions rather than evidence based on strict research criteria sometimes hold sway. This in turn he holds has led to the promotion of interventions that are inefficient. He sums up his answer to this question by saying that, when one's beliefs are put to one side, "no evidence today exists to causally link exposures to measles viruses or vaccination and autism."[99]

He states that all the research evidence in relation to autism, Crohn's disease, and measles exposure was reviewed by a panel of experts called together in 1998 in the United Kingdom by the Medical Research Council. This MRC panel came to the conclusion that "the available virological and epidemiological evidence did not indicate any link between MMR vaccination and bowel disease or autism" (MRC, press release, 24 March 1998). Fombonne also stated that "there are no solid epidemiological data to support the hypothesis of an increased incidence of autism that can be attributed to the relatively recent use of the combined MMR vaccine in the immunization programs in some countries."[99]

More recently, in Washington (April 2000) at a hearing of the House Government Reform Committee, the spotlight was put firmly on "autism and the potential correlation with childhood immunisation." On the panel of witnesses at this hearing was Dr. Andrew Wakefield, of the Royal Free and University College Medical School in London, who testified positively on a linkage between the MMR (measles, mumps, rubella) vaccine and autism, while Dr. Brent Taylor, from the same medical school, who was also a witness on the panel, testified against any linkage. The Centers for Disease Control and Prevention (CDC) witnesses also made clear their position which is "that there is insufficient scientific evidence to allege a link between vaccines and autism."[100]

However, subsequent to this, in response to the serious concerns being expressed by parents and in the light of emerging new hypotheses about vaccines; the CDC and the NIH were instrumental in initiating a three-year investigation by the U.S. Institute of Medicine to look into and report on this whole area of vaccine safety issues. The task force for this undertaking, the Immunization Safety Review Committee, set objectives for this three-year investigation and commissioned papers for its first meeting of researchers in July 2001. Throughout their tenure they expect to issue reports and recommendations.

To return again to the 1996 report, when the working party on the search for the etiology of autism reported back to the State of the Science Conference, there was among them "remarkable consensus at the meeting that autism is a genetic condition" and that "Mapping studies should be undertaken to identify the genetic loci [see glossary] that contribute directly to the disorder. The familial relative risks are sufficiently large to indicate the action of genetic factors and estimates of the number of loci involved are on the order of 3–6."[101]

When writing more recently on the same subject, Dr. Eric Fombonne noted "the view shared in 1998 by most researchers in autism is that genetic factors do play an influential role in the etiology of autism. In fact, the evidence points towards autism being one of the psychiatric disorders most influenced by genetic factors, the heritability estimates for autism being much higher than those typically reported for conditions such as schizophrenia or manic-depressive psychosis."[102]

Of all the chromosomal abnormalities found in association with autism, the most commonly described in recent studies is that involving the proximal long arm of chromosome 15 (15q11–q13) in patients meeting strict criteria for Autistic Disorder.[103]

As a result of the findings of The Human Genome Project (see glossary), which has produced its first rough draft of the human genome sequence (February 2001), experts agree that information is now sufficiently advanced to set about planning mapping studies in order to identify the genetic loci (places or sites) that contribute directly to autism. There would appear to be about thirty thousand to forty thousand protein-coding genes in the human genome as opposed to earlier estimates of approximately one hundred thousand, but it could be many years before the final number is known.[103A] However, based on the evidence to date it is expected that autism, because it is genetically complex, will not follow a simple Mendelian pattern of inheritance (see under genetics in glossary) but will prove to be an example of genetic heterogeneity (meaning that a number of genes act independently to confer risk for autism). In planning these mapping studies it is thought that the best strategy would be to focus on families with more than one affected member.

With regard to Asperger syndrome, since Hans Asperger himself suggested that this condition was more common in family members, particularly fathers, there have been a number of case reports noting the presence of AS in first degree relatives. In recently reviewing the literature on this, one particular study states that while there is evidence from clinical reports of an increased incidence of Asperger syndrome in fathers in particular, this is not backed up by controlled studies.[104] The authors consider this to be a clinical impression that must be seen in the light of a hypothesis until it can be verified. These researchers are at present conducting an intensive study of Asperger syndrome subjects and immediate family members on a battery of neuropsychological and psychiatric assessments. This is an ongoing study that applies direct assessment, and the results, they hope, may help to clarify the relationship of AS with other conditions.

Research into the genetics of autism is now moving forward at a fast pace. In March 2000 an international meeting took place in Italy that was attended by almost all genetic genome researchers working on autism throughout the world. Encouraged by the success achieved in other disorders, there is now a considerable commitment among the research community to finding the genes involved in autism.

NEUROCHEMISTRY

As already indicated, results from brain research point to altered development of the brain from before birth.[82] Because of this there would now seem to be some consensus among researchers that autism can be viewed as a disorder of brain cell (neuron) organization. Therefore the next logical step is to study the role of neurochemicals in controlling the development of the brain. Consequently research is now centering around neurochemistry. What is neurochemistry? It is the study of the molecules called neurochemicals that send signals within nerves and between nerves (see under neurone in glossary). A neuron is a nerve cell. Anything that affects the development of the brain is likely to be long lasting because a change in neurochemicals in one cell may lead the next cell to be changed in its developmental course, and this in turn will change other cells.[105] Findings from research strongly support the involvement of neurochemicals in autism. They are suggested to play a significant part in the condition.[106]

This leads to the question of which neurochemicals are the important ones. Serotonin is one such neurochemical, and it has received much attention in recent years. Thirty-five years ago the first study showing an increase in whole blood serotonin levels in some children with autism was undertaken, and thirty-five years later the mechanism of how this happens and the significance of it have still not been worked out. What has been shown fairly consistently though, is that about a quarter of autistic children and adolescents do have an increased level of serotonin in the blood. However, the correlation of this with levels of serotonin in the brain remains unclear.[66] When these high blood levels of serotonin were artificially lowered in chemical trials by a number of researchers, no significant improvement in behavior or learning problems in the children involved was brought about. The picture is further complicated by the fact that many other medical conditions, including chronic schizophrenia, mental retardation, and motor neuron disease, can also show high blood levels of serotonin.[23] In a recent comprehensive overview entitled "Psychopharmacology in Autism," Dr. Luke Tsai gives an update on serotonin research in autism and suggests that low availability of brain tryptophan could be one of the possible mechanisms implicated in why the functioning of serotonin is altered in autism. He does, however, point out that as yet no consistent correlation has been discovered between the symptoms and behaviors seen in autism and blood serotonin level. He concludes that both the importance of elevated levels of serotonin and the mechanism of how this arises remain unresolved in autism.[106]

Filipek refers to a recent landmark study that measured serotonin synthesis in seven autistic boys using PET (see under brain imaging in glossary). The team who conducted this study found decreased serotonin synthesis in the frontal cortex and thalamus and increased serotonin synthesis in areas of the cerebellum. Filipek indicates that in children without autism, between the ages of three and six, serotonin synthesis is more than twice the normal adult figure, and that it decreases to adult level between the ages of six to ten. She further refers to a personal communication from the same source which has also found that, in contrast to this normal developmental pattern of serotonin synthesis in the average child, children with autism show an almost opposite pattern. This team of researchers have found that in autistic children serotonin synthesis is low below six years of age, and then increases little by little until, after eight years of age, it reaches figures which are much higher than that found in the control group.[13]

Looking at serotonin from the genetic perspective, one recent report, as previously mentioned, suggests an association with autism of a short variant of the serotonin transporter gene (5-HTT) promoter.[67] This result is from a study of eighty-six autistic children and their parents.

A second neurochemical that has received a lot of attention is dopamine. There are many studies that indicate an abnormal functioning of dopamine in children with autism. However, the results have been conflicting and contradictory. Homovanillic acid (HVA), which is the end product of dopamine breakdown, has been studied in both cerebrospinal fluid and urine. Again the results are conflicting, with different studies showing both normal and elevated levels.[23] After a careful consideration of the research studies on dopamine in autism, Tsai indicates that HVA levels have not been shown to "correlate" with any autistic symptoms or behaviors. However, he notes, stimulant medication, which is a dopamine agonist (see glossary) has been found to exacerbate preexisting symptoms of aggression, hyperactivity, and stereotypies in children with autism. In view of this he considers that it suggests a role for dopamine in the symptoms of autism. In referring to L-Dopa, which is a precursor of dopamine, he indicates that since the studies of the early 1970s, which had negative findings, there has been no further clinical trials of L-Dopa in people with autism.[106]

The study of neurochemistry is hugely complex. Dr. Edwin H. Cook of the Department of Psychiatry and Pediatrics at the University of Chicago, in his report to the State of the Science Conference, depicted very clearly the problems they are up against when he summed up this situation: "Since autism is due to alterations in the normal development of some neurons, all neurochemicals active in the brain during development of relevant structures, including the amygdala, hippocampus and cerebellum are suspect. Because the hippocampus is such an active area of the body during development, it was chosen as the best place to find a large number of expressed genes. Over 3,000 expressed genes were found in the developing hippocampus."[105] He goes on to explain that the number of theoretically possible "neurochemical candidates" amounts to in excess of 100,000 because each of these genes can have at least one and often "several protein products." All of which adds up to the fact that the perplexing enigma of autism would be easier to solve if there were only a handful of neurochemical candidates.[105]

Cook then outlines a number of approaches, one of which is that proposed in the genetic studies. This is to set up a genome-wide study of families where two relatives, probably sibling pairs (e.g., brothers), are affected. Once the genetic loci (sites) are identified, it is expected that each locus would correspond to a protein that would be abnormal. It could be abnormal in either the amount of protein or in the way it functions. This in turn would lead to a change in its overall chemical functioning.[105]

Research in autism, as in any other disorder or illness, is costly in terms of time and finance, so it is necessary to plan future studies very carefully. One of the first of these sibling pair analysis studies using the most recent advances in molecular biology techniques has now reported back.[107] It reveals that there is a suggestion of the implication of chromosome 7 in autism. Another research study also reports findings implicating chromosome 7 and more particularly a gene on chromosome 7 known as Hoxa 1 (a small gene containing just two protein-coding regions).[108] This gene produces a protein that regulates the activity of other genes, and when the first neurons are being formed in early pregnancy, this gene is active in the brainstem. It is not active in any tissue after this early period of gestation. The clue to this research came from a little known fact that about 5 percent of children who had been victims of the morning-sickness drug thalidomide developed autism. Patricia Rodier hypothesizes that a gene that is active only during development would be well placed to account for a congenital disorder like autism because if the gene is active throughout life, problems would be expected to increase with age, whereas autism appears to be stable after childhood.

The research team involved in this study went on to discover two variant alleles of Hoxa 1 in people with autism, one of which produces a protein slightly different from that produced by the normal gene, the other involving a change in the physical structure of the DNA in the gene. They point out that Hoxa 1, as already predicted, is only one of the many genes involved in autism and that if present it may or may not express itself. This means that its presence in an individual does not necessarily lead to autism. Their preliminary data show that the variant allele occurs in well over one-third of those who do have autism and in about one-fifth of those who do not have autism. Also, they have found that the allele is not present in almost two-thirds of people with autism so that other genetic factors must be involved. They are continuing now to search for other variants of Hoxa 1 because it is known that most genetic disorders arise from multiple deviant alleles mutated from a single gene.[108]

The State of the Science Conference offered great hope for the acceleration of the pace of research into autism. As well as gathering together the top experts in the field to pool their resources and supplying funding for research, the NIH is inviting comments from scientists, clinicians, and families regarding proposals. They are especially interested in financing programs that will test significant hypotheses already established about autism. The turn of the millennium is an exciting time in autism, with the possibility of new discoveries and a concentrated effort of this nature is already yielding very significant results. Perhaps we will not have to wait for too much longer for a real breakthrough in autism.

Three years after the 1995 conference the NIH Autism Coordinating Committee, in conjunction with major medical and professional academies and parent research organizations, again sponsored a working conference on the State of the Science in Autism: Screening and Diagnosis. The aim of this conference was three-fold: to look closely at the whole question of diagnosis and screening in autism, to get a clear picture of the facts already known about research, and to plan future research.[18] One of the top priorities for the future at the conference was the search for the elusive "ultimate diagnostic indicator," a biological marker (or markers) that would mark out autism unequivocally from other disorders. At present there exists no such biological marker or no medical test that will do this. The search for this "holy grail of unequivocal diagnosis is a work in progress"; it is the ultimate goal.[18] A whole range of possible indicators are being targeted and explored, and there has been a substantial investment in this area because future treatment strategies will revolve around it.

A second important area focused in on at this conference was the question of how to improve the diagnosis of comorbid disorders, including psychiatric disorders, which, if present, can greatly alter the course of autism and contribute heavily to a poor outcome. The conference concluded that this is of special importance in adults with autism because these are treatable disorders that frequently are not detected. Attention was also drawn to the need for systematic research into sensory processing abnormalities in autism. Over the years the distortion of sensory perception has been well documented clinically, but the neurological basis for it is unknown, and as previously pointed out, there is a paucity of basic research in this area that could contribute to early diagnosis and treatment. The role of gene/environment interactions in autism was emphasized. This research will need to identify trigger factors such as toxins, viruses, immune deficiencies, or infections. If these are known, preventative measures can be developed.[18]

Six months after this State of the Science Conference, a historic meeting was held in January 1999, when a consensus was reached concerning diagnostic criteria for autism based on up-to-date research evidence. Out of this arose a document of Practice Parameters.[12] This very comprehensive, in-depth document, written by nineteen of the top specialists in this field, analyzes past diagnostic and screening criteria and formulates future criteria. They call for two different levels of investigation, the first of which would be carried out on all children in order to identify those at risk for atypical development. The second would, using specialist evaluation, then follow up on those at risk children, would differentiate those with autism from other developmental disorder groups, and would decide on the optimum type of intervention for each child.

This team then elaborates in detail on how the evaluation at each level should be carried out, laying down very specific guidelines for professionals. It places great emphasis on the fact that autism must be seen for what it is; that is, a medical disorder, and that suitable medical and therapeutic intervention must not be denied to patients under the "rubric of 'developmental delay' or mental health condition." It also emphasizes that "professionals must learn to provide more than a diagnosis and a telephone number for government services to parents." In addition, it stresses, the basic fundamental need for increased educational input at the preservice level for all the disciplines involved with autism, from the trainees in psychiatry, pediatrics, neurology, and psychology, to those involved in speech and language pathology, on to the areas of public health, occupational therapy, and early childhood education. The team stressed that in all of these areas there is a need for vastly increased knowledge regarding the symptoms of autism, the needs of autistic people, and what the outcome is in autism. In conclusion it sums up:

It is the consensus of this Panel that the role of medical professionals can no longer be limited to simply the diagnosis of autism. Professionals must expand their knowledge and involvement to be better able to counsel families concerning available and appropriate treatment modalities, whether educational, empirical, or "just off the web." In addition, professionals must be familiar with federal law which mandates a free and appropriate education for all children from the age of 36 months, and in some states from zero to three as well.[12]

CHAPTER 12

IS THERE A CURE FOR AUTISM?

The answer is "No." Autism is still thought of in terms of being a life-long condition. Rutter (1999), in an overview of the interplay between research and clinical work in autism since the time of Kanner's first diagnosis in his summing up conclusions, expresses the opinion that as yet "no cure is even remotely on the horizon."[7] So we turn to the question of intervention. As we have seen from the preceding pages, it is reported that a small percentage of children appear to spontaneously outgrow autism. Other children, given the right kind of intervention at the right time, would appear to be able to develop normally from then on. We have seen that the earlier these programs are started, the better the outcome, because there is evidence to show that pathways in the brain can be modified by environmental molding at a young age. All of which brings up the question of the importance of early diagnosis.

A recent U.K. survey of close to 1,300 families with autism, in describing their diagnostic experiences, revealed that the average age of diagnosis was around six years old. This was in spite of the fact that the average age at which parents were first alerted to the fact that something was not quite right with their child's development was about a year and a half. They had sought help, on average, when the child was a little over two years old.[109] Less than 10 percent of this group was given a diagnosis at the first consultation, which was with a general practitioner or health visitor. The remainder was referred on to another professional. Here a little over one-third

was given a formal diagnosis, a quarter was referred on to a third professional, and another quarter was told either that there was not a problem or
that it was not necessary to take further action or to return if the situation
did not improve. About a fifth of all families revealed that they had problems
in obtaining this referral; some had to pay, others to exert considerable pressure. Of those parents who were referred on to subsequent professionals,
almost one-third reported that virtually no help was offered, while a further
third saw the principal benefit as being help with education. The final diagnostic label in almost half the cases was autism, and in about one in seven
it was Asperger syndrome. When asked for their views on the diagnostic
procedures, half of the families reported not being satisfied, while a third
reported that they were satisfied. In the column dealing with what was the
greatest source of help to parents over time, almost half reported that this
came from two sources: (1) the educational system, and (2) other parents
and parents' organizations. Slightly over one-third named the medical health
care profession.

In summary, the authors of this report, while acknowledging that the age
at which diagnosis is made is improving, conclude that professionals at all
levels "must" give serious consideration to whatever concerns parents might
have about their child's early development and be prepared to refer them
on quickly to suitable facilities. They state that having to wait for five years
or more for a diagnosis is unacceptable. They also affirm that if professionals
are not able to give a specific diagnosis of autism, they should avoid, if at
all possible, using terms such as a tendency to autism or features of autism.
In addition, they hold that while diagnosis may be a vital step, it is not
sufficient in itself. They stress the parents' need for support and help of a
practical nature, especially in the early years. This, they feel, could have a
significant influence in reducing "challenging behaviors" as the child grows
older, in addition to alleviating anxiety and stress in the family.

Dr. Lorna Wing, another U.K. professional writing at the same time and
in a similar vein, states: "A common mistake made by those lacking relevant
experience is to assume that the child's behaviour is due solely to parental
mishandling, especially since the children often have an alert and attractive
appearance. For accurate diagnosis it is essential to ask the right questions
systematically, listen to the parents with great care, and treat them and their
information with respect."[6] Wing continues: "Autistic-spectrum disorders
have profound effects on the lives of the individuals who are affected and
their families. Their difficulties are often intensified by lack of recognition,
even denial that autism exists, among some medical and other professional
workers."[6]

To revert again to the question of early intervention, why do early intervention programs produce significant improvement in some children with
autism while others do markedly less well? We have seen that dietary intervention has highlighted the possibility of partly digested proteins (peptides)

interfering with the learning process. There also is a theory that these peptides may play a role in interfering with brain maturation and may have an inhibiting affect on the breakdown of other peptides in the body.[64]

Another factor at work in the autistic equation revolves around the abnormal processing of sensory stimuli. The sense of hearing is the sense most likely to cause severe problems. Clearly it is going to be very difficult to respond to any special education program if you are tormented by loud sounds (hyperacusis), cannot regulate the effects of sound, find that all sounds are scrambled, are unwittingly screening out certain frequencies of sound, cannot select from the environment the important stimuli to focus on, cannot exclude background noises, or have a delayed unsynchronized reaction to processing some sound stimuli. Some children with autism even become fixated on sound (like John K. with helicopters). It has been found possible to have hyperacusis in one ear and normal hearing in the other. Also, all of these difficulties are not fixed and can fluctuate over time and can go undetected.

One of the first researchers in the field to document the importance of the connection between hearing and voice was Dr. Alfred A. Tomatis, an ear, nose, and throat specialist.[110] In his research he found that when a person's hearing is artificially filtered to produce blind spots, then the voice is modified in a corresponding way. This led him to the conviction that the "voice can only produce what the ear hears." In order to treat the patients who consulted him with hearing and voice difficulties, he developed an apparatus called the "Electronic Ear." This involved getting the ear to adopt a self-listening position by regulating the bones of the middle ear, the malleus and stapes, to bring about tension in the eardrum. His theory is that when the ear is able to hear the lost or damaged frequencies correctly, then the voice regains the ability to produce them. Because these two organs are interconnected, changes in the ear will affect the voice and changes in the voice in turn will affect the ear. He found this approach to be successful for treating many of the cases he encountered in his practice.

He also suggested that a well-functioning listening ear should be able to attune itself to the entire spectrum of sound and should be able to identify the source of a sound. He held that the right ear was involved with measuring the highest frequencies and the left ear with the lowest, and he stressed the importance of establishing dominance in the right or directing ear for competent ear/voice control. Tomatis puts forward the idea that the primary function of the ear is that of charging the cortex of the brain with electrical energy. He held that high frequency sounds, which are rich in high harmonics, have a greater power of stimulation for the cortex. Since its first inception in the early 1950s the Electronic Ear has been constantly updated in the light of ongoing research.

The Tomatis method is practiced in a number of authorized facilities throughout Europe and America by a professional trained and certified by

Dr. Tomatis. It involves a series of diagnostic evaluation tests, as well as ongoing monitoring to assess progress. The procedure has both an active as well as a passive component. The active involves oral sound training, speaking, and singing; the passive involves listening to the sounds of music and voice through the Electronic Ear.[110]

Another pioneer in the field of auditory therapy is Dr. Guy Berard. Berard's work came to prominence in the United States in 1991 after the publication of a book entitled *The Sound of a Miracle* by Annabel Stehli.[111] This book told the story of Stehli's daughter Georgiana who had been diagnosed as having autism and who had an extreme sensitivity to sound—so sensitive, in fact, that she could "hear her blood rushing through her veins." When Georgiana was eleven years old, she was treated with auditory integration therapy (AIT) in France by Berard. This treatment enabled her to overcome her extreme sensitivity to sound and thereafter she began to develop normally. As was to be expected, this story sparked off an intense interest in AIT. Anecdotal evidence for AIT varies from reports of children whose behavior, sound sensitivity, and language use have improved, to those whose behavior, sound sensitivity, and language have worsened, to those who report no change after treatment.

What does AIT consist of? It involves ten hours (usually given in 20 half-hour sessions) of listening through headphones to specially selected music tracts that have been electronically filtered and modified. Before the treatment begins tests are carried out in order to identify any peak frequencies at which hearing may be more acute. The AIT apparatus is then adjusted to dampen down or filter out these peak frequencies. Filters can be further adjusted if required by evidence from a second hearing test. The expected result at the end of the treatment is that all sound frequencies will be registered with equal clarity, and peaks will be eliminated.

The first AIT study reviewed here included eighty children and adolescents (4 to 17 years), with autism and Asperger syndrome, and they were followed up for a period of twelve months.[112] All children showed sensitivity to sound ranging from either mild to severe. They were randomly allocated to either an experimental group (AT) or a structured listening group (SL). The SL group listened to the same music, but it was not filtered. The results of this study reported that the children in both groups, that is, in both the AT and SL group, showed improvement after one month on all scores, and this was maintained at twelve months. They also reported improvement in behavior and severity of autism in nearly three-quarters of each group. At six to twelve months after the experimental intervention, an improvement in both performance IQ (PIQ) and verbal IQ (VIQ) was found. As Bettison indicated, this was unexpected because as she pointed out IQ is one of the factors that has been shown in the past to remain stable over time in people with autism. In addition, she reported evidence from the scores on the Sound Sensitivity Questionnaire that the intervention reduced sound sensitivity in the children and also reduced some of their abnormal responses to sound. There was, however, no untreated control group included in this study.

Bettison considers it possible that "variety and a wide frequency range in music have the same effect as the electronic modifications." She also considers that this would make sense "if the abnormal responses to sound result from deficiencies in arousal, orienting responses, or attention." She concludes that "because both auditory training and the control condition resulted in similar improvements, it is not certain what led to these effects." She stresses the need for further research in this area.

It is necessary to emphasize here that Bettison issued a note of caution as to whether auditory training is suitable for all children with autism because of the fact that two children, one with a diagnosis of psychiatric disturbance and the other with severe emotional disturbance, were reported to have become significantly more disturbed after the listening. She considers that this suggests that auditory training or other intensive listening programs should not be undertaken by children with these diagnoses.[112]

Although hyperacusis is well documented clinically, there is a lack of scientific research on figures for how many autistic people actually suffer from acute sound sensitivity. One questionnaire based on findings taken from in excess of seventeen thousand copies of a diagnostic questionnaire returned by parents of autistic children throughout the world showed, on analysis, that about 40 percent of these children exhibited some symptoms of sound sensitivity.[113] Another parent questionnaire, recording the prevalence of sensory processing abnormalities in autism, documented a 100 percent positive result. This study related to the first two years of life of a number of young children with autism, all of whom had auditory processing abnormalities. By contrast, in the controls for this group, a little over one-tenth of the developmental delay group (matched for IQ, age, and sex) and none of the typical development group (age, and sex matched) showed auditory processing abnormalities.[113A]

The second reviewed study on AIT gave the results of treating nine children with autism (ages 3 to 16; IQ 35–70). These children had been evaluated prior to the treatment on standard autism tests and at post-treatment evaluation nine months later the only improvement shown was a slight decline in the ABC sensory score. The authors conclude from this open pilot study that their results "do not provide any support for a positive effect on autistic symptoms." They also consider that the moderate reduction in the sensory score could be a chance finding.[114]

A third study provided AIT and a placebo version of it, which consisted of inactive headphones but surrounding music played in the room to sixteen children attending special education schools. Treatments were given approximately four months apart so that seven of the children received AIT first, while nine received the placebo version first. Four months later the reverse obtained. Raters were unaware of the order of treatments. Ratings of problem behaviors and direct behavioral measurement were followed up over a period of fourteen months. These authors report that the data showed that the children, either as individuals or as a group, did not benefit from AIT. From their results they conclude that AIT, for which families can pay up to £1,250, "cannot be recommended for children with autism and problem behaviors."[115]

In a recent overview of five AIT studies, including two discussed here (Bettison and Gillberg et al.), Dawson and Watling concluded that the existing empirical evidence arising from these studies provided "no, or at best, inconclusive support" for the use of auditory integration training in autism. They further point out that the American Academy of Pediatrics in their position paper of 1998 underscored this position.[33]

The final study researched was questionnaire based.[116] These authors sent questionnaires to the parents of 150 children who had received AIT, requesting information on the results of the treatment. They point out that "because AIT is relatively untested, most discussions about it at this point are purely speculative, lacking a strong theoretical base. It is not known whether the training works for all children with autism, nor has unequivocal scientific evidence been provided that it works for any."[116] They then discuss the limitations of questionnaire-based studies and the degree of bias that will inevitably be involved, as parents desire to see positive changes in their children, particularly when sacrifices of time and money are involved. Nonetheless they believed that parents might provide insights that would help other parents and professionals to make judgments concerning how efficacious AIT is at a time when it is still in the experimental stage.

They looked for information in five areas—"language use, behavioural control, social interaction, sound sensitivity and attention span." Just over a quarter of the parents (42) responded. An analysis of the results showed that in language use nearly 79 percent noticed positive changes; of these, 17 percent were minor changes only; the remainder noticed no change. In behavior control, half the parents noticed positive changes; a further quarter reported only minor improvements; 10 percent reported no change; while 15 percent reported a worsening of behavior. In one of these cases the child became so seriously aggressive and self-injurious that he had to be placed in care. This behavior was described by the parents as "new behavior" for the child. With regard to sound sensitivity, 85 percent of parents noticed an improvement following AIT, and 15 percent noticed no change. The figures for attention span are similar, with 85 percent noticing improvements, 12.5 percent no change, and 2.5 percent regression. In social interaction 86 percent noticed some positive changes, a quarter of which were ranked as minor, and the remainder noticed no change.

Various comments accompanied the returned questionnaires including those with regard to the reduction in sound sensitivity, noting how one child was able to discard his ear plugs after AIT while another reported that "his head didn't hurt anymore," and a third stated "we're using household appliances again after having stopped for almost three years." One parent reported that he "loves trains, but before AIT he couldn't stand their whistles. It doesn't bother him anymore." Another noted "not playing the records so loudly as before . . . I think he is tuning into others' speech more often."

The authors of this report conclude:

Auditory integration training is still in the early stages of implementation. It may eventually go the way of a number of other miraculous treatment hopes for autism. At this point, all we can say conclusively is that the results are inconclusive. It does seem that the benefits some parents attribute to AIT are sufficiently strong, specific, and life-significant to encourage other parents to seek treatment for their children. On the other hand, such results should be interpreted with caution because of the possibility that they could be explained by factors other than AIT.[116]

Subsequent to the publication of this paper one of the authors, Dr. Nickola Nelson of the Department of Speech Pathology and Audiology at Western Michigan University, had occasion to ponder the whole question of the issues raised by so-called miracle treatments for autism (treatments that are not recognized by mainstream medical establishments) and the dilemma faced by parents.[117] She highlights the fact that parents often feel desperate following their child's diagnosis and as a result will put themselves through enormous expense, hardship, and sacrifice in an effort to procure any kind of treatment for their child rather than give up without a good fight. Even the most unlikely interventions will be tried. She quotes one parent expressing it as "Credulity is an elastic element, capable of stretching in proportion with need." In discussing how this situation can be improved, Nelson argues for better relations between parents and professionals. "We also believe that professionals can serve as better consultants to parents when parental viewpoints are considered, and that professional attitudes associated with 'protecting' parents from seeking certain treatments for their children are patronizing and inappropriate."

She writes that similar thoughts were echoed earlier by Dr. Ralph Maurer in his capacity as chairman of the Autism Society of America's Professionals' Advisory Committee when he observed that "professionals have breath of experience, and parents have depth." He comments further: "Each can learn from the other, but for either to learn requires a dialogue, and a dialogue requires mutual respect."

In her article entitled "Clinical Research, the Placebo Effect, Responsibility to Families, and Other Concerns Stimulated by Auditory Integration Training,"[117] Nelson also deals with the dilemma of the clinicians. She comments that "For many professionals the ethical dilemma is acute between choosing to provide AIT in the absence of clear evidence of its effectiveness, and the alternative of declining to assist families who believe that AIT might make a major difference in their child's life."

Going on to discuss research procedures, she records that in standard research procedures the test of efficacy of any treatment is generally considered to be the double-blind control group study. This is known as the gold standard. This type of study is designed to give one group of patients the treatment under experimental testing and to give a similar group (called the control, which has been cross-matched for number, age, sex, severity of condition, etc.) a placebo treatment. For example, if a drug is being tested, the experimental group will get the actual drug, but the control group will get a similar looking but inert pill that does not contain any pharmacologically active substance. This pill is called a placebo. Only the controller of the experiment will know which group or individual is getting which. This is where the word *blind* comes in. It is done to prevent personal bias entering the experiment and to make it as objective as possible.

The word placebo comes from the Latin verb "to please." Its use in medicine dates back to the time of Hippocrates, the Father of Medicine, and his great medical school at Cos in ancient Greece. It was Hippocrates who established the healing principle of "the laying on of hands" in order to draw out the energy resources of his patients in the fight against disease. Throughout the centuries placebos were commonly used in medicine as treatments for many medical conditions and diseases with very good results, even in pain control during surgical procedures.

The placebo effect is well recognized in modern medicine, where it has been found that about one-third of patients in a clinical trial of a new antidepressant will respond to the placebo version alone.[51] Also the rate of response has been found to be even higher in the case of clinical trials of anti-anxiety agents. Overall it is not unusual for a placebo effect to occur in about half of the patients in any study of a medical treatment—so much so that the U.S. Food and Drug Administration has mandated that a placebo group or other control group must be included in the clinical trials of any new medication. This is to establish how effective it is before it is placed on the market.[51]

To return again to the paper of Nelson's, she asks what brings about a placebo response and reviews research showing that the answer would appear to lie in the patients' own expectation of what the placebo treatment might do for them. Those who had an active, positive approach to it exhibited a sense of control over the treatment. These were the people who responded well to it. Conversely, those who were passive in their approach, had a negative attitude, and doubted the value of the treatment responded less well. In discussing the role of the placebo effect in AIT, Nelson asks "How does belief in a treatment influence its apparent and real efficacy?" She further ponders, "If faith and sacrifice were not called for, would treatments yield equal benefits?"

She answers these questions by discussing a further possibility. If the family had a dramatic increase in their expectations for a child's improvement, might not this then influence change in that child, particularly when that child has a malfunctioning sensory processing system? This, in turn, begs the question as to whether the autistic condition is really as stable and uncontrollable as it appears to be.

Nelson's paper provides much to reflect upon. Her in-depth analysis seriously considers many ethical, methodological, and professional responsibility issues that surround controversial treatments like AIT.[117] She concludes:

Parents need to be included in the conversation, not as passive advisees, but as active participants in the search for understanding about the meaning of efficacy. In addition, an open dialogue should supplement the private one that is often relegated to the closed conversations of the peer review process. By opening the discussion of controversial clinical treatments such as AIT, a balance is sought for coping with the dilemma raised at the beginning of this letter—that is, we should seek to balance an open-minded willingness to consider alternate explanations for new treatments (even those with no plausible theoretical base) with a healthy scepticism in our continued pursuit of meaning and empirical support for clinical activities.[117]

One final consideration to be addressed is the safety of AIT. Some specialists are hesitant to recommend AIT because they believe that it is not safe.[118] These concerns came to the fore after a study indicated that the output levels from the Audiokinetron were in excess of the federal guidelines for exposure to sound. These output levels, however, were only obtained at the maximum setting of the Audiokinetron.[119] Subsequent research confirmed these results when measuring the output from two Audiokinetrons and two BGC AudioTone Generators as measured in the ear canals of twenty-four adults. Also, as was similar to the previous study, when normal-use settings were set for each machine, this greatly lowered the maximum output levels. These lower levels were held to be within the sphere of acceptable risk. Lucker points out that by employing lower settings for the equipment, safety of listening conditions "may be achieved." Therefore he concludes that "AIT practitioners should feel more secure that they may not be exposing their subjects to possible permanent hearing-loss risk *if* [that author's italics] they employ lower settings on the equipment." In addition to this, he feels that constraints should be put on manufacturers so that all future models of their equipment contain only the lower settings.[118]

Still staying with perceptual disorders as one of the other factors in the autistic equation, we turn our attention again to the question of face perception as documented under Mark R. and referred to subsequently in the work of Dr. Digby Tantam and colleagues.[44] There has been a build-up of information in the literature over the last ten years on this issue, giving evidence that abnormal face processing is found in autism. Some autistic children have been found to sort faces in photographs by using the hats or glasses worn by people rather than relying on facial expression. They have shown difficulty labelling facial expressions, such as anger, joy, surprise, and so forth. When given the task of finding the misfit face among a group of faces, they have performed worse than the control group. They have also been found to have problems with matching gesture and facial expression. Conversely, they were found to be much better at matching upside-down faces than were controls, and they appeared to rely more on features in the lower part of the face for recognition than on the contour of the face as a whole.[44] All the studies looked at, with one exception, where "faces in the flesh" were involved, have used either photographs or video material in their research procedures.

Some researchers have attributed these perception disturbances to the developmental delay that is associated with autism. Others see them more in terms of being part of a general perceptual disorder. It has long been suggested that physiognomic perception, that is, perceiving inanimate objects as real people, might be a factor operating in autism. There are also indications that many autistic children treat people as if they were objects, and there is no doubt whatsoever that Mark R., in his early childhood, found no distinction between people and inanimate objects.

Recently a case of physiognomic perception in a young, autistic, Japanese woman, who in her drawings substitutes Kanji characters (Japanese ideogram/alphabet figures) for the faces of her figures, has been described.[120] The figures are perfectly drawn, but in place of the face these Kanji ideograms appear. This patient has been preoccupied with collecting these Kanji characters since childhood and uses them to depict different emotional expressions. One set will depict laughter, another anger, and so on. The author, Kobayashi, is familiar with other similar cases of physiognomic perception in her practice and, quoting Dr. Edward Ornitz and Dr. Edward Ritvo, she suggests that this mode of perception in autism might "represent perceptual inconstancy." She also notes that "such a phenomenon would seem delusional to us."[120A]

There has over time been some controversy in the literature as to whether, in autism, faces are processed in a similar manner to other visuospatial stimuli or are in fact mapped onto face-specific brain systems. This issue has been raised in a recent study of face recognition in autism and related disorders.[121] These researchers refer to the appeal of studying the "social deficits in autism" by approaching the problem from the angle of the deficits in face perception. They also point to the expanding knowledge of brain systems that are involved in the recognition of faces. In reviewing the literature published over the last twenty years on research into deficits in facial recognition, they comment on the conflicting results obtained, as some researchers have found deficits while others have not. They point to the different methodologies used, which cause confusion and make comparisons more difficult. Also, as they had discovered, most studies reviewed investigated deficits in adolescents and adults. This gives rise to the question as to whether young people with autism might in fact have a face processing difficulty in their younger years that could improve with age, as they develop compensating strategies, even though some evidence of a deficit could remain. For their study they chose three groups (34 in each group) of young children who were matched on nonverbal mental age as well as on chronological age. One-third were children with autism, one-third were children with pervasive developmental disorder not otherwise specified (PDDNOS), and one-third were children with non-PDD disorders. They found "pronounced deficits" in facial recognition in the autistic group in relation to the other two groups. The children with PDDNOS did not show face recognition deficits, and this result had not been expected.

These authors speculate that as children progress in years, they may become more skilled at processing facial recognition as they adopt compensatory tactics. They bring out the possibility that in autism faces may be processed in the same manner as other visuospatial stimuli and may not map on face-specific brain systems. In this paper they cite preliminary data, obtained by their group, which appears to point to the fact that "brain activation patterns specific to face recognition might map on structures usually involved in other forms of visual spatial stimuli (e.g., inanimate objects), rather than on the unique structures proven to be associated with face perception."[121]

This preliminary data has now been published and an analysis of the results has shown that in a sample of people with autism and AS significant differences were found in the pattern of brain activation during face discrimination when compared with controls.[122] It was found that in the autism group there was significantly greater functional activation in the inferior temporal gyri (ITG) and less functional activation in the fusiform gyrus (FG) (see glossary) than in the control groups when viewing pictures of faces. The fusiform gyrus, a temporal lobe structure, is one brain region traditionally involved in face perception in normal individuals. Among the control groups the ITG was the area showing most association with object discrimination. Therefore these authors conclude that their results suggest that the perception of faces in autism is more like the perception of objects in people who do not have a social disability. This study was based on using functional magnetic resonance imaging (fMRI) (see under brain imaging in glossary) to measure changes in blood oxygen level–dependent (BOLD) contrast in fourteen high-functioning individuals with autism or Asperger syndrome and two groups of matched normal controls (14 in each group).[122]

Another recent study to investigate face perception has come up with similar results.[123] This latter study found that all tested patients with autism showed either reduced functioning or no functioning in the fusiform gyrus during the task of perceiving faces in pictures. By contrast, the normal controls for this group showed strong functioning in the fusiform gyrus when undertaking the same tasks. Speculating on the cause, these authors suggest that it could be due to structural abnormality in the fusiform gyrus in individuals with autism or it could be due to underdevelopment of this structure arising from lack of experience with faces. They indicate that this leads to the fact that testing such hypotheses could provide critical information and could answer such questions as to whether intensive training in face processing leads to normal activity in the fusiform gyrus or "would a response to faces occur in a completely unexpected brain region." If this were so it would provide important information regarding brain "learning patterns" in autism and would highlight *intact* brain areas in autism. As they go on to suggest, there is now considerable potential for monitoring such brain activity and using it to design and evaluate better intervention treatment strategies that have a biological basis for individuals with autism.[123] The above two studies are the first of their kind.

And what of the orthomolecular or megavitamin and mineral approach as an intervention in autism? The orthomolecular approach is of the opinion that medical and psychiatric conditions can be treated by providing the patient with the best possible nutritional needs for mind and body. It is based on the assumption that some illnesses occur because specific nutritional needs are lacking. Ever since the discovery of the fact that diseases like scurvy, pellagra, and beri-beri were caused by vitamin deficiency and were treated successfully with the right vitamins, the use of vitamin therapy has become established. However, it has to be kept in mind that large doses of any nutrient can be toxic to the body.

The subject of the use of megavitamins and minerals as an intervention treatment in autism is a controversial one. The research into it has fallen prey to the problem that dogs much of the research in autism, that is, different studies use different protocols so that it lacks standardization. Not all of the studies looked at used the double-blind, placebo-controlled format. As a result, in many cases in comparing one study with another, one is not comparing like with like, and this is why results can be so conflicting. Before any study of the effects of megavitamin therapy is carried out, the adequacy of the basic diet of the child must be taken into consideration and a baseline established. Otherwise any improvements seen could be due to a deficiency rather than a need for extra vitamins and minerals.

Clinical studies have, over time, shown that some people with autism do have vitamin and mineral deficiencies.[124] These deficiencies could be due to the restricted diets that some people with autism follow or to malabsorption in the digestive system. Lack of essential vitamins and minerals can interfere with hormonal activity in the body as well as the action of neurotransmitters and other metabolic functions.[124] In a review of vitamin therapy in autism, Dr. Theodore Page states that vitamin B6 (pyridoxine) has been the "best studied and most successful," adding that several well-designed studies have shown favorable effects from pyridoxine, and that these effects are increased by taking magnesium in conjunction with it. The improvements recorded are improved social behavior, improved language, reduced aggression, and increased interest in the environment.[65] Conversely, Dr. Leon Sloman, director of psychopharmacology at Clarke Institute of Psychiatry in Toronto, has noted:

Vitamin B6 is relatively safe compared to other commonly used psychotropic drugs. However, in massive doses (200mg/kg/day) vitamin B6 can produce nerve damage in animals. Sensory neuropathy in humans has been reported following high-dose pyridoxine treatment. The side effects of megavitamin therapy (with vitamin B6 as one component) are (1) withdrawal reactions after the vitamin therapy is abruptly discontinued; this includes behavioural deterioration and seizures; (2) sensory neuropathy; (3) interactions with phenytoin and possibly other drugs; (4) gastric distress, nausea, and diarrhea; (5) excitability, irritability, and sound sensitivity; (6) enuresis and daytime incontinence; (7) increased autistic symptoms or hyperactivity; and (8) insomnia. It is conceivable that a subgroup of autistic children have a metabolic defect resulting in increased requirements for one or more nutrients, but, because the overall benefits of vitamin B6 and magnesium in PDD have not been established, their routine use cannot be recommended at this time.[125]

Now a new study has been initiated that hopes to come up with some clearcut information on autism and treatment with multivitamin/mineral supplements. This study will follow a double-blind, placebo-controlled format and will test a supplement designed for people with autism. It contains a mixture of vitamins, minerals, and herbs. The people involved are twenty-five children ages three to seven, and they are being evaluated on "medical history, therapy approaches, diet, behaviour, language, social skills, sleep and gastrointestinal issues." Vitamin and minerals levels in each child will also be assessed and reviewed. This study is being undertaken by Dr. James Adams, a parent/professional and a team at Arizona State University, in partnership with the Southwest Autism Research Center and The Greater Phoenix ASA Chapter.[124]

Finally, what part does secretin play as an intervention therapy in autism? Secretin is a small peptide hormone secreted by the cells in the wall of the small intestine when acidified food enters it from the stomach. Its purpose is to stimulate the pancreas to produce alkaline pancreatic juice and to stimulate the liver to produce alkaline bile. These alkaline fluids then neutralize the highly acidic food contents coming in from the stomach. On October 7, 1998, NBC's *Dateline* broadcast a story relating to the use of secretin in a young boy with autism who suffered with vomiting and chronic diarrhea. After receiving secretin as part of a diagnostic work-up for his gastrointestinal condition, this child was reported to have shown a dramatic improvement in some of his symptoms of autism within a few short weeks. Prior to that, a clinical report in one of the professional journals indicated quite significant improvement in the behavior of three young children with autism within weeks of receiving secretin, also for gastrointestinal problems.[126] In neither case had an improvement in autistic symptoms been expected. This finding sits uneasily in the context of the current understanding of autism. It has been speculated that secretin might have a central brain stimulating effect, but this remains unclear and unverified.

As a result of the *Dateline* story, there has been a large number of inquiries to clinics and professionals world-wide for information on secretin and requests for the "therapy." In view of this, researchers are advising that the hormone not be tried until proper double-blind, controlled trials have been carried out. Such trials are necessary to evaluate the clinical efficacy of treatments. Anecdotal reports of the effect of the hormone on people who have been given injections range from improvement in symptoms, to a worsening of symptoms, to a single report of first time grand-mal seizures.[127] One recent written report from a mother documents her son's regression after treatment with secretin and issues a warning. He became "increasingly frustrated and anxious," his aggressive episodes worsened, and his perseverative behavior became almost continuous. She felt as if he had "regressed six months." In addition her eight-year-old son developed severe bowel constipation problems.[128]

The American Academy of Child and Adolescent Psychiatry has issued the following Policy Statement on secretin.

Secretin in the Treatment of Autism
Discussed and Revised by the Autism Committee on October 29, 1998
Approved by the Council on March 3, 1999

Secretin is a polypeptide neurotransmitter involved in digestion. This agent has been approved by the Food and Drug Administration for use in the diagnosis of gastrointestinal problems in adults; repeated use has not been approved by the FDA. Several anecdotal reports have suggested that secretin may ameliorate some of the symptoms of Autism and one open study of three children has been reported. The mechanism of action is unclear; there are not yet appropriate controlled studies which support the use of this agent, nor has it been determined that it is safe for repeated administration. Accordingly, the use of this agent should be considered unproven and experimental.

Given the severity of Autism, parents and family members are often willing to try treatments that promise improvement, but are unproven. Such treatments are usually based on anecdotal reports that are often unsubstantiated by more rigorous research; the short term change reported may be nonspecific and unsustained.

Families should be helped to make informed decisions about their use of alternative or nonestablished treatments, including careful consideration of risks and benefits.

The American Academy of Child and Adolescent Psychiatry supports the study of all promising treatments by well designed research.[129]

The National Institute of Mental Health also issued a statement on secretin along similar lines, and they are advising parents not to pursue treatment with it for their children other than as part of controlled research studies. They add that the safety and possible benefits of secretin can only be assessed through careful research (March 1999).[130]

One of the first of these clinical trials of secretin has now reported back.[127] The results have found that the hormone was no more effective than a placebo in improving the symptoms of autism. This particular study involved fifty-six children with autism from ages three to fourteen. Half of these children received a single dose of synthetic human secretin, and the other half received a placebo (a harmless saline solution). The results showed that there was a "decrease in the severity of symptoms" in both groups of children, thus showing no advantage of secretin over the placebo. This study, however, as the authors pointed out, had certain limitations. It was a single dose; synthetic secretin was used; the study was short term. By contrast, most of the anecdotal reports of the effects of secretin were based on the use of biological (porcine) secretin. Further clinical trials are now under way to test secretin to learn how effective it is at different doses: whether biological secretin is better than synthetic secretin; what particular symptoms of autism it is most effective for; and whether more than one treatment is necessary.[127]

CHAPTER 13

❧❧❧❧

CAN OTHER MEDICAL CONDITIONS COEXIST WITH AUTISM?

The answer is a very definite "Yes." They are called comorbid conditions. Some of them are organic conditions, while others fall into the category of psychiatric and/or behavioral conditions. Epilepsy is one of the medical conditions that has a stronger than normal association with autism. As previously indicated, about one-third of all children with autism will develop seizures, and the estimated prevalence of epilepsy by adulthood is on the order of 20 to 35 percent.[131] This is in contrast to a rate of 0.5 percent among the general population.[23] Seizures are more common among the severely mentally retarded people with autism than among the more mildly retarded. However, epilepsy has also been documented relatively often among high-ability autistic people. The rate of epilepsy in Asperger syndrome has been described as being on the order of a few percent.[23] Filipek and her associates, in commenting recently on epilepsy in autism, stated that all types of seizures may be seen, but the more prevalent seem to be partial complex seizures. This team emphasizes that "Any behaviors such as staring, cessation of activity, or aggressive escalations associated with confusion should trigger a high index of suspicion of complex partial seizures in autistic individuals."[12]

Another medical condition associated with autism is fragile X syndrome. Early reports of this noted a high incidence of association (up to 25%) but newer studies report a much lower incidence of the order of 3 to 7 percent. Other large studies show no association. These differences in figures would appear to be a measure of the different methods of analysis used, with the newer technique of "molecular genetic analysis" giving the lowest results.[12] Fragile X syndrome is thought to be among the most common causes of mental retardation. In the general population the prevalence is about 1 in 1,000 males and 1 in 2,000 to 2,500 females. Also 1 in 700 females is thought to be a carrier.[132] There is an association between the syndrome and a fragile site on the long arm of the X chromosome at Xq27.3. Consequently the gene is not producing protein.[132A] The intellectual impairment in individuals affected by the condition varies from severe to mild. The treatment therapy of choice for the learning impairments associated with fragile X syndrome is sensory motor integration.[132]

Tuberous Sclerosis Complex is another of the medical comorbid conditions associated with autism. Figures for the number of autistic people who have comorbid tuberous sclerosis are of the order of 0.4 to 3 percent.[12,22] It also is a genetic disorder. The condition results in a faulty protein that produces abnormal cells during the development of the tissues. This, in turn, gives rise to abnormal growths of tissue in some organs of the body. The brain, heart, kidneys, and skin are the organs most affected. This condition gives rise to a variety of physical and mental problems that vary greatly in their expression.[133]

The behavioral and psychiatric symptoms associated with autism include ritualistic, obsessive/compulsive behaviors, self-injurious behaviors, acute and chronic anxiety with panic attacks, apparent absence of emotional reactions, hyperactivity, poor attention span, sleep abnormality, night rocking, agitation, abnormalities of mood, and psychiatric preoccupations. As Tsai points out, up until recently these were looked upon as being associated features of autism. Now, however, more researchers are arguing for the need to recognize them as coming into the category of comorbid neuropsychiatric disorders.[106]

There is a difference between the ritualistic, obsessive/compulsive behavior seen in autism and the type of obsessive/compulsive disorder (OCD) seen in the general population. Wing makes the distinction between true obsessional neurosis and the repetitive interests and activities of Asperger syndrome when she points out that people with AS are not aware of the illogicality of their rituals and they do not resist them.[34] This is in contrast to classic cases of obsessional neurosis where there is full awareness of how illogical these behaviors are. Szatmari also compares the rituals and compulsive behaviors of children with AS with the behaviors of children in the general population who have obsessive/compulsive disorder. He comes to the same conclusion, commenting that the key feature of true obsessive/compulsive disorder is that it is experienced as "ego-dystonic or alien."[134] He indicates that with Asperger children such behaviors can stem from high levels of arousal. In his opinion, if careful attention is paid to the circumstances surrounding these rituals, for example, anxiety-provoking situations, they can often suggest that the resulting behaviors fall into the category of pervasive developmental disorders rather than obsessive-compulsive disorders.[134] When discussing the same subject, again in Asperger syndrome, Tantam states that in his clinical practice he will review his diagnosis of Asperger syndrome if the individual does not show ritualistic or repetitive behaviors. The reason for this is that he regards such activities as almost always arising as a result of anxiety in individuals with this disorder and that anxiety almost invariably accompanies Asperger syndrome.[135] He quotes research as showing that the rituals in OCD and those in AS can be differentiated on the basis of the higher incidence of fear thoughts and autonomic activity found in OCD.

Szatmari, writing again later on this same topic, stresses that it is important to make a distinction between the "obsessive *interests*" found in AS children and the "obsessive *thoughts*" seen in OCD.[73] He indicates that AS children have a very narrow sphere of interests and that although these are alluded to as obsessive the child himself does not regard them as unreasonable; quite the reverse, because they help to reduce anxiety and give the child enjoyment. He quotes other research as showing that the compulsions and obsessions found in autism are not as elaborate as those in OCD and also that they tend to be more stereotyped and concrete.

Self-injurious behaviors (SIB) include head banging, wrist and finger biting, face slapping, and eye poking. These behaviors are very distressing for both the children and their parents, and some children do very serious damage to themselves. It was originally thought that this type of behavior was present only in those children falling within the handicapped range of intelligence, but it is now known that such behavior is also often seen in autistic children with normal intelligence. A few studies have given figures for the prevalence of SIB in autism. These range from about one quarter to almost one half. Tsai states that research has not achieved effective medication therapy for self-injurious behavior.[106]

Many experienced workers in the field comment on the all-pervading high anxiety levels experienced by individuals with the autistic spectrum disorders. Szatmari, in discussing anxiety in AS, indicates that "elective mutism" (silence) "can be seen in conjunction with this disorder, particularly in the preschool years. In this situation children with Asperger's syndrome develop a phobia about speaking in social situations and are overwhelmed by feelings of anxiety." He adds that "both generalised anxiety disorders and specific social phobias can occur in children and adolescents with Asperger's syndrome" and that "these anxiety symptoms are often extremely distressing to the child."[134] The question of social phobia comes up for discussion again later. Tantam, writing more recently, states that anxiety disorders in AS are very common expressions of distress and may not be easy to diagnose, as they may tend to show up in the form of an increased severity in the expression of the core syndrome, particularly in the increase of rituals.[135] He considers that the expression of severe anxiety states in AS, caused, for example, by the threat of facing a serious life change, may give rise to agitation states that in turn may lead to confusion and behavior changes. He indicates, quoting from other sources, that acute anxiety states of this nature may correlate with "cycloid psychosis" or may be associated with first-rank symptoms of schizophrenia. (The misdiagnosis of AS/HFA for schizophrenia has already been discussed.) Tantam also draws attention to the fact that symptoms of catatonia may occur and that in some cases the above psychotic incident may be attributed to bipolar affective disorder. However, he notes that in other cases they would appear to be true anxiety psychoses. Finally, he states that these psychotic episodes normally have a good outcome.[135]

The autism literature documents that a certain percentage of children exhibit, for no apparent reason, sudden, severe temper tantrums; unexplained eruptions of anger; screaming spells; inexplicable crying periods; or, on the other hand, periods of complete inactivity. These have been looked on as being part of the general condition of autism and seen in terms of a worsening of both behavior and condition. Recently Dr. Angel Diez Cuervo, former medical director at the Hospital Institute San Jose in Madrid, has discussed these behaviors in terms of a possible link between neurological disorders and some subtypes of autism:

> Without allowing the problem to get out of proportion we would like to highlight that, in the case of children with autism who do not show any clear signs of epilepsy, but who do have periods of complete inactivity, abrupt, vegetative manifestations, inexplicable bursts of anger, unprovoked screaming or crying fits, a slight suspicion of brief affections of consciousness, psycho motor automatisms, etc., we need to complete full neurophysiological assessments, although an initial absence of any anomalies is the most frequent result. Only in rare cases do we succeed (after repeated examinations) in detecting specific alterations which confirm the suspicion of a participation of the frontal lobes and/or temporal lobes and the limbic zones linked to these episodes.[136]

This author points out that it has been proven that the right therapy using suitable medication, and in specific cases, surgery, can eliminate or reduce these behaviors, even though the basic core characteristics of autism will remain. He comments that at the present time two definite conclusions can be drawn; namely, "1) all neurons are potentially epileptogenic and 2) everyone has a convulsion threshold." If intense excitatory stimulation (e.g., hypoglycaemia or electric shock) affects an individual, reducing the normal threshold, it can trigger a downward convulsion, and the subject is more likely to have a brain seizure. He adds that what would be considered normal stimulation for the average person might, because of genetic vulnerability, cause a convulsion in a person with autism.

In recent years Dr. Diez Cuervo and his colleagues have carried out studies (biochemical and morphological) on the brains of individuals with autism and individuals with epilepsy (or those with both disorders) and have discovered similar alterations in them. They point out that these

experimental studies showed clearly that these alterations are phenomena which arise, in a parallel fashion, when the epileptic foyer is developing before epileptogenic activity begins. They are not the consequence, but the origin, of the critical activity. Therefore, the epileptic fit is the consequence of neuronal hyperactivity in a reduced neuronal population with an increase in the neuroglia.

He sums up by stating that this explanation would clarify why the action of many different pathological factors (e.g., infection, alteration in the immune system, imbalance in neurotransmitters, a deficiency of oxygen in the brain) on the central nervous system can give rise to alteration, and would also explain the mechanism at the origin of these fits.[136]

All of the foregoing considerations lead to the question of treatment. In his brief report to the State of the Science Conference, Dr. Luke Tsai of the Developmental Disorders Clinic at the University of Michigan Medical Center addressed the extent of comorbid psychiatric disorders in autism and posed the question, How frequently do they exist?[137] He answered it by admitting that shared observations among clinicians reveal that they are loathe to make added psychiatric diagnosis in nonverbal autistic individuals who would not be capable of providing information. This is compounded by the absence of sound and dependable diagnostic implements that could be applied to less able people with autism. He argues that if many of these psychiatric and/or behavioral symptoms can be looked on as symptoms of comorbid psychiatric conditions the data indicates that medication can be an effective as well as a safe extra treatment for some of the symptoms occurring in autism. He sums up by writing that much still remains to be accomplished, and that research should now concentrate on formulating sound and suitable diagnostic measures by which comorbid psychiatric disorders can be identified in people with autism.[137] As we have seen outlined in the previous chapters this work has begun.

The major psychiatric disorders of depression (unipolar) and manic depression (bipolar) can coexist with the autistic spectrum disorders. How prevalent are they, how severe are they, and how do they respond to treatment? Recently one group of researchers got together all published cases in an attempt to answer some of these questions.[138] In a review of the literature they found seventeen such cases. In this sample, fourteen of the fifteen for whom figures were available were in the mentally retarded category of IQ, and in the overall sample the age range was from four years to forty. Almost half of the sample were female. Overall eight individuals had depressive-like episodes only; four had manic-like episodes; four had both manic and depressive episodes, and one had mixed affective episodes.

Asking the question, Can affective disorders (see glossary) be diagnosed in people with autism? they answer it by stating that the behaviors noted fitted into the category of the three essential features described for affective disorders. These are the presence of vegetative signs and symptoms, a change in how the patient views himself, and a change in the prevailing mood. They also noted that the changes in behavior occurred in episodes and responded to suitable medication.

In discussing the results of their review, the authors point out that it is not known how common mood disorders are in unselected cases of autism. It is not known whether they appear in the same frequency as in the general population or perhaps greater, and how they may vary with age and/or IQ. In many of the cases studied in their review, the effects of the mood disorder were severe; severe enough to threaten the patients' placement at school, at home, or in the workplace. One patient, who had to be placed in care for two years due to aggressive outbursts, was able to return home after treatment of his affective disorder. In other cases there had been severe symptoms of hyperactivity, aggression, and SIB, and these symptoms had either disappeared or improved greatly after treatment. Also in some cases, there had been a marked improvement in the ability to function and a reduction in autistic features after treatment. All cases reported at least "a partial response to treatment for mood disorders." All manic episodes needed treatment with more than one medication, whereas depressions could be treated with a single medication.

These authors maintain that research is needed to check out whether in fact the conditions described in these papers actually represent true affective disorder. That they do would be supported by the findings of some workers in this field.[139,140] This team found that the rates of major affective disorders and/or anxiety disorders among the relatives of autistic people were higher than what would be expected in the general population. In one study they found an incidence of about one in seven for treated affective disorders among the brothers and sisters of autistic people. The estimated population rate for this is 2.6 percent. In another study of anxiety disorder and major depressive disorders, this time of parents, they found an increased rate of anxiety disorder of almost one-quarter among the parents of autistic people when compared to a rate of three per hundred among the parents of Down syndrome persons. Also, the rate of major depressive disorders among the parents of children with autism was over a quarter, almost double that found among the Down syndrome parents. In addition, they found that the first depressive episode occurred before the birth of the autistic child in over three-quarters of the parents affected by the major depressive disorder. These and other studies point to the fact that a relationship may exist between genes underlying autism and those underlying affective and/or anxiety disorders.

A more recent study entitled "Autism, Affective Disorders and Social Phobia" by Susan L. Smalley, James McCracken, and Peter Tanguay of the

Department of Psychiatry at the University of California carried out a very thorough investigation of thirty-six families with an autistic child and found that almost two-thirds had a first degree relative diagnosed with major depressive disorder and 39 percent had a first degree relative diagnosed with social phobia (see glossary).[141] The control group was made up of families with a child having a genetic condition but not autism. In this control group only one-fifth had a first degree relative with major depressive disorder, and 5 percent had a first degree relative diagnosed with social phobia. All of these figures add up to a frequency of major depression of almost 40 percent among 96 first degree relatives of autistic people compared with just over one-tenth found among 45 relatives of the control group. The occurrence of social phobia among the relatives of the autistic group was almost ten times more common than that found among the relatives of the control group. In addition, the majority of the parents affected with a major depression had had the occurrence of the first depressive episode before the birth of their autistic child, and all parents with social phobia had their first occurrence of this also before their child was born.

Studies of twins have shown that social phobia has a strong link with genetic inheritance. In discussing their findings these authors consider that "Taken together, these family studies suggest that autism, major depressive disorder, social phobia, and possibly substance abuse show a familial association." Also, there was evidence that higher rates of social phobia "may show a stronger familial association with autism in the absence of mental retardation than autism with comorbid mental retardation."

The substance abuse referred to here is alcohol abuse or dependency and drug abuse or dependency (over one-fifth among parents of autistic patients as compared with none in the control group).

Having pointed out that it is unclear how major depression and social phobia are related in these families they sum up with:

These findings confirm the work suggested by previous investigators that autism and major depression are familially associated. Furthermore, our data suggest that social phobia may be a specific anxiety disorder associated with autism, particularly in a subset of families in which autism occurs in the absence of mental retardation. This finding is intriguing given that a core criterion for autism is an abnormality in social relationships. While this familial relationship *may* be genetic, elucidation of a genetic underpinning requires additional research using alternative strategies, such as complex segregation analysis and gene mapping. (From "Autism, Affective Disorders, and Social Phobia" by S.L. Smalley, J. McCracken, and P. Tanguay, *American Journal of Medical Genetics*, Copyright © 1995 Wiley-Liss, Inc., Reprinted by permission of Wiley-Liss, Inc., a subsidiary of John Wiley & Sons, Inc.).[141]

With regard to Asperger syndrome, a number of suggestions in the literature link it with bipolar disorder, but most of these are based on small numbers of cases. There is, however, one larger study where an investigation of fifty-one individuals (ages 3 to 35 years) with a diagnosis of autism or pervasive developmental disorders was undertaken (17 of whom fitted the diagnosis of AS), which found that the incidence of bipolar disorder in families positive for AS was 6.1 percent. This figure is very much greater than would be expected in the general population.[142]

Gillberg and Coleman, in commenting recently on how research has begun to uncover some of the underlying medical conditions that show up with the distinctive pattern of autism behavior, discuss infantile autistic bipolar disorder (IABD) as a disease entity of autism. Certain criteria define IABD. There is regression after an initial period of normal development; classical criteria for autism must be met; the core autistic symptoms, as they unfold in the young child, must show an obvious mode of cycling; the presence of a family history of bipolar disorder or major depression in first or second degree relatives must be present; and finally, no dysmorphic features, no seizures, or neurological dysfunction can be present.[23A]

They further state that it could be argued that the patients who present with these symptoms have both autism and bipolar disorder but they stress that it is one disease only and cannot be separated into two. They further elaborate that the cycling pattern occurs in the core autistic symptoms themselves as they wax and wane, and that the characteristics of IABD also include obsessive traits and special abilities and presents within the first thirty months of life. They stress that this particular group should not be confused with other groups of children with autism who during childhood have depressive episodes and sometimes manic episodes that present at a later stage. This latter group, they note, results in two separate comorbid diseases that is autism in conjunction with later onset bipolar mood disorder or depressive disorder. They record that the IABD children are not a common group but that many large specialized autism clinics have seen a very small number of them.[23A]

To what extent is schizophrenia associated with autism? People with autism can develop a superimposed schizophrenic illness later in life. The incidence of this, however, would appear to be small. Hans Asperger himself found that of his two hundred cases, only two developed schizophrenia in later life.[143] This is a rate of 1 percent, the same as in the general population. Tantam found schizophrenia among 3.5 percent of his sample, but because this sample was based on referred cases, it was likely to contain a higher than average number.[43] In the past many cases of Asperger syndrome/high ability autism have been given a mistaken diagnosis of schizophrenia. In drawing attention to this fact of mistaken diagnosis, Wing considers that the main difficulty arises because some workers define schizophrenia loosely while others have a more strict definition.[34] She highlights the "marked contrast between the vague woolliness of schizophrenic thought and the concrete, pedantic approach found in Asperger's syndrome," adding that "Unless they have a superimposed schizophrenic illness, people with Asperger's syndrome do not experience thought echo, thought substitution or insertion, thought broadcast, voices commenting on their actions, voices talking to each other, or feelings that external forces are exerting control over their will, emotions or behaviour."

Moving on to the question of "magical thinking" in Asperger syndrome, Wing notes that although some people become preoccupied with their own imaginary world and may be said to have delusions or hallucinations, these experiences are probably "better termed 'over-valued ideas.'"

Szatmari discusses in detail the condition of childhood schizophrenia and comments that it is obvious that some of the features of AS overlap with some features of schizophrenia.[73] For example, he draws attention to the fact that the speech patterns of children with AS may sound "disorganized," and that it is possible to judge some autistic behaviors as "catatonic." Also, when under extreme pressure a child with AS may have thoughts and ideas that could be mistaken for delusions and that it is not always easy to make the distinction between real hallucinations and pseudohallucinations. Another complicating feature, as he points out, is that the developmental background of children with schizophrenia can be similar to that of AS, with a history of poor relationships with their peer group, a narrow range of interests, and a habit of withdrawing from social situations. Szatmari illustrates the key features that can be used in differential diagnosis, stating that the "psychotic" symptoms of children with AS are fleeting and generally last hours or at the most days and that removal of the extreme stress under which they arose will resolve them. By contrast, the psychotic symptoms seen in schizophrenia need to last "for a full month" unless, of course, they are being treated with medication. Finally, as he points out, the age of onset is different, the presence of true psychotic symptoms usually occurring later in schizophrenia—generally after nine years of age—whereas in PDD children the developmental abnormalities occur before five years of age.[73]

One final question to be addressed is the similarities between Asperger syndrome, high-functioning autism, and schizoid personality disorder. In "Schizoid Personality in Childhood," Dr. Sula Wolff, formerly of the Department of Psychiatry at the University of Edinburgh in Scotland, who has worked for over thirty years in this area, discusses in detail the links between high-functioning autistic people, people with Asperger syndrome, and people with schizoid personality disorder and considers whether they should be on the autistic continuum. She writes: "Yet the concept of an autistic spectrum is valid. Well-functioning autistic people and severely impaired people with schizoid personality disorder, and AS as defined in ICD-10, have much in common." But she considers it more of a problem as to whether the phrase *autistic spectrum disorder* should be used to include the full gamut of closely related conditions from autism and Asperger syndrome to schizoid personality disorder.[143]

What are the defining features of schizoid personality disorder? There are certain core features: Those affected remain emotionally detached, lacking in empathy for others; they are loners; they show increased sensitivity and can develop paranoid thinking; they can talk either too much or too little; they have a rigid mental set and are single-minded in their pursuit of their own special interests; they have an unusual style of communication and a unique style of imagination.[143]

Wolff draws attention to the fact that there would seem to be close similarities between children with schizoid personality disorder and the group of children described by Asperger under the term autistic psychopathy in 1944. However, these former children do not completely fulfill present-day diagnostic criteria for Asperger syndrome, either in WHO (1992, 1993) or APA (1994). She points out that their disabilities are not quite so severe and their future outlook is much more optimistic than that of individuals presently receiving a diagnosis of AS.

Moving on to discuss the relationship between schizoid personality disorder and schizotypal personality disorder, Wolff reveals that in a follow-up study of a group of children over three-quarters of the schizoid boys and girls in the group in adult life fulfilled the criteria for DSM-III schizotypal personality disorder. In addition, by the age of twenty-seven, 5 percent of this group had developed a schizophrenic illness. This is in contrast to 0.31 to 0.49 percent developing schizophrenia by that age in the general population. This fits in with a genetic link between schizotypal personality disorder and schizophrenia. Questioning the relationship, if any, between Asperger syndrome and schizotypal personality disorder, Wolff points out that this remains unclear. She then explores the relationship between Asperger syndrome, as presently diagnosed, and schizoid children, pointing out that the children with autistic psychopathy as originally described by Hans Asperger were less impaired than those now diagnosed with AS under present-day criteria. She comments that much of the research into how affected people function psychologically has worked on the assumption that AS and HFA are equivalent as to diagnosis. She also mentions the doubt that has been cast on the accounts by Hans Asperger in relation to the giftedness and occupational achievements in later life of some of his cases.[21]

Commenting on the treatment needs of schizoid children, Wolff writes that families need to be informed that neither they themselves nor the child have caused the problems and that the personality impairments are likely to continue. She also states that treatment strategies should respect the child's solitariness, as efforts to make him sociable can lead to failure. Rather, the family and school should work to adapt to the child's needs for his own space and to allow him the freedom to follow his own special interests. With regard to the role of psychiatrists and psychologists, she says that they will best fulfill this role by acting as an advocate for the family and the child, easing their way through the school years and beyond into higher education and the work force. They should also be prepared to liaise with the law if the child gets into trouble and explain the need to avoid any custodial setting that would revolve around "noisy and aggressive group living."[143]

Finally to the question of schizophrenia. Schizophrenia is an illness that affects 1 percent of the population at some time during their lives. It is a severe mental disorder, and many professionals think that it is a group of illnesses rather than one specific illness. The symptoms can vary from one person to another. Chemical imbalance, due to dysfunction of the brain, is increasingly being highlighted by recent research into schizophrenia. In similarity with autism, schizophrenia is now being looked at in the light of a neurodevelopmental disorder with a partially genetic basis. It is thought that several genes are involved.[143] Results from another study that compared autism, schizophrenia, schizotypal personality disorder, and PDDNOS on the basis of language deficits found considerable overlap between these four groups.[143A] Other researchers in this field found that over one-third of children with schizophrenia showed autistic symptoms.[144]

The symptoms of schizophrenia involve a disturbance in thinking, in keeping contact with reality, and in responding emotionally. The patient may become disturbed by delusions and hallucinations and may hear nonexistent voices from strange sources. Some clinicians and researchers now divide the symptoms into type A positive (paranoia, bizarre thinking, hallucinations, and delusions) and type B negative (withdrawal, loss of initiative and drive, blunted and inappropriate emotions). Is there a cure? There is no cure, but there is intervention in the form of prudent use of medication to suppress the psychotic symptoms and reduce anxiety. This, coupled with good social support and a positive psychological approach to rehabilitation, improves the prognosis. Research over the years has shown that about a quarter of those who develop schizophrenia will recover and never have another episode. A further half will have recurring episodes but with the right treatment will be able to return to their normal life in between. Unfortunately, the remainder will not recover and will need regular psychiatric care.

And to conclude, How does schizotypal personality disorder manifest itself? Szatmari, in his discussion of both schizoid personality disorder and schizotypal personality disorder, points out that the latter differs from the former because of the presence of other symptoms such as magical thinking and peculiar beliefs, illusions of perception, feelings of depersonalization and derealization, and uncommon speech patterns. While stating that these additional symptoms are similar to psychotic symptoms at a subthreshold level, he notes that several studies have indicated that these two disorders in adults are related genetically to schizophrenia. There is, however, he points out, no evidence that this holds true for *"children"* with these two disorders.[73]

CHAPTER 14

❧❧❧❧❧

AUTISM AND CURRENT ISSUES IN BRIEF

In Short, What Is Autism?

To answer this we go to the definition of autism as it appears in *The Advocate*, December 2000, The Newsletter of the Autism Society of America.

Autism is a complex developmental disability that typically appears during the first three years of life. The result of a neurological disorder that affects the functioning of the brain, autism and its associated behaviours have been estimated to occur in as many as 1 in 500 individuals. Autism is four times more prevalent in boys than girls and knows no racial, ethnic, or social boundaries. Family income, life-style, and educational levels do not affect the chance of autism's occurrence.

Autism interferes with the normal development of the brain in the areas of social interaction and communication skills. Children and adults with autism typically have difficulties in verbal and non-verbal communication, social interaction, and leisure or play activities. The disorder makes it hard for them to communicate with others and relate to the outside world. They may exhibit repeated body movements (hand flapping, rocking), unusual responses to people or attachments to objects, and they may resist changes in routines.

Over one half million people in the U.S. today have some form of autism. Its prevalence rate now places it as the *third* most common developmental disability—more common than Down syndrome. Yet most of the public, including many professionals in the medical, educational, and vocational fields, are still unaware of how autism affects people and how to effectively work with individuals with autism.[145]

What Percentage of People with Autism Fall within the Mentally Handicapped Range of IQ?

In the past the majority of documented figures for intelligence in autism showed that about three-quarters of the autistic population fell within the mentally retarded range. Now, however, the scene is changing, and anecdotal evidence suggests that many individuals with autism are faring much better than was the case in the past due to changes in early diagnosis and intervention, educational treatment, speech therapy, better services at a younger age, behavioral intervention, and more individual community support for parents and children. All of these changes are reflected in the more recent studies of children with autism in the third generation (children born after 1974). The group most likely to change are those with IQs in the 50 to 70 range.[146] It is, however, necessary to point out here that there is a question mark over the validity of using standard measures of intelligence testing to assess cognitive ability in people with autism. Such measures are of their very nature open to criticism.[147] The multidisciplinary Consensus Panel, which recently produced the Practice Parameters for autism, states in its recommendations for future research that it is obvious that the tools presently available to ascertain the "cognitive and neuropsychological" abilities of people with autism have "significant limitations." Consequently they are calling for research efforts to concentrate on the development of well-founded, soundly based alternatives.[12] Other considerations aside, the acute anxiety alone that can be brought on as a result of being placed in a test situation and having to maintain concentration over a considerable period of time can result in this high-anxiety population not performing to the best of their abilities.

What Percentage Are Nonverbal?

Up until recently and based on older studies, it was accepted that one-third (some studies quote one-half) of all autistic children do not acquire speech. But in line with what is written here, this also is changing and more recent studies are showing different findings for children with autism in the third generation. These range from 14.5 percent to 28 percent nonverbal, across four different studies.[146]

What Is the Ratio of Males to Females?

The figure for this has traditionally been reported at approximately 3:1 to 4:1. However, it now seems that the ratio appears to vary with IQ, ranging from 2:1 with severe dysfunction to more than 4:1 in those with average IQ.[12] Some researchers feel that fewer females with normal IQs are diagnosed with autism because they may be more socially adept than males with similar IQs.

What Percentage Are Hyperactive?

The figures for this range from anything between a third and a half.

How Many People Have Additional Comorbid Disorders?

While there would appear to be no epidemiological studies in this area, the figure is thought to be as much as 50 percent. These include epilepsy, sensory dysfunction, aggression toward themselves (SIB) or others, bipolar mood disorder, depression, and anxiety. All of these will contribute to the relatively poor outcome documented for many people with autism.[147] One preliminary study has suggested that the risk factor for developing comorbid affective disorder could be as high as one-third.[148] This research was based on a study of thirteen individuals with autism (average age 18 years), and it was found that 33.3 percent of this group had been treated for affective disorder. No diagnosis of manic depressive disorder was present. The question of comorbid disorders is an area that urgently needs research.

Overall, What Percentage of People with Autism Fall into the High-Functioning Range?

Schopler and Mesibov reported that of their over two thousand clients with autism in North Carolina, approximately 30 percent would be classified as high-functioning.[149]

Is There a Correlation between Repetitive and Stereotyped Behavior and Abnormality of the Cerebellum?

As the authors of this research under review indicate, the average young child, when placed in a new environment, will eagerly explore it. By contrast the young autistic child will generally fail to do this or will investigate only a small proportion of the available new stimuli. In this new study that under-exploration of the environment has been correlated with structural abnormality of cerebellar vermis lobules VI-VII. (This was pointed out before in the discussion on sensory integration). In addition, it appears that the greatest abnormality in these lobules is found in children with the highest incidence of repetitive and stereotyped behavior.

These authors also point out that this finding is consistent with "a large body of evidence from animal studies." They suggest that "potentially" then defects in cerebellar vermis lobules VI and VII may be enough to cause impairment in exploratory behavior. They point to new fMRI studies that indicate that different regions of the cerebellum are specialized for different functions and note that further systematic research will need to be carried out to find if and how different regions of the cerebellum, in addition to the vermis, are responsible for a "role in deficits in exploratory behavior in autism."[123]

What Is the Most Consistently Reported Cognitive Defect in Autism?

Dr. Courchesne and Dr. Pierce of the Department of Neurosciences at the University of California classify attention abnormalities as falling into this category and state that they are also the most thoroughly investigated by neuroimaging studies. Indicating that it has been shown that in the normal brain the capacity to pay attention involves "a complex network of brain structures including the cerebellum and parietal lobes," they add that neuroimaging studies of patients with autism have shown defects in these areas, which are involved with the ability to disengage attention, to orient attention, and to shift attention. Patients with this type of abnormality are slow to disengage attention and by the time attention has been disengaged the information necessary to discriminate between different sensory stimuli has often disappeared. These authors also indicate that patients with autism and this type of impairment will be slow and inaccurate in shifting their attention back and forth between different stimuli such as sight and sound.[123]

What Is the Most Exciting New Finding in Research at this Point in Time?

On May 3, 2000, at the annual meeting of the American Academy of Neurology, details were given of a ground-breaking pilot study that released information about possible "biological markers in the blood of new born infants who later developed autism and mental retardation." These researchers had found higher levels of four specific brain proteins in the blood of 95 percent of newborn children who were later diagnosed with autism and mental retardation. They selected proteins that are known to participate in regulating growth and development of the brain during pregnancy and proteins that are known to be involved in long-term memory, in learning, and in reacting to sensory stimuli. Their results showed significantly higher levels of two neuropeptides—vasoactive intestinal peptide (VIP) and calcitonin-related gene peptide (CGRP)—as well as two neurotrophins—neurotrophic factor (BDNF) and neurotrophin-4 (NT4)—in the blood of autistic children and children with mental retardation when compared with the levels in the control group of children or in children with cerebral palsy. These results refer to only one point in time—the newborn period. The children with autism and the children with mental retardation without autism had the same result. All the children in this study were born between 1983 and 1985, and each group contained approximately sixty children. This research will provide some clues for identifying which genes may be important in the development of autism and mental retardation.[150] The results of this landmark study are currently being replicated by the same laboratory using a new set of blood samples from children diagnosed according to DSM-IV criteria.

How Common Is Autism?

The earliest studies that used the original definition of Kanner noted a prevalence for typical infantile autism of 4 to 5 per 10,000, which is approximately 1 in every 2,000 people. If, however, autism is diagnosed on the basis of the "broader clinical phenotype and improved clinical recognition," then the figure rises to an estimated rate of 10 to 20 per 10,000, or 1 in every 500 to 1,000 people.[12] Private data quoted in that paper showed a prevalence of 1 in 500 children in a zero-to-three early intervention program and also mentioned another study that found a prevalence rate of 1 in 333 children for autistic disorder and 27.1 extra cases per 10,000 for the autistic spectrum disorders.[151] Filipek and her colleagues from which these figures are taken state that these latter figures require confirmation in a future study.[12] A figure of 26 to 36 per 10,000 was reported for Asperger syndrome in school-age children.[152] These latter authors also quote Wing as suggesting that the rate of autism spectrum disorders may approach 1 percent of the school-age population.

There Is Currently an Impression that the Incidence of Autism Is Rising. Is This True?

Twenty-three studies published before 1998 with very large sample sizes but with different diagnostic criteria and study methods reported the prevalence of autism to be between 0.19 to 2.11 per 1,000. Three recent studies published after 1998 have listed the prevalence of autism to be between 3.08 and 6 per 1,000. In addition, a fourth study, which was released by the American Centers for Disease Control and Prevention (CDC) in April 2000 (which listed the above-mentioned studies), found a prevalence of 4 per 1,000 (1 in 250) for the strict definition of autistic disorder, and 6.7 per 1,000 (1 in 150) for autistic spectrum disorder. This sample was taken from a total population of 8,896 children, ages 3 to 10 years living in Brick Township, New Jersey, during 1998. All children were diagnosed according to DSM-IV diagnostic criteria. A local parents' group had requested this investigation because they had suspected that there might be an unusually high rate of autism in this small community of 77,000 people. The CDC examined whether environmental factors, such as the municipal drinking water supply, water from a local river, and underground water beneath a landfill might have contributed to the apparent increase in autism. Certain chemicals were found in the water but it was concluded that neither children nor mothers were exposed to levels that would be likely to cause adverse health effects.[153]

What Could Be the Cause of This Increase (Real or Apparent) in the Incidence of Autism?

A number of factors have been suggested such as improved diagnostic methods, wider diagnostic criteria being used, greater awareness of these disor-

ders, or maybe a genuine change in incidence. As Dr. Wang, a parent/
professional, a pediatric neurologist and molecular geneticist, and the author
of the above-mentioned report, comments, the real unknown factor is
whether there are certain children who have a genetic susceptibility to autism
but who will only develop it if they are exposed to certain environmental
factors. In addition, he directs attention to the fact that research into environmental factors is difficult because there are so many, they are so varied,
and they can interact together. He emphasizes that sound, rigorous scientific
research in this area is needed to identify possible factors that could interrupt
the normal development of the nervous system in those with a genetic susceptibility.[153]

Is It Clear Yet How Genes Interact with the Environment to Cause Autism?

It has been known for a long time that genes exert an influence on behavior,
both normal and abnormal. We have also seen that autism is genetically
complex. That means that no single gene or even a combination of genes
will have the final say as to whether somebody will or will not have autism.
To develop this issue further, we turn to the Mental Health Report of the
Surgeon General of the United States:

> Rather mental illness appears to result from the interaction of multiple genes that
> confer risk, and this risk is converted into illness by the interaction of genes with
> environmental factors. The implications for science are, first, that no gene is equiv-
> alent to fate for mental illness. This gives us hope that modifiable environmental risk
> factors can eventually be identified and become targets for prevention efforts. In
> addition, we recognize that genes, while significant in their aggregate contribution
> to risk, may each contribute only a small increment, and, therefore, will be difficult
> to discover. As a result, however, of the Human Genome Project, we will know the
> sequence of each human gene and the common variants for each gene throughout
> the human race. . . . For example, once we know that a certain gene is involved in
> risk of a particular mental illness such as schizophrenia or autism, we can ask at what
> time during the development of the brain that particular gene is active and in which
> cells and circuits the gene is expressed. This will give us clues to critical times for
> intervention in a disease process and information about what it is that goes wrong.
> Finally, genes will provide tools for those scientists who are searching for environ-
> mental risk factors.[51]

Are There Suitable Services Available for People with Autism Spectrum Disorders?

All of the foregoing information adds up to the fact that the autism spectrum
disorders are not rare but have a higher incidence in the childhood population than Down syndrome, spina bifida, cancer, and diabetes.[12] They are
now a pressing public health problem for which services urgently need to
be provided, but because of the negative perception of autism, government

agencies are often not willing to spend the resources necessary to provide such services. In the last analysis then, a higher incidence of autism will only mean that we are likely to see further generations of children with autism being denied their legal rights as citizens to take their place as full members of society. Now is the time to send a clarion call to government to allocate the necessary resources for intervention/education, medical care, and community services. Obviously a range of services will be required to meet the varying degrees of autistic impairments. While the needs of the more severely affected may be more obvious, it is not generally appreciated how crippling so-called mild autism can be. A report to the State of the Science Conference pointed out that the three subgroups who had the greatest difficulty getting services to suit their needs were (a) those with acute behavioral problems, who may or may not be nonverbal; (b) those suffering from severe and ongoing anxiety, many of whom are high-functioning; and (c) those who are intellectually capable but who nonetheless are challenged by autism.[147]

In a recent review entitled "Outcome in Adult Life for More Able Individuals with Autism or Asperger Syndrome," Dr. Patricia Howlin of the Department of Psychology at St. George's Hospital Medical School in London concentrates on a number of long-term follow-up studies that document the life styles of groups of high-ability people on the autistic spectrum.[154] She concludes that it is not easy for people in this category to succeed well in adult life. The necessary specialist support systems that should be in place are not there for this group with the result that they are forced to depend largely on the family circle when it comes to finding accommodations and employment. She comments also on the demands of our society which require conformity and do not make allowances for people who are different, pointing out that such pressures can lead to anxiety and stress, which in turn may lead even to psychiatric breakdown. She targets three areas where improvement is necessary in order to ensure that high-ability people will be given the opportunity to use their natural skills and talents. They are (1) suitable educational facilities; (2) assistance with accommodations and living skills; and (3) a social network support system.

She also mentions that there is a need to improve "clinical expertise" and not only in the area of early diagnosis, but also in the area of both recognizing and treating psychiatric conditions in adults, because the impression gained from clinical experience is that if these conditions are not diagnosed and treated promptly, then it can be very difficult to change the patterns of behavior that had become ingrained during the course of the illness. These patterns of behavior can linger on long after treatment has improved the patient's general condition, and this is a very undesirable situation that could be avoided. Finally, she stresses the need for more research into this area of comorbid psychiatric disorders on two levels: (1) to provide more knowledge for clinicians on how psychiatric disorders present themselves in this population, and (2) to gain increased understanding of how best to deal with them from the viewpoint of both medication and psychological intervention strategies.[154]

Another U.K. professional picks up on the need for services when he writes that professionals must now admit that their responsibilities to their patients with Asperger syndrome go far beyond just establishing the diagnosis in childhood. He outlines the type of effective service needed, listing factors such as assessment both from the medical and functional point of view, in addition to psychoeducation and intervention at family level as well as treatment of emotional and behavior problems in both the psychological and the medical field. He considers the most important component of this effective service to be professionals who have an understanding of the "subjective experience" of Asperger syndrome, so that they are in a position to react appropriately to the successes and failures that can occur in the life experience of individuals with Asperger syndrome.[135]

Where to Now in Autism Research?
Dr. Marie Bristol-Power of the National Institute of Child Health and Human Development at the NIH, in "Research in Autism: New Directions," begins by stating that scientific studies have now produced unquestionable evidence that "autism is a biological disorder." She indicates that because so many factors, for example, genetic, immunological, neurological, and perhaps environmental, have been shown to be involved in autism, it would be too simplistic to suggest that all cases of autism could be explained by a single cause and that autism, because of its great diversity among people, might be best thought of as being a class of disorders. She considers that solving the puzzle that is autism is more akin to "peeling an onion," removing "one layer at a time," and draws attention to the fact that in the past year a significant gene for one of the autism spectrum disorders (Rett's syndrome) has been identified. She notes that there are now under way large-scale studies of families with more than one child with autism and promising research on candidate genes, for example, chromosome 15q11–13 or the serotonin transporter gene, is being carried out. She also indicates that research into the understanding of brain function and structure had yielded very significant results into both the strengths and weak points of functioning in autism. Some of this research into the strengths suggests that the fundamental brain functions are undamaged in autism but that the major difficulty for individuals lies in coordinating these resources for the purposes of undertaking complicated tasks. Another research center has come to the same conclusion with regard to the area of auditory function processing. Following on this, yet another center has shown that it is possible to teach fundamental skills in areas such as attention and pre-attention.

Dr. Bristol-Power moves on to the area of animal research, which has shown that it is possible in animals to recover certain functions in spite of serious brain damage. Also, other findings in animal studies suggest considerable development of neurons from birth right through to adulthood. All of this has led to a complete turning around of present thinking with regard to the dexterity with which the method of operation of neurons can be molded and the effect of a stimulating environment on both basic biology and behavior. Dr. Bristol-Power sums up by writing that it is researchers who are willing to take on new challenges and theories that have proved to be testable who will inevitably carry out the best research and that they will also have to be "humble enough" to admit that there are limitations to both the profession's "methodologies" and "knowledge."[155]

PART IV

SOME PEOPLE

Had I the heavens' embroidered cloths,
Enwrought with golden and silver light,
The blue and the dim and the dark cloths
Of night and light and the half-light,
I would spread the cloths under your feet:
But I, being poor, have only my dreams;
I have spread my dreams under your feet;
Tread softly because you tread on my dreams.

"He Wishes for the Cloths of Heaven," William Butler Yeats (1865–1939)

CHAPTER 15

◆◆◆◆◆

AUTISM FROM THE
INSIDE

One of the most extraordinary facts about autism is that the word seems to be almost entirely synonymous with children, autistic children. One rarely if ever hears or reads the words, autistic adults. As if the children with autism were expected to vanish at adolescence and never grow up. But grow up they do, and their poignant accounts of their struggles to come to terms with living in our world have offered some of the greatest insights into autism. While scientists and researchers can approach autism from the outside and look in at it, they come from a different perspective. Autistic people, on the other hand, have the microscopic view. Autism belongs to them. It is their world; they live in it; so who should know it better? Over the years many of these talented people and their parents have let us into their lives when they describe what it is like to have autism and to walk beside it.

One of the earliest of these books is the *The Siege: The First Eight Years of an Autistic Child*, by Clara Claiborne Park, which documents the first eight years of life of her autistic daughter Jessy.[2] Another mother who gives insights into her daughter's life is Susan Moreno. Susan writes about Beth's progress through school and college years in her article on "A Parent's View of More Able People with Autism."[156] Jane Taylor McDonnell writes an account of her son Paul in *News from the Border*; the book contains an afterword by Paul himself.[3] Charles Hart in *Without Reason* describes what it is like to have lived with two generations of autism.[157] And there are many more accounts from all over the world.

But perhaps the best known are the writings of Dr. Temple Grandin whose two books are on the autism best-seller list. Her first book, entitled *Emergence Labeled Autistic*, was published in 1986 and was written in cooperation with Margaret M. Scariano.[158] *Thinking in Pictures* was published by Grandin herself nine years later.[159]

Dr. Grandin is well known because of her achievements in the world of animal science and her dedicated work in the field of autism. She graduated with a Ph.D. degree in the field of animal sciences and is an assistant professor at Colorado State University. In addition, as one of the world's foremost experts in the design and construction of livestock handling facilities, she runs her own business. She has written well over a hundred papers on this very specialized subject and travels throughout the world lecturing on her work.

Her two books are classics in the field of autism and provide valuable insights into the condition. Her life story is documented in both books and in her writings. In them she tells of her frustration, as a young child, at not being able to speak. From an early age she could understand every word spoken to her but could not get the words out to answer. Screaming was the only way she could communicate. At age three a speech therapist entered her world and has been described by her as the professional of most consequence in her life.

In discussing her sensory perception difficulties she writes about her acute sensitivity to sound and touch, describing her hearing in terms of being similar to having a hearing aid with the volume stuck on super loud and comparing it to an open microphone that picks up everything.[160] As a young child she learned to shut down her hearing and withdraw from most noises, often acting deaf. Even today she still finds that sudden loud noises hurt her ears like a dentist's drill hitting a nerve. She also suffered from tactile overload because the nerve endings in her skin were supersensitive. Rough textured clothes caused torture. This oversensitivity to touch led her to design her own device to help her overcome it because she wanted to get the good feeling of being hugged, but when people hugged her she felt overwhelmed by the stimulus. When very young she often daydreamed about a mechanical device she could get into that would apply comforting pressure that she herself could control. In this way she would be able to stop the stimulation when it became too intense.

Eventually she built her own squeeze machine. This device was completely lined with foam rubber, and the user had control over the duration and amount of pressure applied. This reduced her oversensitivity and enabled her to tolerate being touched. Several squeeze machines are now in use at sensory integration clinics in the United States, and therapists have found that some autistic children will immediately use the machine, while others are so sensitive they avoid it. These latter children also avoid other activities involving touch, such as being rubbed with different cloth textures.

In discussing how her thought processes work, Grandin describes her thinking as being entirely visual, saying that for her there is no language-based information in her memory. She says that thinking in language and words is foreign to her and that she thinks entirely in pictures. She compares it to playing tapes in her imagination. To retrieve facts she has to read them off a visualized page of a book or run an imagined video of some previous event through her mind. This method of thinking, she observes, is slower because it takes time to run the videotape in her imagination.[159]

In this connection she points out that Albert Einstein was a visual thinker who relied on visual methods of study and that his theory of relativity was based on visual imagery of moving boxcars and riding on light beams. She adds that when in high school Einstein failed his language examination and indicates that his family history includes a high incidence of autism, dyslexia, food allergies, giftedness, and musical talent and that he himself had many autistic traits.

Being a visual thinker has been a great asset to Grandin in her career as a livestock equipment designer. She can visualize a video of the finished equipment in her imagination. She can then run tests in her imagination to see how the system will work under different conditions. She also writes that as a young child visualization enabled her to understand the words and imagery of the Lord's Prayer. To understand the word "trespass" she envisaged a do not trespass notice on a neighbor's property; to gain a concept of the "power and the glory" she visualized high tension electric towers and a vivid multicolored sun.[160]

In discussing her ability to adapt to the world and the work environment, she admits that she has suffered since adolescence with anxiety, sometimes very acutely. She describes her panic attacks and how she has dealt with them, admitting that her brain has raced like a car without a regulator. This nervous pattern was cyclical throughout the day, being worst in the late afternoon and early evening, dying down late at night and early in the morning. The pattern was also seasonal, peaking in the spring and again in the autumn. She devised a two-prong attack to fight the "nerves." One was to minimize or withdraw from outside stimulation, the other to get intensely involved in activity. This latter had a calming effect so much so that she often wrote three articles in a night. When she was typing at this pace, she felt calmer. But in time the nerves began to affect her health, and it was then she decided to do something about it.

At this point she did some research into medication and found that a very small dose of an antidepressant worked like magic. She has stayed on this very small dose since then and reports that gradually during the last ten years, while taking the medication, the nerve relapses have become milder and milder and farther and farther apart. She compares taking the medicine to adjusting the idle screw on a car's carburetor so that it does not race but runs at normal speed. Now she reports that she is no longer driven.[159]

Grandin has devoted a large part of her life to lecturing, studying, writing about, and probing the causes and conditions of autism. Acknowledging that there are many different autism subtypes, she considers that the brain abnormalities that cause each subtype may be different and suggests that a medication that works for one subtype may be useless for another. She also points out that some people with autism are calm and will probably not benefit from medication. In her brief report to the State of the Science Conference, Grandin wrote of her concern about the necessity for research on sensory processing problems in autism.[161] She also emphasized the need to research the best therapies for sensory dysfunction, stressing that research in this area may explain why intensive behavior programs will work with one child and will fail with another.

Autism is indeed a complex condition showing many faces and facets, and people with autism are as diverse from each other as are people in the general population. Because it is a spectrum disorder it varies widely and while the severe negative aspects of it are well documented, the strengths are not often recognized. In his book *An Anthropologist on Mars*, neurologist Dr. Oliver Sacks analyzes in-depth many aspects of autism and provides new insights into high-functioning autistic people.[8] He describes his visit to an autistic family, the B.s, where both parents are highly gifted. The older son, like the parents, has Asperger syndrome, and the younger son has classic autism. He gives us a glimpse into their life, their thoughts about themselves, and their sense of identity:

It was only after I had settled down that I noticed the well-used trampoline, where the whole family, at times, likes to jump and flap their arms; the huge library of science fiction; the strange cartoons pinned to the bathroom wall; and the ludicrously explicit directions, pinned up in the kitchen—for cooking, laying the table, and washing up—suggesting that these had to be performed in a fixed, formulaic way (this, I learned later, was an autistic in-joke). Mrs. B spoke of herself, at one point, as "bordering on normality," but then made clear what such "bordering" meant: "We know the rules and conventions of the 'normal,' but there is no actual transit. You act normal, you learn the rules, and obey them, but. . . ."

"You learn to ape human behavior," her husband interpolated. "I still don't understand what's behind the social conventions. You observe the front—but . . ."

The B.s then, had learned a front of normality, which was necessary, given their professional lives, their living in the suburbs and driving a car, their having a son in regular school, and so on. But they had no illusions about themselves. They recognized their own autism, and they had recognized each other's, at college with a sense of such affinity and delight that it was inevitable they would marry. "It was as if we had known each other for a million years," Mrs. B said. While they were well aware of many of the problems of their autism, they had a respect for their differentness, even a pride. Indeed, in some autistic people this sense of radical and ineradicable differentness is so profound as to lead them to regard themselves, half jokingly, almost as members of another species ("They beamed us down on the transporter together," as the B.s liked to say), and to feel that autism, while it may be seen as a medical condition, and pathologized as a syndrome, must also be seen as a whole mode of being, a deeply different mode or identity, one that needs to be conscious (and proud) of itself.[8]

Because most of the literature on autism is extremely negative, it is important and enlightening to see the positive compensatory aspects of it highlighted in this fashion.

In his discussion of Temple Grandin's attitude to being autistic, Sacks made similar comments:

Temple's attitudes seem similar to this: she is very aware (if only intellectually, inferentially) of what she is missing in life, but equally (and directly) aware of her strengths, too—her concentration, her intensity of thought, her single-mindedness, her tenacity; her incapacity for dissembling, her directness, her honesty. She suspects—and I, too, was coming more and more to suspect—that these strengths, the positive aspects of her autism, go with the negative ones. And yet there are times when she needs to forget that she is autistic, to feel at one with others, not outside, not different.[8]

It was Temple Grandin who coined the term *An Anthropologist on Mars*. In discussing her ability to empathize, she has said that she could understand "simple, strong, universal" emotions but was stumped by more complex emotions and the games people play. "Much of the time," she adds, "I feel like an anthropologist on Mars."

This theme of being an alien in a strange environment has been emphasized by a number of high-ability young people with autism, and there is no doubt but that the loneliness of their child as he grows older, can cause more sadness to a parent than any other aspect of the condition. In the earlier years just to be around other children can be enough, when the reciprocal interaction of play and games will tide the young autistic child over the barrier of integration. At this age, wrapped in his aura of *autistic aloneness*, he may have little awareness of those around him whatever the reason, perception difficulties or otherwise. But when he moves on into his early teenage years this awareness of others begins to dawn. By this time he has found himself sufficiently to want to reach out, but it is as if there were an impenetrable barrier between himself and them; a transparent wall that he can look through but cannot surmount. Unfortunately but understandably, except in rare cases, there is little reaching out from the other side, and frequently the pain of rejection is added to the loneliness of isolation. This is a hard lesson for both the young person and his parents to learn, and they can feel very helpless in the face of it. This is so well expressed in the following letter written by a mother about her teenage son:

We are fortunate that our son has always attended a regular school. He has even taken gifted math and science classes the past two years in junior high. Yet, this bright boy cannot verbally relate a simple personal experience or engage in a friendly conversation. In his pre-school and elementary years, he was quite content to be alone, to draw endless maps and mazes, happy in his private bubble. However, recently some gradual changes have been occurring. After so many years, he now wants friends, and seems to be experiencing loneliness for the first time in his life. Yet using the phone to call a friend is a sometimes insurmountable task. After years of not even recognizing that another human being was in the same room, he is now beginning to look outwards to people for the first time and not knowing how to reach them brings frustration and sadness not only to him, but to me.

He hasn't the vaguest idea how to initiate a new friendship. He can only watch from afar and hope that someone approaches him. This is very painful in the junior high years when social relationships are so critical, and his behavior is so often misunderstood.

How do you teach a 14-year-old those basic social graces we think of as second nature? He often does not respond when even someone he knows well says "Hi"! He has trouble choosing from a restaurant menu and requesting his selection from the waitress. "Please" and "Thank you" are usually forgotten. He rarely asks questions or even appears to be curious about people. Yet he wants to be with others and included in their activities. Their rejection has caused him to withdraw into isolation again.

Trying to be "normal" has been so painful. As thrilled as I am to see that he is finally reaching out, I remember the happy, carefree boy who lived in a private world, and I cry to watch the sad, vulnerable teenager who has taken his place.[161A]

It is quite a challenge to organize friendships in the teenage years. It is easy to provide playmates for toddlers and young children but as their ages move into double figures the former playmates fall away, one by one, as they mature and forge ahead, widening the gap between themselves and their peers with autism. So what can parents do to improve this situation? The answer is *much*, and now is the time to use all available resources. It is the time to get the extended family and friends to rally around; friends' children are a great source of companions; it is time to tap into church and community services, summer courses, and camps; the time to partake in after school activities, scouts, swimming classes, canoeing, music groups, art classes, pottery courses, metalwork, woodwork, radio-controlled model clubs, chess clubs, astronomy societies, venture sports, and ham radio groups. The latter provides great opportunities for improving and fostering communication. If these activities are not present in your area, get together with other parents and set them up. It is the time to consult professionals and educators for help and support. As the child moves further on into the teenage years, one can organize peers as companions; they can be great friends to accompany to sporting events, and to join with in outdoor pursuits. This can be done on a voluntary basis or on a paid basis. It is of course very important to choose reliable people who are well known to you and to assess them carefully. It is also very important to keep them fully informed with regard to any difficulties that might arise with the autistic young person. The young people of the present generation are very socially conscious, and they have a great sense of responsibility to those not as fortunate as themselves. Generally, when asked they prove willing to lend a hand, and they themselves can benefit greatly from the experience. Implicit in all of the above, of course, is the fact that these activities will have to be tailored to the level of functioning of the young autistic person.

We are all shaped by experience; the experience of childhood and youth being the foundation for adulthood. These are the years when depression can set in if a young person is left alone and lonely, feeling rejected, looking on uninvolved, as the world seems to pass him by and he becomes more and more conscious of his differences and saddened at his inability to do anything about it. At present, while there are no figures for the incidence of depression among the autistic population, it is known that 5 percent of the general population will experience a major depressive illness during their lifetime.[162] Recent figures from the U.S. Department of Health and Human Services on mood disorders in general show that in any one year about 7 percent of the population suffer from mood disorders, and that they are among the top ten causes of world-wide disability.[51] Depression is more than twice as likely to affect women than men. The principal symptoms of major depressive disorder are depressed mood and loss of interest or pleasure.[51] Other symptoms vary greatly from person to person and include some of the following: sleep disturbance (too much or too little), weight changes (too much or too little), fatigue and loss of energy, impaired concentration and memory, anxiety symptoms (e.g., panic attacks), feelings of worthlessness or excessive guilt, and suicidal thoughts.

For some autistic people who may develop depression, professional help and medication will be necessary. Anecdotal evidence has shown that acceptance and inclusion, such as becoming more integrated into the community, also helps greatly; then self image begins to change and the future looks brighter. The poem "Darkness" written by Mark R. affords a glimpse into the soul-shaking desolation experienced in severe clinical depression:

Darkness

Darkness, darkness, oblivion,
Hope gone, leading in despair.
In this black pit I lie
Swallowed up in darkness.
No light, just final gloom.
Worse than a total occultation
No life, no joy, no happiness
All just a dream.
In the cold light of reality

You try to strive.
But loneliness and isolation overwhelm.
Ten thousand feet under
In a mine, injured, lifeless.
In a river deep in the murky waters
No way up, weighed down
By some invisible force or millstone.
Burnt.
In a cemetery in a grave
Once alive, now dead and gone.

For high-ability people with autism life can pose additional problems. They face choices and sometimes dilemmas and one of them is having to make the decision to either openly admit their autism or to stay silent and take a different route, walking the fine line between two worlds. In other words, to try to "pass." The following text of an autism conference speech depicts this dilemma as expressed by Perry Hoffman. It is called "Man with a Briefcase":

I observe the man with the briefcase and I wonder, "Where is his destination? What kind of life does he have?" Neatly dressed in business attire, he seems to me to be very important. The man with the briefcase probably drives a car, wears good clothes, engages in regular conversation with his girlfriend or spouse. Does the usual things with his wife and children. He is clean—polished. Smooth. Slice of Jimmy Stewart Americana. Down to earth, all-American guy. I'd love to meet him. Wouldn't anyone?

I look at the man with the briefcase with envy. I want to be just like him. One thing is for certain—he's not autistic. You won't hear echolalia from this man. He doesn't need routine. Doesn't need time for Judge Wopner at 6:30 like Rainman. I sit in my room a prisoner to my autism. Mom and Sis doing their loving best to get me out. I wanted to get out—really get out. I wanted to love, to feel, to connect. But, I couldn't. I was stuck. So I continued to look at the man with the briefcase and say, "How do you do it? What's your secret to relationships?"

Flashback—December of '78. Cute red head girl caught my eye. Looking to impress. If she liked me, I would get boarding pass to real world. Closer to having a relationship. Closer to my dream of becoming the man with the briefcase. Closer to being a regular guy.

Through my shyness and awkwardness, I summoned the courage to get her number. I did it. I had arrived. I started becoming a pen pal to her. She started telling me intimate details about her hopes, dreams, and aspirations. Perhaps this was an opportunity to tell her what I was—that I was autistic.

Wrote about autism in Christmas card. Days and nights passed. No response. Was it something I did or said? I turned to my friend and he decided that we should go over to her house. In excited anticipation, I bought her a little Christmas gift.

When we arrived, I looked into her soft sweet face. Upon seeing me, she turned to my friend and said loudly, "Now why did you have to bring him and his autism

over here?" I was devastated. The Christmas present I had for her shook in my hand.
I walked to the nearest garbage can and threw it away.

"Boy was I stupid," I said, crying. "Why in God's name did I have to tell her that
I was autistic as a child?"

From that point on I denounced my autism. I buried it, vetoed it, denied it, cursed
it, exorcised it by putting a stake in its heart. I never tried harder to become the man
with the briefcase. Read the *New York Times*. Glanced at the *Wall Street Journal*.
Personified cool, like Miles Davis and Frank Sinatra. Be suave like a Tom Cruise.
Be a sophisticate like Denzel Washington. Observe how the regular people act at
singles clubs and parties. Act like a business man. "Good morning sir—pleased to
meet you. Here is my card. Let's negotiate the deal."

Man with a briefcase. Man with a position. Man with a condo. Man with a red
Ferrari in his driveway. Bring him into a social circle and he'll astound you with his
facts and figures. Man who knows leader of Ghana and Greece. Man who knows
Troy Aikman's passing percentage. Man who knows the exact number of games Cal
Ripkin played. He's the foremost expert on relationships. Go ask him. One thing's
for certain—he's not autistic. Ain't no echolalia from this man!

I tried to act like the man with the briefcase. Took on intellect and coolness. Raised
hand in classroom—decorated language with sophisticated tongue. Impress friends
with my knowledge of restaurants, art, movies, music, books, and sport. Goal: to
become multi-cultured man.

Bury autism in layers. Don't reveal anything. Deny my past. Always remember to
be phoney and plastic. Don't be true to yourself. The man with the briefcase would
do it that way. One thing's for certain—he's not autistic. Doesn't need time for
Wopner at 6:30 like Rainman.

I was slowly dying. There were days I truly wanted to end it all. If any days were
good, I didn't deserve it. I shouldn't be happy. Autism teaches you that—because it's
a life sentence. In my jail, the nights were always cold, dark, and lonely. Relationships
were going nowhere.

By the time I hit my late twenties, I had enough of the carnage, the hate and the
self-pity. Perhaps there were autistic people who pretty much went what I went
through. Instead of absorbing, let me give—let me share—let me help others who
were stuck in their own darkness.

Fast forward to '96. Clinton in Whitehouse. Chicago Bulls rule NBA. *Independence
Day* in the cinema. WWW Dot Com universal language. Man offers experience and
help to parents. Man seeking to guide and teach others.

Today I write this to all my autistic friends to say, "Yes, I have been there. Did
that. My story is your neighbor's story. Our story is Temple Grandin's and Donna
Williams'. It includes all the speakers at the conference. It also includes the four-
year-old who is about to be diagnosed with autism. It's all about us."

We've all had that awkward moment. From that heartbreaking dating experience
to that personal rejection. It hurts. It stinks big time. We want to love, cherish, heal,
and champion our partners. We can do these things. I know we can! People, though,
just won't give us that second look because we are/or were autistic.

I said good-bye to the man with the briefcase a long time ago. I have my own life
to worry about now. Facing up to myself is indeed rather scary. I don't know where
this will lead me. I still feel quite alone. I feel practically naked that I revealed so
much. Every person I tell constitutes great risk for me. Will they accept me, hug

and embrace me, or will they run away—afraid of what I was? I ask myself in the realm of relationships: Is this an act of courage—or blind faith?

Mel Gibson's "Wallace" character in *Braveheart* said "Every man dies, but not every man truly lives." If that's the case, let me truly live. To work, to play, to engage in a conversation with a friend, to go off to faraway places, to share a pizza with someone special. I can do that. You can do that. As a matter of fact, we can all do that.[163]

On Saturday, March 11, 2000, several hundred people gathered in Westchester County, New York, for a Celebration of Hope—an evening to celebrate excellence in the autism community. The evening featured special awards for three individuals whose personal achievements and contributions to the autism community represent excellence in a variety of forms. They were Dr. Isabelle Rapin, Mr. Perry Hoffman, and Dr. Arnold Gold. Amidst all the awards and celebration the highlight of the evening was the standing ovation Perry Hoffman received as he finished a stirring and inspirational speech about his own experience with autism.[164]

CHAPTER 16

PARENTS' PERSPECTIVE

Sometimes—rarely, but sometimes—
when I see his dark eyes flash with pleasure upon
hearing a well-known opera's little-known cabaletta;
when the intensity of his look tells me that,
amidst green hills and far horizons,
he has zoomed-in on a distant antenna;
when the dimple in his tanned cheek twinkles,
and I suspect he is remembering a gaffe of Donald Duck;
when I look at him, his grey sideburns
delineating his beautiful, balding head—
I wonder: What if, over forty years ago, that
chromosome had not been quite so fragile:
that quirk in his central nervous system
had not condemned him to a lifetime
of depending upon the good will of others?
What would he have been like now?
Sometimes—rarely now, but sometimes—
helpless with love, helpless to defend his future,
feeling my soul drowning in a lifetime
of unshed tears, I think FOOL! Enough of
"what-might-have-been!" This being, your son,
sensitive to the beauty of sound,
has greeted you with joy; had brought you a most

extraordinary gift:
   himself

"Jonathan at Forty," Bernice Singer,
from *The Early Years of the MAAP*, p. 128.

And finally what of the parents of young and not so young people with
autism, who walk beside their loved ones through the good times and the
bad? How do they cope? How do they endure? What is life like for *them*?

In 1965 two graduates with Irish roots and ancestry met at Washington
University in St. Louis. Each had come there to study for a Ph.D. degree
in English. Some years later they married and there was nothing in either
of their backgrounds to prepare them for the fact that their first child would
have autism. Like all families who struggle to adjust and come to terms with
an intellectual handicap, they discovered "the humanity that runs far deeper
than the success and achievement we are all thought to value."

Because I had a child like Paul, I was forced to confront my deepest prejudices.
Beneath all the other differences which might define human beings, there was one
which for me was unquestioned, and that was intellect. Living all my adult life in an
academic environment, I had never been forced to consider that intellect is not the
same as merit, it is not the same as virtue. It is a gift of nature as surely as any other.
We don't ask for our intelligence and we certainly can never do anything to deserve
it. It is simply given, a gift.

At first I almost wanted to divest myself of my own privileged mind because I felt
so guilty about taking away my son's. I drank myself into oblivion every evening,
blotting out both the consciousness of my pain and also my privileged mental capacity
to feel that pain in all its complexity. But over time, I began slowly to redefine what
I took to be our common humanity. I realize we are all only a car accident away
from mental incapacity. People who are mentally handicapped are in no way essen-
tially different from the rest of us. Our intelligence may seem to be an inherent part
of ourselves, but it simply resides in our bodies tentatively and always in grave danger.

To get to this place I had to move away from self-sacrifice, and from guilt, over-
responsibility and inner conflict.[3]

These words were written by Dr. Jane Taylor McDonnell in *News from
the Border*, the border being the edge between autism and normalcy.[3] This
is a very honest, human story of family life as it revolves around the upbringing of an autistic child, the struggle to come to terms with the condition; and the ongoing, eversearching quest and battle for proper medical and
educational help. It will sound a resonance with every family who lives with
autism as it grapples with the same issues and faces the same conflicts. Paul,
then twenty years old and a high-ability young man taking college-level
classes, has written his own account as an afterword to the book.

Recognizing Paul's difficulty with speech, his struggle to express himself,
and his lack of comprehension, his parents sought expert help from an early
age. They were fortunate at this period of their lives to live in England,

where they were accepted into an innovative program being initiated by Great Ormond Street Children's Hospital. Paul became one of six, three- and four-year-olds who were to have the sole undivided attention of their own special teacher with the back-up help of other childhood specialists, including a speech consultant. This program was devised to educate professionals about the speech difficulties encountered by these children and to construct ways of overcoming them. Because of Paul's involvement in this program, his mother received in-depth insights into the whole process of speech development that, as an educationalist herself, she shares with her readers.

At the start of the program the director explained that its underlying theory of how language was learned was connected with attention control. Their research had shown that children with delayed language development commonly have poor attention control and that this slows down intellectual development. In addition, a child's ability to learn is limited if he insists on being inflexible. In the first year of life babies are easily distracted, and their attention will be held by whatever happens to be the most powerful stimulus at the time. In the second year the child's attention will be focused on what he himself wishes to do, and he will not easily be shifted or redirected. At the third stage the child is not yet able to integrate two channels of attention at the same time, but with the help of adult control he can be taught to shift his attention from what he is doing onto a verbal command or to another direction, and then back again to his task. At stage four the child will learn to control his own attention. The specialist then went on to explain that at stage five the child can carry on a task and cope with taking directions at the same time. For school attendance they prefer children to be at stage six, when they can fully integrate two channels of attention at the same time. This is the level expected of children in a large classroom. After his two terms at the center Paul had made remarkably good progress, and the staff forecasted that he should be able to attend a regular school at the usual time. As his mother stresses, these teachers had given him a precious gift because by helping him to gain some control over his attention, to focus his attention at will, and to shift focus, they had helped him to learn how to learn.

During his teenage years Paul grappled with the trauma of a poor self-image and the subsequent depression following it. This depression was long lasting and severe enough to warrant medical intervention, counselling, and medication. As Paul's mother accepts, it was his intelligence that allowed him to see he was different, that his mind was flawed, and paradoxically, it was the great progress he had made that put him at risk for self-hatred and depression. In her book she faces the classic dilemma of all parents, including those of Mark R., who set out to "normalize" their autistic child:

All through Paul's childhood, I had struggled with this dilemma: Should I work hard on "normalising" him, and in so doing, risk teaching him that he was not normal when he failed or fell short of standard expectations? Or should I appreciate and value his differences and thus permit him to remain trapped in oddity, in loneliness? If I pushed him too hard to be like other children his age, wouldn't I simply be teaching him the deeper lesson that he was flawed?[3]

Every parent raising an autistic child faces this dilemma. Is there a choice? No. This is a dilemma without a choice; without an alternative because the alternative is too unthinkable. Yes, it is difficult to live on the borderland between two worlds. Courage, tenacity, and perseverance are needed by any young person facing the challenge, but these qualities are very evident in the writings of young adults with autism. They are part of the strengths of autism, the alternative face of it that is rarely talked about. Yes, there will be difficulties adjusting and adapting, but with the right kind of help and support, young people can learn to come to terms, to build on their strengths, to accept where they are, and where they are coming from, and then move forward.

So, where is Paul today? All throughout his young and adolescent life he had had a fascination with maps and weather conditions. This was (at the time of his writing) being channelled toward a career in meteorology. He drove himself to his community college every day and worked two or three nights a week. He was on the board of directors of The Twin Cities Autism Society. In conjunction with his mother, who is a Board Member of the Autism Society of America, he gives presentations at national conferences. He has many friends. Summing up, he writes:

Today, things are much easier for me. I go to Inver Hills Community College, where I'm working for my associate of arts degree. I am very hopeful about my future. I've taken some very difficult classes in geography, but I have passed all of them with a fairly decent grade. . . . This past October, I gave a talk in front of nearly three hundred people up in the Twin Cities about my autism. I was very pleased to have the opportunity to tell everyone about myself. For the first time in my life, I felt good about myself. I talked about what autism felt like for me, and I told some funny stories. My talk was about ten minutes long. After I talked, I answered questions. I found it a little hard to answer some questions, but I did so in the best way that I could. On the whole, this talk was a very big success for me. My talk brought tears to the eyes of many. It was a big step forward for me.

As I look back on my life so far, I see that I have been very brave. There were many obstacles for me to cross. Sometimes I felt like giving up. At times there seemed to be no hope for me at all. Now I see that there is a lot of hope for me. I've made it this far, and I'm NOT going to give up.[3]

The Siege, written over thirty years ago, was one of the first personal accounts of autism. Dr. Clara Park, an English professor at Williams College in Massachusetts has also written articles and lectured on autism. *The Siege* is a remarkable book—remarkable for the period in which it was written and for the insights it gives into the day-to-day development of an autistic child. This book has changed the lives of many parents because of its ability to illuminate the nature of the autistic handicap and its intelligent rationalization of autistic behavior. Clara Park's ability to look behind the behavior, to get to the core cause of it, and to then channel it into constructive progress is impressive. Her secret is rooted in her careful observation of her daughter's day-to-day approach to her world, her documentation and intelligent analysis of it, and her ability to draw logical conclusions from it. These could then be translated into a strategy for using it, or changing it to make progress. Here, using the pseudonym "Elly" for her daughter, Jessy, Park gives a glimpse into her own thinking:

Of all Elly's inabilities, which should be taken as primary? Should we do what seems natural and emphasise the most striking symptom, the isolation-in-self which gives the autistic condition its very name? Or do the phenomena call for deeper scrutiny? Should we posit some defect profounder than all these which would explain them all—some inability of the brain, perhaps, to decode its perceptions or render them usable? Might the new individual, faced with a world in which an unreadable welter of impressions obscures even the distinction between objects and human beings, wall itself up as a defence against the anarchy outside? Psychologists formulate the question in their own language: Which is primary, disorder of affect—roughly, feeling or emotion—or dysfunction of cognition? But even for psychologists the answer is years away.

It is fortunate, then, that one needs no answer in order to go to work. Which is primary? It is an analytical question. In the living whole, nothing comes first. Work done on any one of Elly's inabilities affected the others. Every game we played, every exercise we devised to extend Elly's use of her body, her eyes, her ears, her voice, her mind, worked in addition to breach that jealously guarded isolation which for those who lived with her remained the most obvious and the most terrible aspect of her condition.[2]

The Siege is all the more remarkable when one considers the climate of opinion at the time it was written. It was written at the height of the psychogenic theory of autism and was first published in 1967. Now, over thirty years later, *The Siege* has had a number of reprints, is distributed worldwide, and has been translated into other languages.

The trauma of looking for professional psychiatric advice in the climate of the 1960s and the treatment parents of that era received are well illustrated by Clara Park. They had gone looking for help, expecting to meet "wise and sympathetic" people; instead they found it easier to reach Jessy, imprisoned behind the walls of autism, than to reach the professionals who were proposing to treat her. In the same city where they went for help, the director of a clinic for children with autism was writing at the time that one of his biggest obstacles in treating these children was the resistance their parents put up when told that they themselves were the cause of the condition.

By contrast, kindness, wherever she met with it, was what disarmed and unnerved her. This is something that will strike a chord with any parent who has reared a child with autism. There is so much misunderstanding about their behavior, so many embarrassing situations to be apologized for, so much censure to be endured that:

> One is less vulnerable to pain than to understanding and kindness. One develops defences against slights or insensitivity; against kindness, none. When one has been long in such straits, one has a terrible greed for kindness. Before one feels real pain one may think—I thought—that one would want people not to notice, to aid one in the attempt to carry on—business here as usual. It is not so. Business may seem as usual but it is not. What one wants is that people should know that. What one wants is sympathy, understanding, not tacit but openly given. What one wants is love.
>
> Too much to ask? It is surprising how freely it is given in some quarters while in others it is not given at all. I remember, I think, from those years everyone—every-one—who was kind to me. I should, for I lived on kindness, I consumed it like fuel. . . . I remember from the chill months in England the loud-voiced checker in the local Co-op who called me "ducks" and understood when Elly screamed because she couldn't touch the candy. . . . I remember the man who, when I apologized for some embarrassing caper of Elly's with a muffled "not a normal child," smiled and replied, "Well, I'm not normal myself." My honor roll is long.[2]

In her infancy and early years, in stark contrast to Mark R. who was hyperactive and had no concept of the limit of things, Jessy was passive and was very conscious of the limit of things. She actively sought enclosed spaces. In the fight against Jessy's autism her passive inertia was the biggest obstacle to be overcome and, unlike Mark R., food did not work as a reward or reinforcer:

> What did Elly want enough to meet any conditions for getting it? Not a cookie, not a toy, not a ride in the car. A baby who like a Zen adept acquires the knack of inhibiting its desires approaches something akin to the Zen *satori*. Serene, in perfect vegetative equilibrium, it can be content to do nothing at all. When a creature is without desires the outside world has no lever by which to tempt it into motion.[2]

Inertia, be it physical, mental, or emotional, is a characteristic facet of autism and is one of the most difficult aspects of it to overcome. The key to it is to find the right motivator. Like all motivators, this will vary from person to person. Jessy was fifteen years old before her special motivator was found. She had always possessed special mathematical islets of ability, and when she was fifteen an event occurred that was to provide the ideal motivator for a young adolescent who like Jessy was vitally interested in some aspects of numbers. A young friend came to visit. He possessed the equiv-alent of the modern calculator—a golf counter, worn strapped to his wrist, which could add and subtract up to one hundred. It had been recommended by his clinical psychologist as a way of keeping a point score worked on a reward system to improve his behavior. Points gained earned different rewards and privileges. Jessy was "transfixed" by the counter and she, who rarely throughout her life had ever wanted anything, now *wanted* a similar counter and could hardly wait for its arrival. Almost at once she became vitally interested in initiating a point system and in time just gaining points became a reward in itself. It was in this way that her refusal, "her massive, crippling, inertia," was overcome, quite unexpectedly.

Of Jessy's art, her mother has written elsewhere, affirming that Jessy's painting transmutes her handicap rather than surmounts it. She uses the core, literal, repetitive, characteristics of autism to produce a reality that has been transfigured and turned into something rich and beautiful. She emphasizes that Jessy's art just did not happen, maintaining that in autism development just does not happen, even the development of a natural talent like Jessy's. Rather it was developed in the same way as all her capacities were developed, with support and shaping and encouragement, slowly, step by step.[165]

This highlights the message that in autism development does *not* happen of its own accord, it has to be *caused* to happen. When one intervenes and actively manages the condition and channels the behavior into a constructive pattern of use, development will happen. This can be done either by taking up the behavior and working with it to put it to more constructive use and gradually extending it, or by channelling it. What cannot be changed may sometimes be put to good use. Temple Grandin developed a lifetime career out of what started as an autistic obsession. In Grandin's case her interest in building a squeeze machine to comfort herself led to her career as a designer of livestock handling facilities. Another autistic child developed a fascination with insects in his youth, which bloomed into an obsession. Over time the obsession was channelled into identifying insects. With his acute vision, his obsessive interest in repeated patterns, and his visual thinking, he was the ideal candidate to work out keys to the identification of different insects—groups where no keys to identification existed. Combine this with his repeated, compulsive ability to draw patterns accurately and well, and all the requirements for a successful career in entomology were there. In time this was realized.

To return again to the story of Jessy. The "Jessy girls" were much involved in the remarkable success story of Jessy Park. These were helpers who worked with and sometimes lived with the family. A number of them were art students who taught Jessy many of the skills she has now mastered. In the epilogue to her book Clara Park pays tribute to them and looks to the future:

Other people's children—and our own. Part of that long future which we will not share, which Jessy does not envisage but which we must. Yet we were once told to take one day at a time, and told rightly; one day at a time we have come this far. If this is a success story—and it is—it is *Jessy's* success story, the one she cannot tell, the story of her hard struggle to work and love. *Arbieten und lieben*—to work and love—were these not Freud's measures of success? Jessy has learned to do both, and this changes the possibilities for her future. We cannot look very far ahead, even now; we can only ask questions.[2]

And finally she looks back over the past to when it all began and to the years between:

I do not forget the pain—it aches in a particular way when I look at Jessy's friends, some of them just her age, and allow myself for a moment to think of all she cannot be. But we cannot sift experience and take only the part that does not hurt us. Let me say simply and straight out that simple knowledge the whole world knows. I breathe like everyone else my century's thin, faithless air, and I do not want to be sentimental. But the blackest sentimentality of all is that *trahison des clercs* which will not recognise the good it has been given to understand because it is too simple. So, then: this experience we did not choose, which we would have given anything to avoid, has made us different, has made us better. Through it we have learned the lesson that no one studies willingly, the hard, slow lesson of Sophocles and Shakespeare—that one grows by suffering. And that too is Jessy's gift. I write now what fifteen years past I would still not have thought possible to write: that if today I were given the choice, to accept the experience, with everything that it entails, or to refuse the bitter largesse, I would have to stretch out my hands—because out of it has come, for all of us, an unimagined life. And I will not change the last word of the story. It is still love.[2]

Susan Moreno is the Founder and President of *MAAP*, which produces a quarterly journal for families of *M*ore advanced individuals with *A*utism, *A*sperger's syndrome and *P*ervasive Developmental Disorders. She is also the mother of Beth, a more advanced college graduate who "in addition to being a talented violinist, an all-around musician, and gifted in Spanish and French, has autism." Beth has recently received her master's degree in music and liturgy. *MAAP Services Inc*, founded around sixteen years ago, publishes letters from parents and more advanced autistic people from all over the world, serving to keep people in touch with each other and providing a forum for sharing and exchanging views and information. Letters and essays from high ability young men and women with autism provide invaluable insights into their determination and courage in coping with autism, and much can be learned from reading them. *MAAP* now reaches over 10,000 families in the United States and is being circulated in forty-three other countries as well. "You Are Not Alone" is its inspiring motto. *MAAP Services Inc* hosts an annual conference, and Susan is an international conference presenter who also writes and lectures about autism.

In her writings she discusses the many issues involved in parenting an autistic person, giving insights into the joys and sorrows of the challenge and providing us with much practical advice along the way. Stressing that the first hurdle to be surmounted is getting a diagnosis, she writes of "the shock and mourning that follows":

Next, we faced the issue of *receiving the diagnosis and the shock and mourning that followed*. The staff of the clinic that gave us Beth's diagnosis did so in a compassionate and supportive way. However, I remember that my shock was so great that my ears were ringing and my nose stung as if I had been hit in the head. An odd dialogue continuously raced through my brain: "Don't cry. Don't scream. Don't let these strangers see you crack. Remember to be polite—they are only trying to help." I think my shock was so great because I was one of those parents who had received some information about autism before the diagnosis. I knew that it was a serious, lifelong disability. Dr. Kenneth Moses claims that parents of disabled children go through a mourning process when they learn of their child's disability. It is as if the child they have dreamed about suddenly is missing, replaced by a child with a very different future. I definitely feel that this was the case for Marco and me. Our hearts broke; we felt angry, guilty, and afraid. This unique mourning is not an experience that goes in exact stages and then goes away. It stays with parents on and off and in varying degrees for the rest of their lives. Time and living may resolve it somewhat, but it still resurfaces when least expected.[156]

Having accepted the diagnosis, the next question is where to go to get the best help, and as she points out, basically this search never ends. She considers it very important to read as much relevant information as possible, and in this way to learn about behavior management and put it into practice in everyday living. High on her priorities she lists the teaching of social skills, commenting that there is nothing harder to teach than social skills, and yet nothing more important. It is an ongoing process.

Learning to deal realistically with hope is another of the issues discussed. Articles appear from time to time in the media promoting a new medication or intervention treatment as a so-called cure for autism, and parents wonder if they should try it. She considers that striking a balance between keeping up with this new information and at the same time not holding out any hope for a cure is difficult to handle. She adds that if one decides to try any of these new ideas, to keep in mind that one is just trying out a new intervention or possible therapy that may help some of the aspects of autism, but not to think in terms of a cure. Susan points out that according to Bennet Leventhal and many other leading experts in the field autism as it is currently understood is not curable.[166]

One decision parents agonize long and hard over is the question of the choice of a school. Should it be special education or mainstream education? Obviously this will depend very much on the level of functioning of the young person. For young people of average or even slightly below average intelligence, the choice of mainstream versus special education becomes an option. This choice will depend on a number of factors, including the emotional vulnerability of the child, the ethos of the school concerned, the expectation and personal preferences of the parents. This is a grey area, and there are no black and white answers. Often it is a matter of trial and error. In discussing this question elsewhere Susan had the following thoughts on the subject:

In their attempts to procure teachers who know about autism and who are trained in current teaching techniques which are most effective for children with autism, many parents and professionals have insisted on segregated classrooms for people with autism. In most cases, the least desirable placement for a high-functioning person with autism is a setting which contains exclusively peers with disabilities. The high-functioning person with autism needs and often wants interaction with non-disabled peers. Role models for *positive* peer interaction can be better provided by typical peers, as well as peers with handicaps that do not effect the ability to interact socially (e.g., Down syndrome). Conversely a placement with children who experience similar handicapping conditions promotes an environment which maintains similarities across students. For example, placing students together who experience aggressive behavior will establish a setting which promotes the performance of this problem behavior. Obviously, this type of placement is not desirable. Therefore, a regular education setting is preferable if all other considerations are equal.[167]

Also in this handbook Susan faces what is perhaps the most difficult question of all for parents. What does the future hold? This is the question to which there may be no real answer. It is: What will happen to them when something happens to us? She writes:

Every time my daughter masters a new skill or overcomes an autistic mannerism or behavior, I find myself wanting to believe that she will make it all the way—that maybe someday she will be regarded by that most wonderful and frustrating of all terms, "normal." But then I plant my feet firmly on the ground and realise that autism, as we know it now, is not and may never be a curable condition. I am both comforted and challenged by the fact that there seem to be endless possibilities to what she *can* accomplish. I am grateful for her potential and for what she has already overcome. In the midst of this optimism, I constantly worry about her future and the unknown challenges she must face.[167]

Finally, she encourages us with the good news of the good things that have happened in her life because of her daughter. Her joy in her daughter's achievements, small and large; her appreciation of what the human spirit can achieve, gained from watching her daughter try to help herself with such human dignity; her experience of the human kindness of all the wonderful people who have befriended both her daughter and the family; the solidarity from good friends who have stood by her through the good times and the bad; the blessing of "bright and caring professional mentors" who made themselves available whenever needed. And finally her "exquisite joy in the very, very small things" she will never take for granted again; "peace and quiet"; "smiles and hugs"; and "laughter."[156]

To live with one generation of autism is a challenge to the human spirit; to have lived and worked with two generations is awesome indeed. This has been the life experience of Charles Hart. Two children were born with autism, fifty years apart. One was his older brother and the other his older son. In his book *Without Reason* he traces the development of both against the background of the social conditions of two different eras.[157] His brother, Sumner, was born into the America of the 1920s, and he was almost sixty years old before they had a name for his condition. In that era services for people with special needs did not exist, and Sumner's remarkable mother looked after him entirely by herself for almost sixty years, until shortly before she died when she allowed him to attend a day-care center. After her death Charles Hart became responsible for his brother's care in addition to the care of his own son. This book describes his advocacy, both legal and medical, for better conditions and acceptance for both, and indeed for other people with disabilities as well. In this advocacy he was campaigning for better care at two different ends of the spectrum, the young and the old. His concern for his brother revolved around custodial care with all its attendant problems of unsuitable placements, total lack of training for, and understanding of, the special needs of people with autism, and medical intervention in the form of psychotropic drugs. When his brother became seriously ill due to overmedication, he describes how he dealt with the situation by learning to exert his authority to greater effect. In order to do this he first obtained copies of the hospital records. He then set about making contact with the protection and advocacy agency of the state dealing with protecting the rights of people with disabilities.

His successful advocacy won out in the end, and he describes how at the age of sixty-eight his brother had come to terms with his new life without his mother. Now he lived in shared accommodation with five other adults in an attractive home, and he travelled every day by private transport to a local work center where he earned a weekly wage. Then, at the age when most people are retiring, he was preparing to face a new career as the staff in the center were planning a placement for him in private industry working alongside nondisabled employees.

Charles Hart's son was born into a very different America, the America of the 1970s. In early childhood he received a diagnosis of brain damage, but he was eight years old before his father realized by chance attendance at an Autism Society conference, that the name of his son's disability was *autism*. The family was fortunate in having a wise physician who counselled them with the following advice:

"There is no 'key' to unlock your child from his disability. There is no normal little human being hiding behind some mask of autism. But there can still be progress, even hope for a satisfying life, if you don't let his disability affect the way you feel about him. . . . I've seen people with disabilities suffer from three forms of handicap," he said. "First, there's the natural limitation brought on by the physical or mental impairment. Then there is usually environmental deprivation when others decide the person doesn't need or won't benefit from opportunities. . . . Finally we have what I call the 'tertiary' effect of the handicap, when the person with the disability begins to think he doesn't matter. Of all the effects of handicaps, the third phase is the most disabling. More than anything else," he emphasized, "you must help your child feel good about himself."[157]

Charles Hart's second advocacy then, was on behalf of better educational opportunities for his son. He negotiated long and hard with the educational authorities and finally decided to exercise his legal rights. Spurred on by his knowledge of what years of educational neglect and deprivation had done to his brother, he was determined to fight for his son. He was fighting in a better climate, as his son was one of the first generation of children to benefit from the federal law that required all school districts to provide education for every child, regardless of disability. But he soon learned he had another obstacle to overcome, that of "prejudice and ignorance." He was pioneering a trail similar to that taken by those who challenged the educational discrimination against cultural minority children. He had to challenge those specialists who were using the results of standardized intelligence and performance tests to deny his son his educational opportunities. Against strong odds he won his hearing and achieved his purpose. He has since been involved in organizing workshops for parents of children with developmental disabilities to instruct them in how to use the state and federal programs for the disabled. He also has been employed by the Development Planning Council to research and report on programs for people with autism. From then on he and his wife had found a mission, which was that "since Ted couldn't be changed into a normal child, we had to change society's attitudes toward people like him."

Like Bryan O'B., Ted Hart's thought processes were associational rather than logical, and like Bryan, Ted associated random facts and did not follow the logical principle of cause and effect. In describing his lack of fear of flying, he said that he was not afraid of planes and that this was the reason they flew so high, because he was not afraid of high things. As his father explained:

Ted knew that planes fly high in the air. He also knew he had no fear of heights. In his unique way, unfettered by logic or the rules we call common sense, he had tried to associate these two facts. His conclusion was intensely personal and self-centered: planes fly high because Ted Hart isn't afraid of them![157]

Without Reason gives very keen insights into the disorder of autism; insights into the faulty thought processes that can lead to the lack of understanding of the principle of cause and effect; the absence of common sense and basic logic; the excellent spatial skills; the uneven educational profiles; the distortion of time perception including, like Mark R., the lack of appreciation that time goes in one direction only and many more, including above all, the outstanding deficit in the ability to communicate. Finally, Hart emphasizes the principle of freedom, the freedom we all need to be ourselves.

For Ted, freedom must include the right to be different, the right to be comfortable and to be accepted as a person with unusual interests and social behaviors. Drilling him in the superficial imitation of "normal" mannerisms won't make him a better person or a happier one. As I have prayed for so many years, Let Ted develop to the maximum of his ability, whatever that is, and let the rest of us accept him, whatever he will be.[157]

This is a prayer that will echo in the hearts and minds of many parents and is one to which they will wish to answer "Amen."

And now the final word goes to another parent—Mary Anne Coppola:

Sometimes it seems like it was only yesterday that autism stormed into our lives. And sometimes, especially when I'm tired, it seems as though we've been fighting the Hundred Years War. Some days my greatest wish is that autism were to disappear from my son's life forever, and yet Brian says that autism is who he is, and that is just fine with him. Erasing it would be like loosing his arm or his eye. Strangely enough, erasing it would mean, for me, losing some of the most wonderful experiences I have had in the past 26 years.

Isn't it amazing that something as cruel as autism can actually bring goodness into a family? Just as an irritating grain of sand tricks the oyster into slowly creating a beautiful pearl, the pain of autism has forced me into discovering an unexpected beauty and strength in my life. When Brian was born, I was drafted into a job I didn't apply for, want, or was prepared to handle. I stumbled through motherhood— angry, worried, and scared. But mistakes brought growth, and challenges brought new understanding and appreciation. I stopped crying for what would never be and began to rejoice in what was at hand. God had given me this courageous child whose simplicity and peace would teach me humility and bring me joy.[168]

REFERENCES

1. Piaget, J. (1953). *The Origin of Intelligence in the Child*. Translated by Margaret Cook (1993). London: Routledge & Kegan Paul.

2. Park, C. Claiborne. (1967). *The Siege: The First Eight Years of an Autistic Child*. New York: Little, Brown.

3. Taylor McDonnell, J. (1993). *News from the Border*. New York: Ticknor & Fields.

4. Kanner, L. (1943). Autistic Disturbances of Affective Contact. *Nervous Child* 2, 217–250.

5. Ayres, A.J. (1979). *Sensory Integration and the Child*. Los Angeles: Western Psychological Services.

6. Wing, L. (1997). The Autistic Spectrum. *The Lancet* 350:1761–1766.

7. Rutter, M. (1999). The Emanuel Miller Memorial Lecture 1998 Autism: Two-way Interplay between Research and Clinical Work. *Journal of Child Psychology and Psychiatry* 40, 2:169–188.

7A. Frith, U. (1989). *Autism: Explaining the Enigma*. Oxford: Blackwell Publishers.

8. Sacks, O. (1995). *An Anthropologist on Mars*. New York: Alfred A. Knopf.

9. Sacks, O. (1989). *Seeing Voices: A Journey into the World of the Deaf*. Los Angeles: University of California Press.

10. Ellis, H.D. (1990). Developmental Trends in Face Recognition. *The Psychologist* 3, 114–119.

11. Delacato, C.H. (1974). *The Ultimate Stranger*. Novato, CA: Academic Therapy Publications.

12. Filipek, P.A., Accardo, P., Baranek, G.T., Cook, E.H. Jr., Dawson, G.,

Gordon, B., Gravel, J.S., Johnson, C.P., Kallen, R.J., Levy, S.E., Minshew, N., Prizant, B., Rapin, I., Rogers, S., Stone, W., Teplin, S., Tuchman, R., Ozonoff, S., and Volkmar, F.R. (1999). The Screening and Diagnosis of Autistic Spectrum Disorders. *Journal of Autism and Developmental Disorders* 29, 6:439–484.

13. Filipek, P.A. (1999). Neuroimaging in the Developmental Disorders: The State of the Science. *Journal of Child Psychology and Psychiatry* 40, 113–128.

14. Cytowic, R. (1993). *The Man Who Tasted Shapes*. Abacus. London: Little, Brown and Company.

15. Cesaroni, L., and Garber, M. (1991). Exploring the Experience of Autism through Firsthand Accounts. *Journal of Autism and Developmental Disorders* 21, 3:303–313.

16. Collet, L., Roge, B., Descouens, D., Moron, P., Duverdy, F., and Urgell, H. (1993). Objective Auditory Dysfunction in Infantile Autism. *The Lancet* 342:923–924.

17. Marriage, J., and Barnes, N.M. (1995). Is Central Hyperacusis a Symptom of 5-Hydroxytryptamine (5-HT) Dysfunction? *Journal of Laryngology and Otology* 109: 915–912.

18. Bristol-Power, M.M., and Spinella, G. (1999). Research on Screening and Diagnosis in Autism: A Work in Progress. *Journal of Autism and Developmental Disorders* 29, 6:435–438.

19. Quinn, P. (1998). *Healing with Nutritional Therapy*. Dublin: Newleaf, Gill & Macmillan.

20. Steingard, R., and Biederman, J. (1987). Lithium Responsive Manic-like Symptoms in Two Individuals with Autism and Mental Retardation. *Journal of the American Academy of Child and Adolescent Psychiatry* 26, 6:932–935.

21. Frith, U. (1991). Asperger and His Syndrome. In *Autism and Asperger Syndrome*, edited by U. Frith. Cambridge, UK: Cambridge University Press.

22. Asperger, H. (1991). "Autistic Psychopathy" in Childhood. In *Autism and Asperger Syndrome*, edited and translated by U. Frith. Cambridge, UK: Cambridge University Press.

23. Gillberg, C., and Coleman, M. (1992). *The Biology of the Autistic Syndromes*. 2d ed. London: MacKeith Press.

23A. Gillberg, C., and Coleman, M. (2000). *The Biology of the Autistic Syndromes*. 3d ed. London: MacKeith Press.

24. Pollak, R. (1997). *The Creation of Dr. B: A Biography of Bruno Bettelheim*. New York: Simon & Schuster.

25. Bettelheim, B. (1967). *The Empty Fortress: Infantile Autism and the Birth of Self*. New York: The Free Press.

26. Rimland, B. (1964). *Infantile Autism: The Syndrome and Its Implications for a Neural Theory of Behaviour*. London: Methuen.

27. Sheerer, M., Rothmann, E., and Goldstein, K. (1945). A Case of "Idiot Savant": An Experimental Study of Personality Organisation. In *Psychological Monographs*, edited by J.F. Dashiell. 58, 4. American Psychological Association.

28. Hashimoto, T., Tayama, M., Miyazaki, M., Murakawa, K., Shimakawa, S., Yoneda, Y., and Kuroda, Y. (1993). Brainstem Involvement in High-Functioning Autistic Children. *Acta Neurologica Scandinavica* 88, 123–128.

29. Hebb, D.O. (1958). The Motivating Effects of Exteroceptive Stimulation. *American Psychologist* 13, 109–113.

30. Ornitz, E.M., and Ritvo, E.R. (1976). The Syndrome of Autism: A Critical Review. *American Journal of Psychiatry* 133 6:609–621.

31. Ornitz, E.M. (1985). Special Article: Neurophysiology of Infantile Autism. *Journal of the American Academy of Child Psychiatry* 24, 3:157, 251–262.

32. Sacks, O. (1985). *The Man Who Mistook His Wife for a Hat.* London: Gerald Duckworth.

32A. Sacks, O. (1973). *Awakenings.* London: Gerald Duckworth.

33. Dawson, G., and Watling, R. (2000). Interventions to Facilitate Auditory, Visual, and Motor Integration in Autism: A Review of the Evidence. *Journal of Autism and Developmental Disorders* 30, 5:415–421.

34. Wing, L. (1981). Asperger's Syndrome: A Clinical Account. *Psychological Medicine* 11, 115–129. London: Cambridge University Press.

35. Wing, L. (1998). The History of Asperger Syndrome. In *Asperger Syndrome or High-Functioning Autism?* edited by E. Schopler, G.B. Mesibov, and L. Kunce. New York: Plenum Press.

36. Wing L., and Gould, J. (1979). Severe Impairments of Social Interaction and Associated Abnormalities in Children: Epidemiology and Classification. *Journal of Autism and Developmental Disorders* 9, 1:11–29.

37. Gillberg, C., Steffenburg, S., and Jakobsson, G. (1987). Neurobiological Findings in 20 Relatively Gifted Children with Kanner-Type Autism or Asperger Syndrome. *Developmental Medicine and Child Neurology* 29, 641–649.

38. Gillberg, C. (1989). Asperger Syndrome in 23 Swedish Children. *Developmental Medicine and Child Neurology* 31, 520–531.

39. Gillberg, C. (1991). Outcome in Autism and Autistic-like Conditions. *Journal of the American Academy of Child and Adolescent Psychiatry* 30, 3:375–382.

40. Lotter, V. (1978). Follow-up Studies. In *Autism, A Reappraisal of Concepts and Treatment,* edited by M. Rutter and E. Schopler. New York: Plenum Press.

41. Ozonoff, S., and Miller, N.J. (1995). Teaching Theory of Mind: A New Approach to Social Skills Training for Individuals with Autism. *Journal of Autism and Developmental Disorders* 25, 415–433.

42. Bauminger, N., and Kasari, C. (1999). Brief Report: Theory of Mind in High-Functioning Children with Autism. *Journal of Autism and Developmental Disorders* 29, 1:81–86.

43. Tantam, D. (1991). Asperger Syndrome in Adulthood. In *Autism and Asperger Syndrome,* edited by U. Frith. Cambridge: Cambridge University Press.

44. Davies, S., Bishop, D., Manstead, A.S.R., and Tantam, D. (1994). Face Perception in Children with Autism and Asperger's Syndrome. *Journal of Child Psychology and Psychiatry* 35, 6:1033–1057. Cambridge: Cambridge University Press.

45. Lovaas, O.I., Schriebman, L., Koegel, R., and Rehm, R. (1971). Selective Responding by Autistic Children to Multiple Sensory Input. *Journal of Abnormal Psychology* 77, 211–222.

46. Burke, J.C. (1991). Some Developmental Implications of a Disturbance in Responding to Complex Environmental Stimuli. *American Journal on Mental Retardation* 96, 1:37–52.

47. Lovaas, O.I., Ackerman, A.B., Alexander, D., Firestone, P., Perkins, J., and Young, D. (1981). *Teaching Developmentally Disabled Children: The Me Book.* Austin: Pro-Ed.

48. Lovaas, O.I. (1987). Behavioural Treatment and Normal Educational and

Intellectual Functioning in Young Autistic Children. *Journal of Consulting and Clinical Psychology* 55, 1:3–9.

49. Yarnall, P.A. (2000). Current Interventions in Autism—A Brief Analysis. *Advocate* 33, 6.

50. Rogers, S.J. (1996). Brief Report: Early Intervention in Autism. *Journal of Autism and Developmental Disorders* 26, 2:243–246.

51. U.S. Department of Health and Human Services. (1999). *Mental Health: A Report of the Surgeon General*. Rockville, MD: U.S. Department of Health and Human Services, Substance Abuse and Mental Health Services Administration, Center for Mental Health Services, National Institutes of Health, National Institute of Mental Health.

52. Baron-Cohen, S., Cox, A., Baird, G., Swettenham, J., Nightingale, N., Morgan, K., Drew A., and Charman, T. (1996). Psychological Markers in the Detection of Autism in Infancy in a Large Population. *British Journal of Psychiatry* 168, 158–163.

53. Perry, R., Cohen, I., and DeCarlo, R. (1995). Case Study: Deterioration, Autism, and Recovery in Two Siblings. *Journal of the American Academy of Child and Adolescent Psychiatry* 34, 2:232–237.

54. Maurice, C. (1993). *Let Me Hear Your Voice*. New York: Alfred A. Knopf.

55. Johnson, C., and Crowder, J. (1994). *Autism: From Tragedy to Triumph*. Distributed by Autism Research Institute, San Diego, CA.

56. Quill, K., Gurry, S., and Larkin, A. (1989). Daily Life Therapy: A Japanese Model for Educating Children with Autism. *Journal of Autism and Developmental Disorders* 19, 4:625–637.

57. Hardy, P.M. (1987). The Psychopharmacology of Autism. Presented at the Summer Institute on Autism, Lesley College, Cambridge, MA.

58. Keel, J.H., Mesibov, G.B., and Woods, A.V. (1997). TEACCH-Supported Employment Program. *Journal of Autism and Developmental Disorders* 27, 1:3–9.

59. Van Bourgondien, M.E., and Woods, A.V. (1992). Vocational Possibilities for High-Functioning Adults with Autism. In *High-Functioning Individuals with Autism*, edited by E. Schopler and G.B. Mesibov. New York: Plenum Press.

60. Kaufman, B.N. (1994). *Son-Rise: The Miracle Continues*. Tiburon, CA: Kramer Inc.

61. Kaufman, B.N. (1977). *To Love Is to Be Happy With*. New York: Fawcett Crest.

62. Nordoff, P., and Robbins, C. (1971). *Therapy in Music for Handicapped Children*. London: Victor Gollancz.

63. Reichelt, K.L., Knivsberg, A.M., Lind, G., and Nodland, M. (1991). The Probable Etiology and Possible Treatment of Childhood Autism. *Brain Dysfunction* 4, 308–319.

64. Knivsberg, A.M., Reichelt, K.L., Nodland, M., and Hoien, T. (1995). Autistic Syndromes and Diet: A Follow-up Study. *Scandinavian Journal of Educational Research* 39, 3:223–236.

65. Page, T. (2000). Metabolic Approaches to the Treatment of Autism Spectrum Disorders. *Journal of Autism and Developmental Disorders* 30, 5:463–469.

66. Rapin, I., and Katzman, R. (1998). Neurobiology of Autism. *Annals of Neurology* 43, 7–14.

67. Cook, E.H., Courchesne, R., Lord, C., Cox, N.J., Yan, S., Lincoln, A., Haas,

R., Courchesne, E., and Leventhal, B.L. (1997). Evidence of Linkage Between the Serotonin Transporter and Autistic Disorder. *Molecular Psychiatry* 2, 247–250.

68. Schopler, E. (1996). Are Autism and Asperger Syndrome (AS) Different Labels or Different Disabilities? *Journal of Autism and Developmental Disorders* 26, 1: 109–110.

69. Schopler, E. (1998). Premature Popularization of Asperger Syndrome. In *Asperger Syndrome or High-Functioning Autism?* edited by E. Schopler, G.B. Mesibov, and L. Kunce. New York: Plenum Press.

70. Wing, L. (1991). The Relationship Between Asperger's Syndrome and Kanner's Autism. In *Autism and Asperger Syndrome*, edited by U. Frith. Cambridge, UK: Cambridge University Press.

71. Gillberg, C., and Ehlers, S. (1998). High-Functioning People with Autism and Asperger Syndrome. A Literature Review. In *Asperger Syndrome or High-Functioning Autism?* edited by E. Schopler, G.B. Mesibov, and L. Kunce. New York: Plenum Press.

72. American Psychiatric Association. (1992). *Diagnostic and Statistical Manual of Mental Disorders, Fourth Edition.* Washington, DC: American Psychiatric Association.

72A. World Health Organisation. (1992). *The ICD-10 Classification of Mental and Behavioural Disorders.* Geneva: World Health Organisation.

73. Szatmari, P. (1998). Differential Diagnosis of Asperger Disorder. In *Asperger Syndrome or High-Functioning Autism?* edited by E. Schopler, G.B. Mesibov, and L. Kunce. New York: Plenum Press.

74. Szatmari, P., Bartolucci, G., and Bremner, R. (1989). Asperger's Syndrome and Autism: Comparison of Early History and Outcome. *Developmental Medicine and Child Neurology* 31, 709–720.

75. Szatmari, P., Tuff, L., Allen, M., Finlayson, J., and Bartolucci, G. (1990). Asperger's Syndrome and Autism: Neurocognitive Aspects. *Journal of the American Academy of Child and Adolescent Psychiatry.* 29, 1:130–136.

76. Ozonoff, S., Rogers, S.J., and Pennington, B.F. (1991). Asperger's Syndrome: Evidence of an Empirical Distinction from High-Functioning Autism. *Journal of Child Psychology and Psychiatry* 32, 1107–1122.

77. Klin, A., Volkmar, F.R., Sparrow, S.S., Cicchetti, D.V., and Rourke, B.P. (1995). Validity and Neuropsychological Characterization of Asperger Syndrome. *Journal of Child Psychology and Psychiatry* 36, 1127–1140.

78. Volkmar, F.R., and Klin, A. (1998). Asperger Syndrome and Nonverbal Learning Disabilities. In *Asperger Syndrome or High-Functioning Autism?* edited by E. Schopler, G.B. Mesibov, and L. Kunce. New York: Plenum Press.

79. Volkmar, F.R. (1999). "Can You Explain the Difference Between Autism and Asperger Syndrome?" *Journal of Autism and Developmental Disorders* 29, 2:185–186.

80. Duane, A., Cowdry, R.W., Hall, Z.W., and Snow, J.B. (1996). The State of the Science in Autism: A View from the National Institutes of Health. *Journal of Autism and Developmental Disorders* 26, 2:117–119.

81. Filipek, P.A. (1996). Brief Report: Neuroimaging in Autism: The State of the Science 1995. *Journal of Autism and Developmental Disorders* 26, 2:211–215.

82. Bauman, M.L. (1996). Brief Report: Neuroanatomic Observations of the Brain in Pervasive Developmental Disorders. *Journal of Autism and Developmental Disorders* 26, 2:199–203.

83. Kemper, T.L., and Bauman, M.L. (1993). The Contribution of Neuropathologic Studies to the Understanding of Autism. *Behavioral Neurology* 11, 1:175–187.

84. Folstein, S., and Rutter, M. (1977). Infantile Autism: A Genetic Study of 21 Twin Pairs. *Journal of Child Psychology and Psychiatry* 18, 297–321.

85. Bailey, A., Le Couteur, A., Gottesman, I., Bolton, P., Simonoff, E., Yuzda, E., and Rutter, M. (1995). Autism as a Strongly Genetic Disorder: Evidence from a British Twin Study. *Psychological Medicine* 25:63–77.

86. Steffenburg, S., Gillberg, C., Hellgren, L., Andersson, L., Gillberg, I.C., Jakobsson, G., and Bohman, M. (1989). A Twin Study of Autism in Denmark, Finland, Iceland, Norway and Sweden. *Journal of Child Psychology and Psychiatry* 30, 405–416.

87. Cryan, E., Byrne, M., O'Donovan, A., and O'Callaghan, E. (1996). Brief Report: A Case-Control Study of Obstetric Complications and Later Autistic Disorder. *Journal of Autism and Developmental Disorders* 26, 4:453–460.

88. Konstantareas, M.M., and Homatidis, S. (1999). Chromosomal Abnormalities in a Series of Children with Autistic Disorder. *Journal of Autism and Developmental Disorders* 29, 4:275–285.

89. Weizman, A., Weizman, R., Szekely, G.A., Wijsenbeek, H., and Livini, E. (1982). Abnormal Immune Response to Brain Tissue Antigen in the Syndrome of Autism. *American Journal of Psychiatry* 139, 1462–1465.

90. Todd, R.D., and Ciaranello, R.D. (1985). Demonstration of Inter- and Intraspecies Differences in Serotonin Binding Sites by Antibodies from an Autistic Child. *Proceedings of the National Academy of Sciences U.S.A.* 82, 612–616.

91. Singh, V.K., Warren, R.P., Odell, J.D., Warren, W.L., and Cole, P. (1993). Antibodies to Myelin Basic Protein in Children with Autistic Behaviour. *Brian, Behaviour and Immunology* 7, 97–103.

92. Warren, R.P., Foster, A., Margaretten, N.C., and Pace, N.C. (1986). Immune Abnormalities in Patients with Autism. *Journal of Autism and Developmental Disorders* 16, 2:189–197.

93. Warren, R.P., Foster, A., and Margaretten, N.C. (1987). Reduced Natural Killer Cell Activity in Autism. *Journal of the American Academy of Child and Adolescent Psychiatry* 26, 333–335.

94. Warren, R.P., Burger, R.A., Odell, D., Torres, A.R., and Warren, W.L. (1994). Decreased Plasma Concentrations of the C4B Complement Protein in Autism. *Archives of Pediatric and Adolescent Medicine* 148, 180–183.

95. Warren, R.P., Odell, D., Warren, L.W., Burger, R.A., Maciulis, A., Daniels, W.W., and Torres, A. (1997). Brief Report: Immunoglobulin A Deficiency in a Subset of Autistic Subjects. *Journal of Autism and Development Disorders* 27, 2:187–192.

96. Gupta, S., Aggarwal, S., and Heads, C. (1996). Brief Report: Dysregulated Immune System in Children with Autism; Beneficial Effects of Intravenous Immune Globulin on Autistic Characteristics. *Journal of Autism and Developmental Disorders* 26, 4:439–452.

97. DelGiudice-Asch, G., Simon, L., Schmeidler, J., Cunningham-Rundles, C., and Hollander, E. (1999). Brief Report: A Pilot Open Clinical Trial of Intravenous Immunoglobulin in Childhood Autism. *Journal of Autism and Developmental Disorders* 29, 2:157–160.

98. Plioplys, A.V. (2000). Intravenous Immunoglobulin Treatment in Autism. *Journal of Autism and Developmental Disorders* 30, 1:73.

99. Fombonne, E. (1999). Ask the Editor. *Journal of Autism and Developmental Disorders* 29, 4:349–350.

100. House Government Reform Committee Autism Hearing. (2000). *Advocate* 33, 3.

101. Spence, M.A. (1996). Pathophysiology of Autism: Etiology and Brain Mechanisms. *Journal of Autism and Developmental Disorders* 26, 2:129–134.

102. Fombonne, E. (1998). Preface. *Journal of Autism and Developmental Disorders* 28, 5:349–350.

103. Gillberg, C. (1998). Chromosomal Disorders and Autism. *Journal of Autism and Developmental Disorders* 28, 5:415–425.

103A. International Human Genome Sequencing Consortium. (2001). Initial Sequencing and Analysis of the Human Genome. *Nature* 409, 860–921.

104. Volkmar, F.R., Klin, A., and Pauls, D. (1998). Nosological and Genetic Aspects of Asperger Syndrome. *Journal of Autism and Developmental Disorders* 28, 5:457–463.

105. Cook, E.H. (1996). Brief Report: Pathophysiology of Autism: Neurochemistry. *Journal of Autism and Developmental Disorders* 26, 2:221–225.

106. Tsai, L.Y. (1999). Psychopharmacology in Autism. *Psychosomatic Medicine* 61: 651–665.

107. International Molecular Genetic Study of Autism Consortium. (1998). A Full Genome Screen for Autism with Evidence for Linkage to a Region on Chromosome 7q. *Human Molecular Genetics* 7, 571–578.

108. Rodier, P.M. (2000). The Early Origins of Autism. *Scientific American.* February, 38–45.

109. Howlin, P., and Moore, A. (1997). Diagnosis in Autism. A Survey of Over 1200 Patients in the UK. *Autism* 1, 135–162.

110. Tomatis, A.A. (1991). *The Conscious Ear.* New York: Station Hill Press.

111. Stehli, A. (1991). *The Sound of a Miracle.* London: Fourth Estate.

112. Bettison, S. (1996). The Long-Term Effects of Auditory Training on Children with Autism. *Journal of Autism and Developmental Disorders* 26, 3:361–374.

113. Rimland, B., and Edelsen, S.M. (1995). Brief Report: A Pilot Study of Auditory Integration Training in Autism. *Journal of Autism and Developmental Disorders* 25, 1:61–70.

113A. Dahlgren, S.P., and Gillberg, C. (1989). Symptoms in the First Two Years of Life: A Preliminary Population Study of Infantile Autism. *European Archives of Psychiatry and Neurological Sciences* 238, 169–174.

114. Gillberg, C., Johansson, M., Steffenburg, S., and Berlin, O. (1997). Auditory Integration Training in Children with Autism. Brief Report of an Open Pilot Study. *Autism* 1, 1:97–100.

115. Mudford, O. (2000). Auditory Integration Training: Recent UK Study. *Autism* 4, 3:337–338.

116. Monville, D.K., and Nelson, N.W. (1994). Parental Viewpoints on Change Following Auditory Integration Training for Autism. *American Journal of Speech-Language Pathology.* May, 41–53.

117. Nelson, N.W. (1994). Clinical Research, the Placebo Effect, Responsibility to Families, and Other Concerns Stimulated by Auditory Integration Training. *American Journal of Speech-Language Pathology.* September, 106–111.

118. Lucker, J.R. (1998). Is Auditory Integration Training Safe? *Journal of Autism and Developmental Disorders* 28, 3:267.

119. Rankovic, C.M., Rabinowitz, W.M., and Lof, G.L. (1996). Maximum Output Intensity of the Audiokinetron. *American Journal of Speech-Language Pathology* 5, 68–72.

120. Kobayashi, R. (1996). Brief Report: Physiognomic Perception in Autism. *Journal of Autism and Developmental Disorders* 26, 6:661–667.

120A. Ornitz, E.M., and Ritvo, E.R. (1968). Perceptual Inconsistency in Early Infantile Autism. *Archives of General Psychiatry* 18, 76–98.

121. Klin, A., Sparrow, S.S., de Bildt, A., Cicchetti, D.V., Cohen, D.J., and Volkmar, F.R. (1999). A Normed Study of Face Recognition in Autism and Related Disorders. *Journal of Autism and Developmental Disorders* 29, 6:499–508.

122. Schultz, R.T., Gauthier, I., Klin, A., Fulbright, R.K., Anderson, A.W., Volkmar, F., Skudlarski, P., Lacadie, C., Cohen, D.J., and Gore, J.C. (2000). Abnormal Ventral Temporal Cortical Activity during Face Discrimination among Individuals with Autism and Asperger Syndrome. *Archives of General Psychiatry* 57, April, 331–340.

123. Courchesne, E., and Pierce, K. (2000). An Inside Look at the Neurobiology, Ethiology, and Future Research of Autism. *Advocate* 33, 4.

124. Greater Phoenix Chapter Launches Research Initiative. (2000). *Advocate* 33, 3.

125. Sloman, L. (1991). Use of Medication in Pervasive Developmental Disorders. *Psychiatric Clinics of North America* 14, 1:165–182.

126. Horvath, K., Stefanatos, G., Sokolski, N., Wachtel, R., Nabors, L., and Tildon, T. (1998). Improved Social and Language Skills after Secretin Administration in Patients with Autistic Spectrum Disorders. *Journal of the Association of Academic Minority Physicians* 9, 9–15.

127. First Clinical Study on Secretin Not Definitive. (2000). *Advocate* 33, 1.

128. Klaeger, D., and McDougle, C.J. (2000). Secretin in Autism—A Parent's Perspective. *Journal of Autism and Developmental Disorders* 30, 1:72–73.

129. American Academy of Child and Adolescent Psychiatry. (1999). *Policy Statement: Secretin in the Treatment of Autism.*

130. National Institute of Mental Health. (1999). *Research Units on Pediatric Psychopharmacology Autism Network, Statement on Secretin.*

131. Minshew, N.J., Sweeney, J.A., and Bauman, M.L. (1997). Neurological Aspects of Autism. In *Handbook of Autism and Pervasive Developmental Disorders*, edited by D.J. Cohen and F.R. Volkmar. 2d ed. New York: Wiley.

132. Laxova, R. (1994). Fragile X Syndrome. *Advances in Pediatrics* 41, 305–341.

132A. Oostra, B.A., and Willems, P.J. (1995). A Fragile Gene. *BioEssays* 17, 11: 941–947.

133. Hunt, A., and Shepherd, C. (1993). A Prevalence Study of Autism in Tuberous Sclerosis. *Journal of Autism and Developmental Disorders* 23, 2:323–341.

134. Szatmari, P. (1991). Asperger's Syndrome: Diagnosis Treatment and Outcome. *Psychiatric Clinics of North America* 14, 1:81–93.

135. Tantam, D. (2000). Psychological Disorder in Adolescents and Adults with Asperger Syndrome. *Autism* 4, 1:47–61.

136. Diez Cuervo, A. (1996). The Effect of Epileptic Fits on the Disorder of Autism. *Autism-Europe Link* 19, 2:8–9.

137. Tsai, L.Y. (1996). Brief Report: Comorbid Psychiatric Disorders of Autistic Disorder. *Journal of Autism and Developmental Disorders* 26, 2:159–163.

138. Lainhart, J.E., and Folstein, S.E. (1994). Affective Disorders in People with Autism: A Review of Published Cases. *Journal of Autism and Developmental Disorders* 24, 5:587–606.

139. Piven, J., Gayle, J., Chase, G.A., Fink. B., Landa, R., Wzorek, M., and Folstein, S. (1990). A Family History Study of Neuropsychiatric Disorders in the Adult Siblings of Autistic Individuals. *Journal of the American Academy of Child and Adolescent Psychiatry*, 29, 2:177–183.

140. Piven, J., Chase, G., Landa, R., Wzorek, M., Gayle, J., Cloud, D., and Folstein, S. (1991). Psychiatric Disorders in the Parents of Autistic Individuals. *Journal of the American Academy of Child and Adolescent Psychiatry* 30, 3:471–478.

141. Smalley, S.L., McCracken, J., and Tanguay, P. (1995). Autism, Affective Disorders, and Social Phobia. *American Journal of Medical Genetics* 60, 19–26.

142. DeLong, G., and Dwyer, J.T. (1988). Correlation of Family History with Specific Autistic Subgroups: Asperger's Syndrome and Bipolar Affective Disease. *Journal of Autism and Developmental Disorders* 18, 4:593–560.

143. Wolff, S. (1998). Schizoid Personality in Childhood. In *Asperger Syndrome or High-Functioning Autism?* edited by E. Schopler, G.B. Mesibov, and L. Kunce. New York: Plenum Press.

143A. Baltaxe, C., and Simmons, J. (1992). A Comparison of Language Issues in High-Functioning Autism and Related Disorders with Onset in Childhood and Adolescence. In *High-Functioning Individuals with Autism*, edited by E. Schopler and G.B. Mesibov. New York: Plenum Press.

144. Watkins, J., Asarnow, R.F., and Tanguay, P. (1988). Symptom Development in Childhood Onset Schizophrenia. *Journal of Child Psychology and Psychiatry* 29, 865–878.

145. What Is Autism? (2000). *Advocate* 33, 6.

146. Eaves, L., and Ho, H.H. (1996). Brief Report: Stability and Change in Cognitive and Behavioral Characteristics of Autism through Childhood. *Journal of Autism and Developmental Disorders* 26, 5:557–569.

147. Bryson, S.E. (1996). Brief Report: Epidemiology of Autism. *Journal of Autism and Developmental Disorders* 26, 2:165–167.

148. Abramson, R.K., Wright, H.H., Cuccaro, M.L., Lawrence, L.G., Babb, S., Pencarinha, D., Marsteller, F., and Harris, E.C. (1992). Biological Liability in Families with Autism. *Journal of the American Academy of Child and Adolescent Psychiatry* 31, 2:370–371.

149. Schopler, E., and Mesibov, G.B. (1992). Preface. *High-Functioning Individuals with Autism*. New York: Plenum Press.

150. Scientists Discover Possible Biomarkers for Autism in Infants. (2000). *Advocate* 33, 3.

151. Baird, G., Charman, T., Baron-Cohen, S., Cox, A., Swettenham, J., Wheelwright, S., Drew, A., and Kernal, L. (1999). Screening a Large Population of 18 Month Olds with the CHAT. Paper presented at the Proceedings of the Society for Research in Child Development, Albuquerque, NM.

152. Kadesjo, B., Gillberg, C., and Hagberg, B. (1999). Brief Report: Autism and Asperger Syndrome in Seven-Year-Old Children: A Total Population Study. *Journal of Autism and Developmental Disorders* 29, 4:327–331.

153. Wang, C. (2000). High Autism Prevalence But No Cluster Found in Brick Township. *Advocate* 33, 3.

154. Howlin, P. (2000). Outcome in Adult Life for More Able Individuals with Autism or Asperger Syndrome. *Autism* 4, 1:63–83.

155. Bristol-Power, M. (2000). Research in Autism: New Directions. *Advocate* 33, 4:16–17.

156. Moreno, S. (1992). A Parent's View of More Able People with Autism. In *High-Functioning Individuals with Autism*, edited by E. Schopler and G.B. Mesibov. New York: Plenum Press.

157. Hart, C. (1989). *Without Reason.* New York: HarperCollins.

158. Grandin, T., and Scariano, M.M. (1986). *Emergence Labeled Autistic.* Novato, CA: Arena Press.

159. Grandin, T. (1995). *Thinking in Pictures.* New York: Doubleday.

160. Grandin, T. (1992). An Autistic Person Explains Her Experiences with Sensory Problems, Visual Thinking and Communication Difficulties. *4th Congress, Autism–Europe.* Holland.

161. Grandin T. (1996). Brief Report: Response to National Institutes of Health Report. *Journal of Autism and Developmental Disorders* 26, 2:185–187.

161A. Coppola, M.A. (1985). Residual Autism Newsletter. In *High-Functioning Individuals with Autism*, edited by S. Moreno. Crown Point, IN: MAAP Services Inc.

162. Jamison, K.R. (1993). *Touched with Fire.* New York: Free Press Paperbacks.

163. Hoffman, P. (1996). Man with a Briefcase. *MAAP* IV.

164. ASA and ASAF Host the Celebration of Hope. (2000). *Advocate* 33, 2.

165. Park, C. (1992). Autism into Art: A Handicap Transfigured. In *High-Functioning Individuals with Autism*, edited by E. Schopler and G.B. Mesibov. New York: Plenum Press.

166. Leventhal, B. (1991). The Biochemistry of Autism. Paper presented at the Annual Meeting of the Autism Society of America, July, Indianapolis.

167. Moreno, S. (1991). *High-Functioning Individuals with Autism.* Crown Point, IN: MAAP Services Inc.

168. Coppola, M.A. (1997). Letter to Susan. *MAAP* II.

169. Twachtman-Cullen, D. (1998). Language and Communication in High-Functioning Autism and Asperger Syndrome. In *Asperger Syndrome or High-Functioning Autism?* edited by E. Schopler, G.B. Mesibov, and L. Kunce. New York: Plenum Press.

170. Aarons, M., and Gittens, T. (1992). *The Handbook of Autism: A Guide for Parents and Professionals.* London: Routledge.

171. Biklen, D. (1990). Communication Unbound: Autism and Praxis. *Harvard Educational Review* 60, 3:291–314.

172. Ornitz, E.M., and Naruse, H. (1992). Neurobiology of Infantile Autism. Proceedings of the International Symposium on Neurobiology of Infantile Autism, Tokyo, November 1990. London: Excerpta Medica.

173. Ozonoff, S. (1998). Executive Dysfunction in Autism and AS. In *Asperger Syndrome or High-Functioning Autism?* edited by E. Schopler, G.B. Mesibov, and L. Kunce. New York: Plenum Press.

174. Ozonoff, S., and Jensen, J. (1999). Brief Report: Specific Executive Function

Profiles in Three Neurodevelopmental Disorders. *Journal of Autism and Developmental Disorders* 29, 2:171–177.

175. Smalley, S.L., and Collins, F. (1996). Brief Report: Genetic, Prenatal, and Immunologic Factors. *Journal of Autism and Developmental Disorders* 26, 2:195–198.

176. Maestrini, E., Marlow, A.J., Weeks, D.E., and Monaco, A.P. (1998). Molecular Genetic Investigations of Autism. *Journal of Autism and Developmental Disorders* 28, 5:427–437.

177. Abbott, A. (2001). And Now for the Proteome . . . *Nature*, 409, 747.

178. Hooper, S.R., and Bundy, M.B. (1998). Learning Characteristics of Individuals with Asperger Syndrome. In *Asperger Syndrome or High-Functioning Autism?* edited by E. Schopler, G.B. Mesibov, and L. Kunce. New York: Plenum Press.

179. Bishop, D.V.M. (1989). Autism, Asperger's Syndrome and Semantic-Pragmatic Disorder: Where Are the Boundaries? *British Journal of Disorders of Communication* 24, 107–121.

Appendix 1: Glossary

Aetiology (etiology): This is the name given to the science of studying the precise cause or causes of disease.

Affective disorder: When psychiatric disorders show up as an abnormality of mood or emotion (affect) they are called affective disorders. Depression (unipolar, as the person experiences low moods only) and manic depression (bipolar when the person experiences both low and high moods) are the most serious of the affective disorders. Manic depressive illness is relatively common; approximately one person in a hundred will suffer from the more severe form and at least that many again will experience milder variations of it.[162] Basically it shows itself in the form of recurrent mood changes that feature mixed episodes of mania and depression. The mood disturbance during the manic phase can range from elation to intense irritability and on to the dysphoric condition described under Bryan O'B.

Research in the United States has shown that in any one year about 7 percent of the population suffer from mood disorders and that women between the ages of eighteen and forty-five make up the majority of those with major depression, the principal symptoms of which are depressed mood and loss of interest and pleasure with other symptoms varying considerably from person to person.[51]

Agonist: An agonist is a substance, for example, a drug, which can mimic the action of one of the body's own chemicals to produce the same or similar effect.

Anatomy: This is the name given to the study of the structure of the different parts of the human body, for example, the study of the structure of the nervous system would be called neuroanatomy.

Antipsychotic drugs: These are drugs used to treat serious mental disorders. They are also called neuroleptics, or major tranquillizers. They are used in the treatment of schizophrenia and bipolar disorder and can also be applied to the treatment of the problem behaviors encountered in autism. They can be divided into two groups: (1) the conventional or older neuroleptics, for example, chlorpromazine (Largactil), haloperidol (Haldol), and thioridazine (Mellaril); and (2) the newer atypical neuroleptics introduced into medical practice over the last eight years or so, for example, clozapine (Clozaril), risperidone (Risperdal), and olanzapine (Zyprexa). These newer medications are called atypical because they have a different method of action from the older types. Also, they are considered to have fewer side effects. In addition, they show promise for treating patients who did not respond to the older neuroleptics. There is a growing body of studies in the scientific literature on the use of the older or typical neuroleptics in children and adolescents with autism. Now a number of controlled studies have been set up by the National Institute of Mental Health (NIMH) in the United States to investigate the effects of the atypical neuroleptics in children with autism as part of its research program.

Aphasia or dysphasia: These refer to either a lack of the power of speech or having a difficulty in speaking and in understanding what others say. They are attributed to brain dysfunction.

Apraxia or dyspraxia: Praxis means to do or to perform, and in medical terms praxis refers to the ability to perform skilled movements accurately. The prefix a- means without the ability. It is thought to originate from the person not being able to organize movements due to some disorder of the brain. The prefix dys- means a dysfunction in the ability. In short, praxis is described as motor planning.

Asperger's syndrome (AS): This is also known as Asperger syndrome or Asperger's disorder. As explained in the text, all of the autism categories are now grouped together under the category of pervasive developmental disorders, PDD, but as pointed out in the opening chapter, "The [autistic] spectrum overlaps with but covers a wider range than the category of pervasive developmental disorders in the tenth edition of the International Classification of Diseases (ICD-10)."[6]

Audiogram: This is the record of a test of hearing shown in the form of a graph. It is carried out on an apparatus called an audiometer. This audiometer measures a person's hearing at different sound frequencies. The science of the study of hearing disorders is called audiology.

Autism: Kanner used the term "early infantile autism" for his cases, in this way drawing attention to the fact that the condition was found in early infancy. Now the most common terms used to describe the condition are autism, childhood autism, infantile autism, autistic spectrum disorder, or autistic continuum disorder. Low-ability autism is occasionally referred to as Kanner's syndrome, Kanner's autism, or classic autism, while high-ability autism may be referred to as more able autism, more advanced autism, or high-functioning autism (HFA), that is, autism not associated with mental retardation.

Autoimmunity: This is a condition that develops when the body turns on its own cells and attacks them, thus treating them as foreign bodies. It is not known why this happens, why the body should fail to recognize its own tissues and begin to produce antibodies against them. Autoimmunity is harmful and a number of research studies have shown that it exists in autism.

Body percept: Ayres defines this as a person's perception of his own body, consisting of sensory pictures or maps stored in the brain.

Brain imaging or scanning: The older scanning techniques measured the anatomy or structure of the brain and other tissues, while the newer techniques can measure how the tissues are functioning. The CAT scan, later called CT scan, is a specialized form of X-ray that rotates around the part of the body to be scanned and the images are formed on a computer screen. This produces cross-sectional images of the organ involved. The MRI scan is newer and does not use X rays. Instead, high-frequency radio waves and strong magnetic fields are used to produce the images. It is very useful for examining the tissues of the nervous system. However, neither of the above scans tells us anything about how the brain functions. The newer PET scan is a tool of modern nuclear medicine. Here radioactive glucose is injected into the body, and its pathway is traced through the different areas of the brain as it is used. This highlights the most active areas of the brain at the time. Damaged tissues will show up because they will have used up less of the glucose due to less activity or none at all in these areas. Functional magnetic resonance imaging (fMRI) detects where and when oxygen is being used in the brain as a person carries out different tasks.[123] We have seen how this is used in face perception studies in autism. These newer imaging techniques now allow researchers to study the pathways of specific neurotransmitters, for example, serotonin and dopamine, in the brains of individuals who have autism.[23A] They can detect serotonin receptor levels and establish if they are normal, increased, or reduced.

Cerebellum: The cerebellum is the largest part of the hindbrain. It has long been known to be associated with coordinating muscle activity in the body and maintaining balance. There has recently been a total review of the understanding of the functioning of the cerebellum due to the results of new research into its function. Part of this has come about as a result of research into the role it plays in autism. Recent findings show that it plays a part in higher brain functions, such as learning ability, language, cognitive planning, the ability to focus and shift attention, as well as other functions such as sensory, motor, and face perception.[123] One of the most frequently found abnormalities in autism, with and without mental retardation, is a reduction of the tissue of the cerebellum. This reduction is in the specialized type of neurons called Purkinge neurons. Courchesne and Pierce (2000) give figures for autopsy studies that show that 90 percent of autism cases have reduced numbers of Purkinge neurons in the cerebellar vermis and cerebellar hemispheres. Loss is typically of the order of 20 to 60 percent among different individuals with autism. They indicate that these neurons are very important because, as well as being the principal site of cerebellar "learning mechanisms," they are also the only pathway by which the cerebellar cortex (one of the largest computing systems in the human brain) can communicate with other parts of the brain.[123] Purkinge cells have many dendrites (branches) fanning out from the cell body toward other cells on the surface of the cerebellum and a long axon that runs deep into the cerebellar tissue.

Cerebrospinal fluid (CSF): The transparent fluid that surrounds the brain and spinal cord is called the CSF. Its function is to nourish and protect the central nervous system. It contains salts, enzymes, and glucose sugar. Also it contains some white blood cells.

Cerebrum: The cerebrum is the largest and most highly specialized part of the brain, and it is located under the top of the head. It is divided into four main regions; namely, the frontal lobes, the parietal lobes, the temporal lobes, and the insular cortex. The mantle of it, called the cerebral cortex, has a very enlarged surface area that is thrown into folds leading to clefts called *sulci* and raised portions called *gyri*.[51] Lying underneath the cortex are vast numbers of axons with an outer insulating sheath of white myelin (white matter), and these surround deep clusters of neurons that are grey (grey matter) because they contain the cell bodies of the neurons. Brain processing information is carried on within this grey matter, and the white matter of the axons undertakes the task of communicating the "messages" from one region to another.[51] The many different sub-areas of the cerebral cortex are involved in particular functions; for example, the parietal lobe is involved in the processing of tactile information, while the frontal lobe is involved in motor behavior. The prefrontal cortex, found in front of the brain, is involved with functions such as planning ability and the integration of "cognitive and emotional streams of information."[51]

Cognitive psychology: We perceive knowledge through our senses and we also conceive it through our minds. Our general ability to do this is referred to as cognitive functioning. The branch of psychology which studies the processes involved in such cognitive functioning—the method, for example, by which concepts are formed, how sensations are processed, how the knowledge gained is stored and retrieved, how memory systems operate, how attention is focused and many more—all come within the aegis of the branch of science known as cognitive psychology. Cognitive psychologists design experiments to test different hypotheses similar to what has been described in the work of Frith.[7A] In this way they hope to get a better understanding of how the brain works.

Communication: What is wrong with the communication of people with autism and Asperger syndrome, even the most high-functioning? To answer this we need to look at the components of speech and language.

Speech: Speech is the way in which we deliver information and, as Twachtman-Cullen indicates, it includes such factors as tone, time, pitch, stress, and rhythm.[169] Prosody (e.g., one's voice rising at the end of a sentence when asking a question is an example of prosody) is also involved in speech. In people with autism prosody can be conspicuously lacking, and as a result the voice takes on the form of a monotone with little nuance of feeling and little inflection as described in John K. Consequently, their speech gives little information about the speaker's attitude and emotional state. John K. showed the greatest difficulty when asked to modulate his voice and "talk softly."

Pragmatics: Pragmatics refers to the use of language for the purpose of communicating, and it is in this use of language that people with high-ability autism and Asperger syndrome can be very different from typical language users.[169] This is because pragmatics involves having insight and intuition. These are necessary to make judgments about the listeners' moods, needs, age, status, capabilities, and so forth. Consequently it is very difficult for someone with the type of disability involved in autism, who cannot see faces or has great difficulty processing facial stimuli, to judge age or moods. They must depend on voice. Not surprisingly then, language use can put such people under extreme pressure. To compound the issue further, as Twachtman-Cullen (in reviewing Mehrabain) points out, research experiments have shown that over half the emotional meaning of a message is conveyed through body language, and over a further third of it is conveyed through the tone of voice, while as little as 7 percent is attributed to the actual words used.[169] Even the most able autistic individuals have difficulty using and interpreting body language and voice intonation. This will give some idea of the dilemma and frustration that they face in the whole area of communication. Small wonder then that Temple Grandin referred to herself as "feeling like an Anthropologist on Mars" much of the time.

Semantics: Semantics refer to the content and meaning of words. If meaning is to be shared in normal conversation, each speaker must have a shared understanding of the meaning behind the words they are using.[169] Because Bryan O'B. was not able to properly process the semantics of speech and was not able to take account of context, a word like *fox*, which could have a number of very different meanings, completely upset his literal pattern of thinking. As he lacked word image flexibility, he became fixated on the meaning of a word when he first heard it, and he had to be taught to adapt to the word *fox* being used in a different context. Leo Kanner, in his seminal paper, referred to this word image inflexibility in autism.[4] For autistic people who have difficulty with the semantic elements of language, it may be necessary to teach them the meaning behind the words. Here one is reminded of the parent who told the following story about the literalness of his autistic son. He had always advised his son to "act right" no matter what others did, and his son always assured him that he would indeed always "act right." One day after things had gone very wrong the perplexed father was astonished to hear his son say "And I did 'act right' Dad, like I always do, I turned right at the end of the road."

Depersonalization: This is a state that can occur in severe depression, in severe states of anxiety, and in schizophrenia. Also, as we have seen, it can be induced by sensory deprivation and can occur in autism. During it a person will feel that he has changed in some strange ways, will experience bizarre sensations, will develop a strong sense of unreality, a feeling of not knowing who or what he is. He is no longer grounded. This has been described as occurring in the experiences of Mark R., and there is now some evidence from research that in certain cases it may be associated with a slowing down of blood flow through the brain. Depersonalization can occur in association with derealization. This is experienced as a sensation that one's environment has changed. It is no longer familiar and can become alien and unreal. These conditions are very frightening for the person affected.

Dysfunction: This term implies that the organ, be it the brain or some other part of the body, for some reason is malfunctioning and is not working well.

Echolalia: Echolalic speech is a common characteristic of speech in autism. It is the repetition of the speech spoken by another person as documented under Mark R. Recent research into echolalia suggests that, in contrast to the average child, the autistic child does not appear to acquire language in the normal manner.[170] Instead their acquisition of speech seems to be fundamentally different as they appear to acquire speech by learning by rote certain echolalic patterns that they pick up from the speech of those around them. Over time they can learn to redirect these phrases and adapt them for use in different contexts, thus giving rise to new phrases. Because they are using language by reference to a store of learned phrases that they now adapt to new situations, their language in the younger years is often slow and hesitant, and at times, as they struggle with selecting one out of two or three possible phrases to answer a single question, they can use bits of all three phrases, thus making what appears to be a nonsense of the answer. One such statement of Mark R.'s comes to mind. In trying to impress on his listener how well he knew a certain poem, he struggled with two different phrases. One was "I knew it like the back of my hand"; the other was "I knew it off by heart." What he actually said was "I knew it like the back of off my heart." Over time, however, autistic people become quite adept at choosing the right phrases and fitting them in where necessary so that their language can at times appear quite spontaneous. In the case of Mark R., over a long period of time spontaneous language did in fact arise out of echolalia. Such language does however have a forced, metallic, mechanical quality about it and lacks intonation and inflection. But again, over time, as it becomes more spontaneous and with the help of speech therapy, much can be done to gain the normal nuances of speech. When stressed, the autistic child or indeed adult can often slip back into echolalia again. The simplest form of echolalia used in the first speech of a very young autistic child can take the form of rhymes, slogans, jingles, and so forth, picked up from television, radio, or songs.

Biklen compares the autistic person's speech ability to a "dedicated" computer or language device that has the ability to produce words, phrases, or sentences that have already been introduced aurally. As this speech becomes more advanced, he holds, the person is capable of choosing certain segments and phrases and manipulating these with other phrases to produce intelligible language; although, he considers, this language does not always have the ability to use pronouns and verb tenses correctly.[171]

Electroencephalogram (EEG): This is a recording of the electrical activity from different parts of the brain. The pattern of the recording reflects the activity of the person's brain. There is an extensive literature on EEG studies in autism showing quite variable results. But, as with much of the research in autism, the findings are inconclusive and contradictory. Some researchers have reported that from a half to three-quarters of autistic patients have abnormal EEGs, while others have reported lower figures. All that can be said with any degree of certainty is that abnormal EEGs do occur in some autistic children.[172] This would appear to reflect the extent to which autism occurs in association with different organic syndromes.

Empirical: In medical terms this means relying on experiment, or experience, or observation and not on theory, reason, or logic.

Executive dysfunction: The frontal lobes of the brain are thought to be involved in regulating abilities such as organization, forward planning, selecting goals, flexibility, self-regulation, and inhibition and thus act in an executive capacity.[173]

The results of an impairment or dysfunction in these skills was described under Bryan O'B. In a review of a number of studies on executive functioning in individuals with autistic spectrum disorders, it was found that over 80 percent of these investigations had shown deficits in executive functioning.[173] Ozonoff comments that there is a great paucity of information written on how to manage these deficits. In her own research, she and her associates found that AS subjects performed considerably below age- and IQ-matched controls, and that there was "no significant difference" between the performance of the HFA and AS groups. They consider that this suggests that all autistic spectrum disorders may share these impairments. Ozonoff also indicates that executive dysfunction also occurs in a number of other disorders including OCD, schizophrenia, and Parkinson's disease and stresses the importance of remedial treatment, outlining programs of cognitive behavioral strategies. These include self-management programs; that is, teaching the individual to plan his own behavior, thus handing over the responsibility to the individual himself. Also, the adult must structure the child's environment, in this way providing structure from outside and making it easier to develop executive functioning skills.[173] There is some suggestion from the literature that the executive functions most affected in individuals with autism are those of flexibility and planning.[174]

Familial: This means a disorder can run in families. Often such a trait can be inherited.

Fusiform gyrus: This is a structure found in the temporal lobe of the brain and it has been shown consistently to be involved in face perception in nonautistic people.[123]

Genetics: Genetics is the study of the science of how characteristics are inherited and passed on from one generation to the next. Deoxyribonucleic acid, DNA for short, is the substance of which genes are made. Genes occur on chromosomes rather like beads on a string. With the exception of the ovum and sperm cell, which have twenty-three single chromosomes, every other cell in the human body (somatic cell) has twenty-three pairs of chromosomes.

Genes can be either dominant or recessive, and these are called alleles or the alternative forms of the gene. A dominant gene will suppress the expression of a recessive gene. The recessive gene will still be in the cell but it will not be active. It will only show up in the absence of the dominant gene; that is, when there are two recessive genes in the cell. This is called the double recessive. The work of the cell revolves around making the right proteins for that cell. DNA and its derivative, RNA, ribonucleic acid, contain the code for making the complicated chemicals called proteins. DNA is a large molecule and it is made up of units called nucleotides. Each nucleotide consists of a sugar group, a phosphate group, and one of four different bases. These four bases are called adenine, guanine, thymine, and cytosine. The bases pair together and adenine always pairs with thymine, while cytosine always pairs with guanine. It is the sequencing of these bases that spells out the code for which protein is to be made by the cell. Proteins are made up of smaller building blocks called amino acids. If the amino acids are put together in the right order, then the right protein will be made for that cell, and the system will work well. But sometimes the system goes wrong and an error in the copying of the code creeps in (this is called a mutation), and then the code for sequencing of the amino acids is incorrect, and the building blocks are put together in the wrong order, resulting in the wrong protein being made, or no protein at all being made (null allele). If the mutation occurs in an ordinary (somatic) cell it will die out with the cell, but if it occurs in a reproductive cell it will be passed on to the next generation.

A genetic locus (plural is loci) is the place on the chromosome where that particular gene is to be found. The total genetic material of any living organism is called its genome. The actual genetic material an individual is born with is known as the individual's genotype. It is his/her genetic make-up. The phenotype is the physical expression of these genes; that is, what the individual actually turns out to be like. Autism is a "complex trait," meaning a trait in which multiple genotypes give rise to the same phenotype; that is, genetic heterogeneity and/or multiple phenotypes arise from the same genotype.[175] Estimates of the number of genetic loci involved in autism are of the order of three to four, but up to ten loci are possible.[176]

Simple Mendelian Inheritance: Gregor Mendel, an Austrian, Augustinian, monk who lived in the nineteenth century, is known as the father of genetics. In his lifetime he cross-pollinated tens of thousands of pea plants and identified characteristics due to single genes. Being both a mathematician and a gardener, he worked out some of the basic principles of modern genetics. These are known as Mendel's laws of heredity. Many hereditary diseases, for example, cystic fibrosis (the faulty gene is on chromosome 7), are inherited in a simple Mendelian pattern of inheritance and are due to the presence of a defective gene as a double recessive. As explained above, when this happens there is no dominant gene in the cell to suppress the expression of the defective recessive gene. Other hereditary diseases inherited in this simple Mendelian fashion are due to the presence of a faulty gene that is dominant. In this case one defective gene inherited from one parent is sufficient to cause the disease. Autism, however, does not fall into this category because there are a number of different genes involved and not just different forms of the one gene (alleles). At the present time almost all the medical disorders that are inherited in this simple Mendelian fashion have already been identified as a result of the work of the Human Genome Organization.

Human Genome Organization (HUGO): This refers to the international research project that was set up in 1988 by publicly funded researchers in order to coordinate research efforts in mapping out the entire sequence of genes on all the human chromosomes. It is the most ambitious biological research program ever undertaken and involves twenty working groups from the United States, the United Kingdom, France, Japan, Germany, and China. It was scheduled to last fifteen years but due to new advances in research techniques it will be finished ahead of time. The rough draft of the genome sequence has now been published (February 2001), and there appears to be something on the order of thirty thousand to forty thousand protein-coding genes in the human genome; much less than was originally expected.[103A] This rough draft covers about 94 percent of the human genome but the sequences are not continuous—there are gaps. These gaps could slow down efforts aimed at finding and identifying genes involved in inherited diseases because the first act in locating such genes is to work out which chromosomes they are on and on which region of that chromosome. So the ultimate goal of the project is to close these gaps and to produce a finished sequence. This task may take some time because of the limitations of present technology. One fact already made clear is that the mutation rate (error in the copying of the genes) is about twice as high in males as it is in females, thus showing that most mutations occur in males.[103A]

Now that the work of HUGO is nearing completion a new organization, HUPO (Human Proteome Organization), has been launched globally as researchers are turning their attention to a study of the proteins for which these genes carry the code. This field of research is called proteomics and it is the next logical step after genomics. It is believed that a correlation exists between disease processes and patterns of protein production in cells.[177] This in turn could lead to new treatments.

Hyper-; hypo-: These prefixes have been described before in connection with sensory stimuli in the work of Delacato. Hyper- means above normal and hypo- means below normal.

Hypoplasia: This refers to an organ or tissue whose development is below normal.

Idiopathic: A disease of spontaneous origin is referred to as idiopathic.

Innate: Inborn, inherent, not arising from outside.

Insulin: Insulin is the hormone secreted by the small glands in the pancreas. Its function is to regulate the blood glucose sugar level.

Lesion: A lesion is an area of tissue in the body that has been damaged by disease or injury.

Limbic system: This is the name of the intricate system of nerve networks and pathways in the brain. The limbic system plays a role in moods, emotions, and the expression of instincts. It also has connections with the endocrine system. The three brain areas involved are the hypothalamus, the amygdala, and the hippocampus. The hippocampus, among its other functions, is involved in verbal memory of "time and place for events with strong emotional overtones."[51] The amygdala is involved in assigning emotional meaning to events and with how the body responds to fear.[51]

As mentioned in the text, autopsy studies have shown abnormality in the limbic system in autism. This abnormality related to a reduction in the size of the neurons, but an increase in the density of them.[82] Abnormalities in the limbic system have also been reported in studies of living patients with autism, more especially in the amygdala, which has been found to have a reduced volume. It has been speculated that these abnormalities in the amygdala may be involved in the emotional dysfunction that is found in autism.[123]

Modality: Modality is the word used to describe different forms of sensation, for example, the ability to detect pain is a modality, as is the ability to detect temperature. Sensations such as hearing, tasting, touch, and smell are also classed as modalities. Dysfunction in a modality may be due to malfunctioning of the sensory receptors or to the areas of the brain involved with receiving the messages.

Molecular biology: This encompasses the study of the molecules that are found in living tissues and includes neurotransmitters, proteins, and nucleic acids found in the nucleus of cells, for example, DNA and RNA.

Neurology: Neurology is the branch of medicine that deals with the functioning and diseases of the nervous system. The nervous system is made up of the brain, the spinal cord, and the peripheral nerves. The peripheral nerves contain sensory and motor nerves, and they form the links between the receptors (proprioceptors) that pick up information and feed it in to the central nervous system (the brain and spinal cord) and the effectors (gland or muscle) that carry out the instructions given.

Neurone (neuron): A neuron is a nerve cell. It is one of the basic units of the nervous system. The brain contains approximately 100 billion neurons and many more supporting cells, or glia, because the working of the brain depends on the ability of nerve cells to communicate with each other. While most organs of the body are made up of only a small number of cell types, the brain, in sharp contrast, contains thousands of different kinds of neurons, each with its own distinct individual shape, connections, and chemistry.[51] Each neuron has an enlarged part called the cell body, which houses the nucleus with its genetic material, and it also contains the energy-producing machinery (mitochondria) that drives the cell. Spreading out from the cell body are branches called dendrites through which impulses, or signals, enter the cell body. A longer process, called the axon or nerve fiber, transmits these electrical impulses away from the cell body. The axon may branch into many terminals at its end. Neurons do not connect directly to other neurons. Instead there are small gaps between them across which the impulse must pass. These gaps are called synapses. There are two parts to the synapse. One is called the presynaptic and is to be found on the terminal part of the sending neuron, and the other is called the postsynaptic and this is to be found on the dendrites of the receiving neuron. In between is the synaptic cleft, and it is into this cleft that the chemical messengers called neurotransmitters are released. When neurons are communicating with each other, the impulses or signals travel along the axon by the movement of ions into and out of the cell. This, in turn, causes electrical signals to sweep down through the cell.

When the electrical impulse reaches the end of a neuron it dies out. The neurotransmitter chemicals then carry the impulse across the synapse and cause the next neuron to fire, and so the message travels on. On average each neuron will make over a thousand synaptic connections with other neurons while some cells, for example, a Purkinje cell, will make more than a hundred times that. It is estimated that there may be over 100 trillion synapses in the brain.[51] This intricate pattern of synaptic connections eventually gives rise to circuits, and a single neuron may be part of more than one circuit. These circuits form the substratum for the basis of mental functioning and behavior. "One of the most awe-inspiring mysteries of brain science is how neuronal activity within circuits gives rise to behavior and, even, consciousness."[51].

A number of different chemicals act as neurotransmitters in the body, and there would appear to be about a hundred different neurotransmitters in the brain.[51] Some are large molecules, for example, peptides, while others are small, for example, dopamine. It has recently been discovered that only a small proportion of the cells in the brain actually make neurotransmitters—only one of every 200,000 cells in the brain makes dopamine and even fewer make the neurotransmitter norepinephrine. Serotonin is made by a somewhat larger but still small number of cells. However, each of these manufacturing cells sends its nerve fibers throughout the brain, the net result being that a very small number of neurons influences almost the entire brain. It would appear that these neurons tend to fire at the same time.[51] The drugs used to treat disorders of mood and other psychiatric conditions target these and other neurotransmitters.

Neuropathy (neuronopathy): This refers to any impairment or malfunctioning of the peripheral nervous system. It can be caused by the failure of proprioception described under Mark R. or can be artificially induced by taking enormous quantities of Vitamin B6 (Pyridoxine).[32]

Neurophysiology: The study of the complicated chemical and physical changes that take place within the nervous system is called neurophysiology. Neuropathophysiology is the term used when there is disease involved. The word "path" put before a word or into a word denotes disease. Pathology is the name given to the study of a disease to understand its cause and nature. Physiology is the study of the function of any organ or group of organs.

Nonverbal learning disability (NLD): Almost thirty years ago a particular group of people were described who were not able to understand the significance of many aspects of their environment; for example, they were lacking in the ability to learn and appreciate elements of emotion such as facial expressions, gestures, and signs of affection. Neither could they learn to anticipate or pretend. Their condition was given the name "nonverbal learning disability," and it was thought to imply a basic distortion of their perceptual experiences.[178] Research into this condition is ongoing, and individuals with the condition show a certain distinct profile of assets and deficits. The assets include good rote auditory-verbal skills, verbal memory skills, and good auditory perception. Deficits include visual-spatial organization, nonverbal problem-solving difficulties, and tactile perception problems. With regard to speech, pragmatics and prosody are also impaired. Individuals with this disability also tend to show marked deficits in mathematical reasoning and reading comprehension, as well as poor social perception and judgment. In addition, they seem to experience great difficulty in adapting to new situations.[178] The overlap between NLD and AS has been referred to previously.

Parkinsonism: This is a disease of the brain. It is associated with a deficiency of the neurotransmitter dopamine. Spontaneous movements are poor and restricted, and the patient will have little modulation and inflection in his voice. Over time the face becomes expressionless. Walking movements are shuffling, and there is a tendency to stoop. The commonest symptom is tremor. It can be brought on by the long-term use of some antipsychotic medications.

Pathogen: A pathogen is a disease-causing organism, such as a bacterium or a virus.

Perseveration: One of the commonest tendencies seen in autism is perseveration, excessively persisting at any activity whether in thought or deed. It may stem from an inability to quickly shift the mental focus of attention due to organic dysfunction in the brain. In autism it is associated with high anxiety levels, and it can also be a symptom of obsessive/compulsive disorder.

Pharmacology: The study of the properties of drugs (medications), how they work, and their effects and side effects on the body.

Placebo: An inactive form of treatment either clinically or psychologically, placebo in its own right can be very effective; sometimes it is more effective than no treatment.

Prognosis: A forecast of the outcome of an illness or disorder is called a prognosis. It is based upon the patient's general health; how severely they are affected by the condition, the availability of appropriate treatment, and how they will respond to it; and on previous medical knowledge of the course of such a condition in other patients.

Proprioception: The task of proprioception is to provide a constant stream of information about the position of the body in relation to space at any given moment. The receptors are to be found in the skeletal muscles, in ligaments, and in the balancing organs of the ear.

Psychodynamic theories: The theory of psychoanalysis put forward by Sigmund Freud was the first of the twentieth-century psychodynamic theories. This theory put forward the idea that "behaviour is the product of underlying conflicts over which people often have scant awareness."[51] There were two major assumptions in the theory of psychoanalysis. The first is that much of what goes on in the mind lies in the realm of the unconscious. The second is that we are greatly influenced throughout life by our past experiences, particularly those of early childhood.[51]

Psychosis: A patient suffers from a psychosis when he loses contact with reality and shows some of the following symptoms: delusions, hallucinations, poverty of thought, major thought disturbances, severe alterations of mood, or very abnormal behavior. Schizophrenia, organic mental disorders, manic depression, and serious paranoid states are all classed as psychoses.

Pyridoxine (vitamin B6): This is one of the B complex group of vitamins, all of which function as coenzymes. Enzymes are proteins produced within living cells. They speed up the rate of chemical reactions in the body (they act as catalysts), and normally they bind with coenzymes. If a metabolic disorder is due to a defect in an enzyme this defect may cause poor binding, and as a result enzyme activity will be reduced. If the concentration of the coenzyme is increased, this in turn may bring about an increase in binding and improve enzyme activity.[65] Vitamins cannot be manufactured by the body and therefore must form part of the diet, but they are only required in very small amounts.

Scotopic sensitivity syndrome (SSS): The Irlen Method describes SSS as a problem in perception. It shows itself in the lack of ability to judge spacial relationships; to read letters, numbers, or musical notes with ease; to deal with the glare of bright lights; or to perceive the printed page with ease and comfort. It cannot be detected by standard visual and medical tests. Looking through color may correct this difficulty by altering the timing by which visual information is received and processed.

Semantic-pragmatic language disorder: In describing this condition Bishop states that children with this disorder show delayed language development and also impairment in comprehension. In addition, they show a significant discrepancy in IQ in favor of performance IQ (PIQ). These children also show some autistic features, but she concludes that these are not severe enough to qualify for a diagnosis of autism.[179] In elaborating further on this condition Szatmari indicates that such children use vocabulary and grammar in a near-normal fashion, but that they have substantial difficulty in initiating and sustaining a conversation and in keeping the sensible links that should exist in normal conversation when moving from topic to topic. They also use words out of context. In addition, he points out that they usually have delayed milestones in language and stresses that, due to the scarcity of empirical data on these children, research in this disorder is urgently needed.[73]

Social phobia: This refers to the very strong pathological fear that can arise in some people when they find themselves in social situations. This fear of encountering people can lead to acute anxiety and can cause the person concerned to avoid such situations while at the same time being well aware that their level of fear is unreasonable.

"Soft" neurological signs: When this diagnosis is given it usually means that the standard examination carried out by a medical specialist has shown up nothing abnormal except a slight weakness in coordination. This can show up as an inability to write the letters b, d, and o or caps B, D, and O accurately and with ease; not being able to easily hop on one leg or easily distinguish right from left; or reversing letters and words, for example, writing ton instead of not.

Stereotypies: The repetitive, purposeless movements that are often seen in autism are called stereotypies. They include arm and hand flapping, twirling, twisting fingers, or waving fingers before the eyes, toe walking, and so forth.

Stimulus: A stimulus always creates a response. The stimulus is the cause that provokes a reaction in a cell, tissue, or organ that is sensitive to that stimulus. The eye responds to the stimulus of light and the ear to the stimulus of sound.

Syndrome: In the third edition of their book *The Biology of the Autistic Syndromes*, Gillberg and Coleman discuss in detail the significance of the use of the word *syndrome* and contrast it with the use of the word *spectrum*. They write that it is important and significant to make a distinction between the two; significant, that is, for medical diagnosis, prevention, and therapy. They indicate that in medicine a number of completely different disease entities can take a similar final course of action with the result that they present clinically with similar symptoms. Consequently they resemble each other, and this in turn gives rise to confusion. They state that autism comes into this category, and that because it does not have one etiology or cause, it is not a single disease entity. Drawing a comparison between it and mental retardation, they write that autism is a syndrome or a sequence of syndromes and that these in turn are caused by a number of diverse unconnected, individual diseases.

Turning then to the use of the word spectrum, they record that a spectrum is likely to occur in most diseases and that it describes changes (e.g., with age) or differences *within* the same disease. They consider that the use of the term autistic spectrum is "appropriate" in clinical practice in a patient whose underlying specific disease entity has not, as yet, been diagnosed.[23A]

APPENDIX 2:
ANNOTATED
BIBLIOGRAPHY

Autism is a spectrum disorder with a wide expression, and parents and professionals approach it from different angles depending on their disciplines or on their personal experience of living and coping with the condition. This is a personal list of sources that I found gave most insights into the autistic condition both from the perspective from which I approached it and from the perspective of coming to grips with what autism is and is not. All sources of information referred to in the text are listed under references.

ACADEMIC

Frith, Uta, ed. (1991). *Autism and Asperger Syndrome*. Cambridge, UK: Cambridge University Press. This collection of seven papers, mainly clinical accounts by different authors, also includes Frith's own translation of Asperger's original paper, " 'Autistic Psychopathy' in Childhood" and her account of "Asperger and His Syndrome."

Gillberg, C., and M. Coleman. (1992). *The Biology of the Autistic Syndromes*. 2d ed. London: MacKeith Press. This is a general reference text medically covering all aspects of the condition from diagnosis to brain imaging, pharmacological therapies to genetics, and biochemistry to neuropsychiatry. It is now in its third edition (2000).

Kanner, Leo. (1943). "Autistic Disturbances of Affective Contact." *Nervous Child* 2, 217–250. This thirty-three-page original paper still stands out as one of the best descriptions of the condition in the early years. To read it is to understand classic autism in the young child.

Sacks, Oliver. (1995). *An Anthropologist on Mars*. New York: Alfred A. Knopf. The last two sections of this book are devoted to autism and Sacks deals with it from the historical as well as the individual perspective. On both counts he probes the autistic condition, particularly the area of special intelligences in autism, and casts an enlightening eye over their nature.

Schopler, Eric, and Garry Mesibov, eds. *Current Issues in Autism*. New York and London: Plenum Press. The eleven comprehensive volumes in this series are wide ranging. Each volume deals in depth with a particular aspect of the condition, for example, "Diagnosis and Assessment in Autism" or "Behavioral Issues in Autism."

Wing, Lorna. (1981). "Asperger's Syndrome: A Clinical Account." *Psychological Medicine* 11: 115–129. This is the important pivotal paper which reintroduced Asperger's work into the literature and combined it with a description of Wing's own cases.

SENSORY PERCEPTION ISSUES

Ayres, Anna J. (1979). *Sensory Integration and the Child*. Los Angeles: Western Psychological Services.

Delacato, Carl H. (1974). *The Ultimate Stranger*. Novato, CA: Academic Therapy Publications. Both the above books give insights into how to understand and how to alleviate the distress and behavioral difficulties that can arise from the often gross distortion of perception found in some people with autism.

JOURNALS

Advocate. This is the quarterly publication of the Autism Society of America. Its selection includes, among other items—"Watching Washington," and considers that one of its primary missions is advocating for the voice of the autism community in Washington D.C., overviews of biomedical research, information and exchange, and autism news.

Autism. The International Journal of Research and Practice. This journal, first released in 1997, is produced by SAGE publications in association with The National Autistic Society. Its aim is to concentrate on research of both a practical nature and an academic nature that will translate into improving the quality of life for people with autism.

Journal of Autism and Developmental Disorders. This journal was first produced in 1971 by Leo Kanner under the title of "The Journal of Autism and Childhood Schizophrenia." The journal has a long history of empirical research directed toward solving the problems of autism. It also provides a forum for readers to ask questions.

The Maap. This is a quarterly publication for families of "More advanced individuals with Autism, Asperger Syndrome, and Pervasive Developmental Disorder/ Not Otherwise Specified." It contains letters, questions, answers, articles, poems, art work, book reviews, and information. It could perhaps best be summed up in one word—sharing.

PERSONAL ACCOUNTS

These personal accounts, written by either people with autism or their family members, furnish both image and reality to the academic face of autism.

Grandin, Temple. (1995). *Thinking in Pictures*. New York: Doubleday. Whereas Grandin's first book dealt mainly with her life story, this second book expands into an overview of autism itself in the light of her experiences as a researcher, a writer, and a conference presenter.

Grandin, Temple, and Margaret M. Scariano. (1986). *Emergence Labeled Autistic*. Novato, CA: Arena Press. When this was published in 1986 it was the first book written from the perspective of autism on the inside and was a landmark in its time. It has been translated into a number of different languages and is on the autism best seller list.

Hart, Charles. (1989). *Without Reason*. New York: HarperCollins. This is a story of two families, spanning two generations, and set against the background of two different Americas; that of the early half of the century, when the condition had no name, and that of the latter half when the questions, if not the answers, began to take shape.

McDonnell, Jane Taylor. (1993). *News from the Border*. New York: Ticknor & Fields. A human story of family life as it revolves around the upbringing of an autistic child, which will strike a chord with every family who lives with autism as they grapple with the same issues and face the same conflicts. The book contains a fifty-page afterword by Paul, then a college student, detailing what it is like to grow up on the borders between autism and normalcy.

Moreno, Susan J. (1991). *High-Functioning Individuals with Autism*. Crown Point, IN: MAAP Services Inc. An invaluable practical handbook which gives "advice and information for parents and others who care." It covers the ordinary day-to-day situations, both at home, in school, and in the community that arise in the lives of all families with autism, including such areas as social skills and tips for teachers.

Park, Clara Claiborne. (1967). *The Siege: The First Eight Years of an Autistic Child*. New York: Little, Brown. This was the first family account and the book has an epilogue written fifteen years later. It reaches out to all parents in its guiding example of what can be achieved in autism. It illuminates the condition that lies behind the behavior and gives indepth insights into how to work with it and draw it out.

APPENDIX 3:
RESOURCES

Telephone and fax numbers are correct at press time but may be subject to area code and individual changes.

SOCIETIES AND ORGANIZATIONS

Asperger Syndrome Association of Ireland Ltd (ASPIRE)
85 Woodley Park
Kilmacud
Dublin 14
Ireland
Tel: 353 1 2951389

Autism-Europe
Avenue E. Van Becelaere
26b Bte 21
B-1170 Bruxelles
Belgique
Tel: +32 2 675 75 05
E-mail: autisme.europe@arcadis.be

Autism Research Institute
4182 Adams Avenue
San Diego, CA 92116

United States
Director Bernard Rimland, Ph.D.
Tel: (619) 281–7165

Autism Research Unit (Titles in Autism)
School of Health Sciences
University of Sunderland
SUNDERLAND SR2 7EE
United Kingdom

Autism Society of America
7910 Woodmont Avenue
Suite 300
Bethesda, MD 20814–3067
United States
Tel: (301) 657–0881

Irish Society for Autism
Unity Building
16/17 Lower O'Connell St.
Dublin 1
Ireland
Tel: 353 1 8744684
Fax: 353 1 8744224
E-mail: autism@isa.iol.ie

MAAP SERVICES INC
P.O. Box 524
Crown Point, IN 46308
United States
President Susan J. Moreno, M.A.A.B.S.
Tel: (219) 662–1311
E-mail: chart@netnitco.net

The National Autistic Society
393 City Road
London EC1V 1NG
United Kingdom
Tel: 020 7833 2299

Parents and Professionals and Autism (PAPA)
Knockbracken Healthcare Park
Saintfield Road
Belfast, BT8 8BH
Northern Ireland
Tel: 01232–401729

EDUCATION AND INTERVENTION

Delacato Centre
700 Thomas Road
Northwestern Avenue
Philadelphia, PA 19118–4601
United States
Tel: (610) 828–4881
E-mail: delacato@pond.com

Boston Higashi School
2618 Massachusetts Avenue
Lexington 232, MA 02173
United States

Irlen Filters
Irlen Institute
5380 Village Road
Long Beach, CA 90808
United States

The Option Institute
2080 South Undermountain Road
Sheffield, MA 01257
United States
Tel: (413) 229–2100
E-mail: sonrise@option.org
Web: www.son-rise.org

Sensory Integration International
1602 Cabrillo Avenue
Torrance, CA 90501–2819
United States

TEACCH
The University of North Carolina at Chapel Hill
Division TEACCH Administration and Research
Department of Psychiatry
CB #7180, 310 Medical School Wing E
Chapel Hill, NC 27599–7180
United States
Tel: (919) 966–2174

JOURNALS AND PERIODICALS

Advocate: Journal of the Autism Society of America
See address above

Autism Research Review International: Journal of Autism Research Institute
See address above

Autism—The International Journal of Research and Practice
SAGE Publications
6 Bonhill Street
London EC2A 4PU
United Kingdom
E-mail: subscriptions@sagepub.co.uk.
U.S. orders to be sent to:
PO Box 5096
Thousand Oaks, CA 91359
United States

Communication: Journal of The National Autistic Society
See address above

Focus on Autism and Other Developmental Disabilities
Pro-Ed, Inc.
8700 Shoal Creek Blvd.
Austin, TX 78757–6897
United States
Tel: (512) 451–3246/(800) 897–3202

Journal of Autism and Developmental Disorders
Kluwer Academic/Plenum Publishers
233 Spring Street
New York, NY 10013–1578
United States

LINK: Journal of Autism-Europe
See address above

Maap: Journal of MAAP SERVICES INC
See address above

Naarative
National Alliance for Autism Research
Research Park
414 Wall Street
Princeton, NJ 08540
United States
Tel: (609) 430–9160
E-mail: naar@naar.org

BOOK RESOURCES

Autism Research Institute
See address above

Autism Society of Michigan Bookstore
6035 Executive Drive, Suite 109
Lansing, MI 48911
United States
Tel: (517) 882–2800
E-mail: miautism@aol.com

Autism Society of North Carolina Bookstore
505 Oberlin Road, Suite 230
Raleigh, NC 27605–1345
United States
Tel: (919) 743–0204

Future Horizons
721 West Abram Street
Arlington, TX 76013
United States
Tel: (817) 277–0727
E-mail: edfuture@onramp.net
Without Reason by Charles Hart is available from Future Horizons.

National Autistic Society, United Kingdom
See address above

AUTHOR INDEX

SUBJECT INDEX

About the Author

ANN HEWETSON is both a professional and a parent of a son with high-ability autism. In her professional capacity, she has worked as a research scientist with the National University of Ireland and later as Head of Science in a large public school. She was instrumental in founding the Asperger Syndrome Association of Ireland.